Speaking and Writing, K-12

Speaking and Writing, K-12

Classroom Strategies and the New Research

E 70

Edited by

Christopher J. Thaiss
George Mason University

Charles Suhor
National Council of Teachers of English

National Council of Teachers of English
1111 Kenyon Road, Urbana, Illinois 61801

Book Design: Tom Kovacs for TGK Design

NCTE Stock Number 46244

Library of Congress Cataloging in Publication Data
Main entry under title:

Speaking and Writing, K-12.

   Includes bibliographies.
   1. Language arts—United States—Addresses, essays, lectures.   2. English language—Study and teaching—United States—Addresses, essays, lectures.   I. Thaiss, Christopher J., 1948- . II. Suhor, Charles.
LB1576.S725   1984   420'.7   84-16480
ISBN 0-8141-4624-4

Contents

Acknowledgments

The editors want to give special thanks to the advisors who helped shape these materials, including Betty Blaisdell, Fairfax County Schools, Virginia; Don Boileau, Speech Communication Association; Pamela Cooper, Northwestern University; Joseph Dominic, National Institute of Education; Kathleen Galvin, Northwestern University; Phil Gray, Northern Illinois University; Barbara Lieb-Brilhart, National Institute of Education; Bob Simons, Director of Basic Skills Programs, U.S. Department of Education. Our appreciation also goes to the excellent staff at Dingle Associates, especially Ramsey Sa'di, Marca Piehuta, and Clarence Johnson. The NCTE Editorial Board and Paul O'Dea, NCTE Director of Publications, also offered valued suggestions in the development of the book.

Permission to reprint the following material used in Jana Staton's chapter, "Thinking Together: Interaction in Children's Reasoning," is gratefully acknowledged: the transcripts of the dialogue journals, throughout, are from *Analysis of Dialogue Journal Writing as a Communicative Event,* written by Jana Staton, Roger Shuy, Joy Kreeft, and Mrs. Reed and published by the Center for Applied Linguistics, Washington, D.C. in 1982. The transcript of the "Seeds Lesson" is from *Language Diversity and Classroom Discourse,* written by Ceil Lucas and Denise Borders-Simmons and published by the Center for Applied Linguistics, Washington, D.C. in 1982. The transcript of the "Five Chinese Brothers" story is from the *Quarterly Newsletter of the Laboratory of Comparative Human Cognition* (1979) which is published by the University of California, San Diego, La Jolla, California. The "Pigman" essay and dialogue are from Grant Farley, Wilmington Junior High School, Wilmington, California.

Introduction

In preparing this book for NCTE, as we corresponded and talked with the authors about their revisions, we were continually reminded of the circumstances under which we came to design this project. The professional services firm of Dingle Associates, Inc., under a Basic Skills Improvement grant from the Department of Education, had invited us in late 1981 to create a series of booklets for teachers, K–12, that would translate the most vital recent research in writing and oral communication into useful suggestions for classroom practice. We focused on ways in which teachers can help their students grow as writers and speakers (and readers and listeners). We stressed activities that didn't isolate the language arts into units and didn't sever the so-called "skills" from the content of learning. We wanted essays that would also help teachers explain to parents and colleagues the theory behind the practice; hence, we sought a plain style, as free as possible from the argot of education.

The teachers, researchers, and writers who met to plan the series included Ronald Allen, University of Wisconsin; Don M. Boileau, Speech Communication Association; Barbara Lieb-Brilhart, National Institute of Education; Pamela Cooper, Northwestern University; Joseph Dominic, National Institute of Education; Marcia Farr, University of Illinois—Chicago; Robert A. Gundlach, Northwestern University; Kenneth J. Kantor, University of Georgia; Nancy S. Olson, American Society for Training and Development; Linda J. Reed, CEMREL; Donald L. Rubin, University of Georgia; Jana Staton, Center for Applied Linguistics; Charles Suhor, National Council of Teachers of English; and Christopher J. Thaiss, George Mason University.

Because many of us came from relatively specialized backgrounds in *either* writing or speaking—the very division which we were seeking to eliminate—we saw from the outset that we could not just write our manuscripts and send them for review to a small editorial group. Rather, we had embarked on an interdisciplinary course that would require considerable exchange of perspectives, data, and reading lists, not to mention multiple reviews by the entire group. This continuing conversation among the authors and the other group members led us to be deeply appreciative of our different data and approaches—an appreciation reflected in the authors' mutual reference to each other's chapters that the reader will note in the text.

In addition, all of us found that we could not bring home our ideas to teachers (or make them fully satisfying to ourselves) merely by reporting the findings of others. So we also cited our own experiences to illuminate important ideas, or we identified teachers, observed them and their students, recorded classroom interactions, and studied writing samples. The essays became, in effect, dramatic scenes exemplifying the ideas hypothesized and substantiated by earlier research. A draft of each essay was reviewed by at least one practitioner, usually an elementary or secondary classroom teacher.

The first published versions of these essays appeared in June 1983 as a limited-edition booklet series, *The Talking and Writing Series, K–12: Successful Classroom Practices* (Washington, D.C.: U.S. Department of Education). Since then we have worked with the authors to update lists of suggested readings and, as needed, to revise the texts in accordance with our suggestions and those of the NCTE Editorial Board. This new edition has also allowed the authors to include their latest ideas on these subjects and their freshest examples.

Ordering the Essays

The original goals of the planning group suggest the arrangement of chapters in this volume. There is a general movement in the text, as in many individual chapters, from the actual classroom scene to its analysis in terms of theory supported by research. We have also attempted to keep before the reader the links between writing and speaking; thus, those few chapters that tend to emphasize one or the other appear in appropriate pairings rather than in clusters of articles on the same aspect of language arts.

"Learning Better, Learning More: In the Home and Across the Curriculum," by Ann Jeffries-Thaiss and Christopher J. Thaiss, opens the volume with portraits of four teachers whose students learn facts and explore ideas through an imaginative range of writing and speaking activities. The chapter details these teachers' assignments and their students' interactions. A fifth portrait, the first in the chapter, shows a family at "work" on a "Pioneer Night," in which, again, learning occurs through varied language experiences. Intended for both teachers and parents, this chapter explores situations that exemplify writing and speaking as modes of learning.

"Talking and Writing: Building Communication Competence" (Donald L. Rubin and Kenneth J. Kantor) uses research results and vivid classroom examples to help teachers answer two central questions: what is competent communication and how do I help my students achieve it? Rubin and Kantor show that communication competence means the person's ability to convey different types of messages to different audiences in different, appropriate styles (e.g., intimate, casual, consultative, formal, and frozen). The writers then describe environments which allow children to develop a wide range of competencies in writing and speaking.

Charles Suhor's "Thinking Visually about Writing: Three Models for Teaching Composition, K–12" graphically defines three paradigms—the "content area" model, the "mastery" model, and the "writing process" model—that have dominated the teaching of writing in recent years. He explores the goals, benefits, and problems of these methods and cites key books and articles that represent each. He suggests where and when the particular models are appropriate and argues for the writing process model as the most flexible and the best suited to children's ways of learning.

Barbara Wood, in "Oral Communication in the Elementary Classroom," provides a classification of ways by which teachers help students become better speakers and listeners. Rejecting the conventional notion that the quiet classroom is best for learning, Wood describes for teachers and parents important modes of interaction among students and between student and teacher that enhance the learning of any subject. She devotes special attention to the use of small groups in the classroom, as well as to "milestones" of communicative ability—talking and listening skills that children acquire as they mature.

Following Wood's emphasis on speaking and listening in the early grades is Marcia Farr's "Writing Growth in Young Children: What We Are Learning from Research." This chapter has a double focus: Farr relates, with frequent anecdotes from the authors she cites, the findings of four recent and essential studies on writing development; moreover, she attends to the "how" of these researchers, to demonstrate that the most relevant, accessible research comes from classroom teachers, working alone or in collaboration with research specialists. She describes, and justifies by the results, the methods of the growing number of teacher/researchers whose intimate knowledge of their students increases the significance of their observations.

Jana Staton, whose research on dialogue journals is one of the four projects featured in Farr's chapter, contributes the next essay, "Thinking Together: Language Interaction in Children's Reasoning." With her sharp focus on teacher-student dialogue, particularly through the dialogue journal, Staton clearly illustrates for teachers a powerful technique for helping students grow as critical thinkers and as versatile communicators. Through progressive excerpts from the journals of several students, Staton provides convincing evidence of the value of such interaction.

Nancy Olson's chapter introduces teachers and parents to "Using the New Technologies in Language Communication Education." For the reader not yet familiar with the diverse modes from "interactive video" to videodiscs to word processors, or for the reader well acquainted with one but not all of these systems, Olson's chapter thoughtfully discusses their potential benefits and drawbacks. As evidence, she cites in detail ongoing uses of these different media in schools across the nation and notes the findings of current research. The chapter concludes with a checklist of points to remember when contemplating the purchase of software.

The volume concludes with a pair of chapters that view the child, the teacher, and the classroom in the context of the whole-school curriculum and societal expectations. In "Integrating the Language Arts," Ronald Allen and Robert Kellner begin with a classroom scene in which talking, writing, listening, and reading reinforce one another in the learning of each subject. Then the authors widen their focus to delineate the communication spiral by which the language arts continue to serve as "means, a tool across the disciplines," through a child's school years. They illustrate this model by citing specific schools using the Wisconsin Alternative Curriculum Design.

The final chapter, Linda Reed's "Assessing Children's Speaking, Listening, and Writing Skills," addresses a persistent dilemma faced by teachers: how to persevere in teaching each unique child the program that he or she needs, even as school boards, the media, and parents put ever-stronger emphasis on standardized test performance. Motivated by the research-based conviction that the individual teacher is the more knowledgeable judge of the student's progress, Reed describes criteria by which teachers can best observe, assess, and demonstrate their students' versatility as language users. An actual Chicago classroom is Reed's principal setting as she shows this on-going assessment in practice.

Features to Look For

While one of our major goals in this project has been to make important research accessible to teachers and parents, we have been even more concerned about presenting clearly and colorfully, practical applications of research. We have not attempted to be comprehensive with regard to research because we have chosen more frequently to emphasize such remarkable people as Tom Watson, Tina Yalen, Ted Brockton, Leslee Reed, Mary McDonnell, and Marlene Harris—teachers whose day-to-day work with children not only puts theory into practice but indeed inspires close study. We of course hope that teachers and parents will use the research described and the classrooms presented to enhance their own schools and homes as interactive learning environments: vital centers for study and enjoyment.

Christopher J. Thaiss
Charles Suhor

Learning Better, Learning More: In the Home and Across the Curriculum

Ann Jeffries-Thaiss

Christopher J. Thaiss, George Mason University

Rich Gottfried, who teaches earth science and chemistry at Chantilly (Va.) High School, was asked how much "extra time" he spent having students write essay tests, rather than fill in blanks, and helping them develop group projects, rather than just lecturing. "Extra time?" he replied, puzzled. "It's not extra. That's how I teach, and that's how they learn. Of what use are facts about rocks and elements if students don't learn to think about those facts the way scientists do?"

This chapter is about teachers like Rich Gottfried, who have realized that students learn science—or math, history, or any other discipline—by *talking* about it and *writing* about it, as well as by reading texts and hearing others talk. These teachers apply to practice what researchers in different fields have been preaching for many years: Learning happens when you or I use our perceptions (e.g., through reading or listening) to solve problems important to us, and try to put those perceptions into *words* (spoken or written) so that others can use them and so that we ourselves will understand them.

It is easy to explain why students forget so quickly so much that teachers tell them: it is not that the data are irrelevant or that students lack intelligence; teachers simply rarely ask students to *use* data, except to give it back to them in undigested bits on so-called tests. Educators often defend this type of teaching by saying that it allows them to "cover material." Besides, they say, the students must first "learn the material before they can use it." But, as the teachers and researchers cited here believe, no one learns except by doing: in effect, *using* information precedes really *learning* it.

This chapter describes four classrooms where teachers and students use a treasury of writing and speaking experiences to learn subject matter: a fifth grade, a high school math class, a ninth-grade earth science class, and an eleventh-/twelfth-grade social studies class. Actual classes in progress, teacher discussions on the motives behind their methods, and brief analyses

1

of each class in terms of the theory that supports it are presented. A short list of suggested classroom activities follows each analysis, as well as a short list of suggested reading.

Of course, the classes dramatized are atypical, in that these teachers are doing much more with time and for students than does the "typical" teacher. This chapter does not portray education in America, but learning as it *can* be and *is*—given teachers who understand how students learn best, and who apply that understanding in imaginative, compassionate ways. These classes *are* typical in that they contain students from varied ethnic, linguistic, and economic backgrounds; students "turned on" or "turned off" to school because of their very individual histories, relationships with parents, friends, or former teachers. In other words, the successes of these teachers could happen anywhere.

Because the philosophy demonstrated here is just as important in the home as in school, the first section (by Ann Jeffries-Thaiss) describes and analyzes writing and speaking to learn in a family setting. It illustrates the learning leaps that take place when wit, words, and a little time are applied.

Writing and Speaking to Learn in the Home

> "We aeat cown mele for denr. We made soop. Ther was carrits and celrry with onunyin."
> —Jimmy, age 6
> "I cooked it and added certain spices to obtain a superior flavor."
> —Jeff, age 10

A Pioneer Night, January 1982

Around 4 p.m., the Sunday activities began to wind down. The two older boys, Jeff, 10, and Jimmy, 6, went out into the snow with their father to gather kindling in the tiny grove near their home. Toddler Christopher, 2, was finishing a color-alphabet game with his mother. After wood was laid on the hearth, Jimmy brought in two bowls of snow to be melted for handwashing.

By 4:30, the dinner was underway. Jeff filled the large Dutch oven with water and added dried split peas, lentils, and two frozen chicken wings. Then came the mixed vegetables that Jimmy had cut up and Christopher had placed in a bowl. Soon, the soup pot began to boil, and the first sips of what would turn out to be a delicious broth were tried. Jeff decided to add salt and garlic for flavor. As Jeff stirred, Jimmy mixed ingredients for wheat and cornmeal muffins. Christopher interrupted his wide-eyed gaze with shouts of "Dum! Dum!" (Give me some!)

Jeff: Do you think this needs more spices?

Daddy: (tasting) I think it could use more salt. What do you think, Jimmy?

Jimmy: (tasting) Yup. A little salt.

Daddy: What did the pioneers use to preserve their food?

Jeff: Salt. Yum, I'd love to have some salted ham.

Jimmy: Like the ones hanging at Monticello and Turkey Run Farm!

Mommy: Right, Jimmy. But I'm afraid that it would be salty beyond your imagination. I bet you'd find it tasted terrible by our standards.

Daddy: Where did the pioneers get salt?

Jimmy: In the sea.

Jeff: They'd have to get tons and tons of water just to get an ounce of salt!

Daddy: What about the pioneers who didn't live near salt water?

Jeff: They'd get it from the ground.

Mommy: Do you know what that's called? (No response.) Natural salt licks. They were very important in pioneer life.

While the soup cooked and the muffins baked, the three boys handed their father kindling, which he arranged in the fireplace. The two older boys wanted him to rub two sticks together—"Just like a real pioneer!"—but, though he tried it for a couple of minutes, he acquiesced to expedience and used a match. Candles were also lit as Mommy dished up food and brought it to the table in front of the fireplace. Herbal tea was brewed, and the family settled down to the evening meal and conversation about the lives of Virginia pioneers.

Jeff asked if there were pioneers around Charlottesville (his favorite city), and this question led to a study of the family atlas and the topography not just of Virginia, but of the entire United States. Jimmy wanted to know the distance from Oakton to Chicago (where Jeff was born), and Daddy showed him how to use the mileage legend to figure distance on a map. Christopher finished his meal and asked for more tea. Daddy asked what other drinks Virginia pioneers might have had. Tea and apple cider were voted probable favorites, with coffee an extreme rarity, milk a luxury, and orange juice unheard of.

Christopher began to play with one of the bowls of melting snow and Jeff pointed out that the water looked dirty, almost like mucus. Both Jeff and Jimmy agreed that *they* would not want snow cones made out of this snow.

Mommy asked why the snow was so dirty, and Jeff explained that it was because of all the pollution in the air from cars, trucks, and industry. And Jimmy decided that pioneer children could have eaten real snow cones.

Christopher was nursed to sleep (in true pioneer fashion!). As Jimmy drew pictures by firelight, Mommy suggested a brainstorming session in which everyone would try to name as many things as possible that might have been found in a pioneer home. In no time, the list numbered 102 items, including a Bible, a stickhorse, wooden spoons, lard, and a spinning wheel. Everyone participated, and the more things that were named, the more excited everyone got, wanting to reach the set goal of 100.

A discussion about what the pioneers might have done for fun followed. The children thought of stickball, fishing, hide-and-go-seek, and hiking. Daddy mentioned storytelling and how songs were passed from one generation to the next. He brought out his guitar and accompanied Mommy singing some old folk songs: "Black Is the Color of My True Love's Hair," "Dona, Dona," and Jeff's favorite, "Barbara Allen."

The evening concluded with everyone writing about this special time together. Jeff and his father wrote descriptions, Mommy reflected in her diary, and Jimmy wrote, as a pioneer boy, to an imaginary cousin, "Charley Slikeman," who lived in Philadelphia.

DEAR CWWORLY IT IS VERY COLD.
WE WENT TO THE STREEM TOGIT
KINDALING. WE ROD A LOT!
WE DUG AND DUG. IT WAS HURD,
IT DRID FAST!
WE AEAT COWN MELE. FOR
DENR. WE MADE SOOP. THER WAS
CARRITS AND CELRRY
WITH ONUNYIN. WE DESCRIBED
THEINGS. IT WAS VERY FUN.
WE GOT 100 WRDS ON THE PAPRE
THINGS IN PIANERE HOMES.
I LIKETE THE BERROL AND THE STIKOS
HORS. LOVE JIMMY

Today was pioneer day.
   At about 4:00 o'clock my brother, father, and I colected fire wood.
   After that we made dinner. We had thick vegetable meat soup. I cooked it and added certain spices to obtain

a superior flavor. Also we ate potatoes, which my father prepared and rolls which my brother made. We could not use lights so we burned a candle a candle past 8:00 o'clock. We made a nice, warm fire. So with the dishes clean and the table cleared we just started talking. Then we looked at the Rand McNally. map of Virginia and looked at the places the pioneers would be living. Then we tried to name all the things a pioneer family would have in their house and we just sat around the fire and my parents sang and that's how the night ended.

Analysis

This sharing among family members shows the lively learning that takes place so easily in the home. The family made no elaborate plans for the evening; they simply decided to stop their usual activities at a prescribed time and spend the evening focused on a central theme. The flow of ideas in this illustration follows the boys' natural interests. Ideas "fit" like the many pieces of a jigsaw puzzle, creating a unified learning experience bound to be more easily retained by the children than if ideas were presented and explored in isolated segments according to subject matter. Note the different areas discussed: American history, science, home economics, sociology, communications, music, geography, map reading, drawing, writing, to name a few. The tools used were simple; no expensive equipment was used or needed. Such "hands-on" activities as wood-gathering, cooking, fire-building, drawing, accompanied by the give-and-take between children and parents, provided many natural opportunities for discussion, and were exercises in imagination, logic, and intuition. Music provided not only a lesson in oral history, communication, and social life, but it also enhanced the atmosphere, creating an impression which reading alone could not have provided.

Aaron Stern, in his remarkable book, *The Making of a Genius,* described many such learning sessions with his daughter, Edith, and his son, David. Stern termed his work, "Total Educational Submersion." In the introduction to the reprinted edition of this book, T.E.S. has been described by John M. Flynn (1977): "The methodology is basically an individualized instruction approach—one which takes the child where it finds him, capitalizes on the child's interests, and uses as instructional materials both books and the environment.... I believe that it incorporates a flexibility which is not often present in other current approaches. For example, the method is quite opportunistic in capitalizing on the child's interest." The key word, "opportunistic," accounts for the successes that

Stern enjoyed with his children, and with the many other children that he has worked with over twenty years. Children love to learn. Letting the child guide the parent creates the most fruitful atmosphere for learning.

The use of writing/drawing in this project was not just a means to record; it helped to fuse ideas. Jeff's description of the evening provided him with a chance for immediate reflection (and feedback) on what he did and what he learned. Jimmy's decision to write to an imaginary cousin, "Charley Slikeman" (a name he chose), gave him a chance to organize information and to fantasize about what he would have to say were he a pioneer boy himself.

Thus, writing and speaking were the tools used to question, express, entertain, solve, record, create, amuse, explore, and discover.

Family activities can be organized around any interest a child may have. Pioneer Night could just as easily be turned into a night in a medieval castle, a day in a major league dugout, a trip on Noah's ark, or a day with George Washington. And no extra time needs to be set aside for such activities; every day, parents and their children share much time doing household chores, shopping, driving, standing in lines, and other activities. Any of these times is a wonderful opportunity to probe a child's mind, encourage questioning, spark his or her imagination. Any time can be special for a parent and child to discover together.

More Ideas

Charades is always a wonderful family activity. Have participants pretend that they are historical figures, or have them act out book titles, events, and so forth.

Choose five to six household items (spoon, screwdriver, box, toothbrush, pin). Have each family member try to name as many uses as he or she can for each. Practical uses as well as imaginative ones should be encouraged. For example, a spoon could be the temporary home of a cold virus, a screwdriver could be a lightning rod for a gnome home. This helps push imagination and problem solving to the limit, thus enabling the child to view the world in new ways.

Have children play "newspaper reporter" and interview their parents about their childhood. The child might then write an article based on the interview.

Have a family "letter-write." Everyone writes to a favorite relative or friend. Very young children can draw pictures. All share their work. A variation: each member chooses an admired person—baseball player, actor, politician, journalist—and writes a letter to send to that person. The whole family will enjoy the responses received.

Family spelling bee: After children are quizzed, see if they can stump parents (with the help of a dictionary if necessary). A great game on car trips—with the winner promised a special treat at the next stop.

Play "What would you do if . . ." (you were lost at the airport, saw a dinosaur, met the President, etc.). This game develops imagination and logic.

Each week share current reading interests. "I'm reading _____, and this is why I (dis)like it." For children too young to read, use part of this time reading to them or asking older children to read to them.

Have a round-robin storywriting session. Each family member starts a story by writing an introductory paragraph. Then everyone hands his or her story to another and writes more. If you choose, pass the stories around more than once. Then enjoy the results. For those too young to read and write, a parent or older sibling can read aloud and take dictation, so that everyone can participate.

Encourage children to share their talents with others. A ten-year-old can read on a regular basis at a local nursing home. The nursing home resident has much-needed company, while the child gives and strengthens his or her sense of self.

Suggested Reading

Beck, Joan. *How to Raise a Brighter Child: The Case for Early Learning.* New York: Trident Press, 1967.

Doman, Glenn. *How to Teach Your Baby to Read.* New York: Random House, 1964.

Flynn, John. Introduction to Stern, Aaron, *The Joy of Learning.* North Miami Beach: Renaissance Publishers, 1977.

Judy, Stephen N. *The ABC's of Literacy.* New York: Oxford University Press, 1980.

Segal, Marilyn. *Run Away, Little Girl.* New York: Random House, 1966.

Stern, Aaron. *The Making of a Genius.* 1971; reprinted North Miami Beach: Renaissance Publishers, 1977.

Suzuki, Shinichi. *Nurtured by Love.* New York: Exposition Books, 1969.

Writing and Speaking to Learn in Fifth Grade

Tom Watson's class at Haycock School has been studying the Renaissance. A week ago, the children were asked to assume roles of famous Renaissance figures and to compose one or more entries of a hypothetical diary kept by the person each chose. This day, the children are presenting these diaries. Some will be selected by the students to be read aloud to the entire class; all children will present their individual diaries to small peer groups.

When Watson announces that group work will begin, the children quickly move to familiar areas of the classroom and circle their desks in groups of fours and fives. They begin chattering ("Who did you choose?" "Guess who I am, and then I'll guess you.") even before Watson repeats the often heard instructions: "Remember, make sure that everyone has a chance to read . . . and after each person has read, remember to give him or her some comments about the diary." He adds, "Then as a group, decide on one or two of your diaries that should be read to the whole class."

The groups begin in earnest. The noise level rises, but none of the groups appears distracted by the others. In one group, Melody handles the job of organizer, reminding the group of its tasks and making sure that all are given equal time. Jeff reads first, then the others read clockwise around the circle. As usual, the group reading sparks some talk on wholly unexpected topics. For example, Matt, as Leonardo da Vinci, has just read a series of diary entries about his painting the Mona Lisa. Dylan says: "Hey, I heard that some people think Leonardo painted her in the nude!" [Laughter.] "No really, and they want to strip away the layers of paint, using a computer."

> *Colleen:* They what?
>
> *Jeff:* That's dumb. They'll ruin the painting.
>
> *Dylan:* No, that's why they use the computer. So they could repaint it with the exact colors.

The discussion continues until Melody reminds the others that two diaries have yet to be read. When all have finished and heard comments, it is time for the group to choose one or two diaries to be read to the entire class. Each suggests a different diary as the best, so they call on Watson to settle the quandary. He tells them that they need not decide; rather, anyone may read. This satisfies the group, which now turns its attention to the rest of the class.

Over the next half hour, the diaries of eight luminaries are read: Michelangelo (Arthur), Queen Isabella (Eric), Shakespeare (Anushka), Dante (Dhananjai), and two each by would-be Galileos (Jeff and Michael) and Isaac Newtons (Mitchell and Will). Each reading brings questions and comments from the children. The teacher points out a particularly clever aspect of each reading: for example, Dante's relief at having finally finished the *Divine Comedy* and Shakespeare's keeping a newspaper review of his first production! The two Galileos point up different and equally remarkable facets of his biography: the first, his brilliant astronomical discoveries; the second, his excommunication and threatened execution by the Catholic Church.

Now, the teacher transforms the discussion into a brainstorming session for the project based on the diaries: dialogues. These will be written and delivered by pairs of students, each continuing in his or her chosen character. Over the next week, the children will develop the dialogues, with some class time allotted for the writing. Each pair will have a choice of purposes: either to debate which of the two characters made the greatest contribution to civilization or to show how each one epitomized the "spirit" of the Renaissance.

Facilitating this second thrust is one purpose of the brainstorming. As the teacher explains, "I'd like you to think of adjectives we could use to describe the spirit, or mind, of the Renaissance." Soon, the board is covered with terms. Among them are: *complex, reborn, curious, primitive —compared to now, creative, smart, discovering, powerful, adventurous, determined.* Now, the teacher takes the thinking another step: "I want you to look over the list and try to find three that seem to encompass all of them." Dylan suggests "complex, reborn, and interested"; Ellen says "interesting, adventurous, and discovering." After each suggested trio, the teacher asks the student to explain his or her choices. "Discovering" provokes a substitution: "I like Ellen's list," says Jeff, "but I think *powerful* should replace *discovering*. Without power no discoveries would have been made." Thus, an issue is raised: What is the relationship between power and discovery? For five minutes, different views are exchanged, with at least a dozen students contributing fresh perspectives. Could Isabella have funded Columbus without the power to do so? No, but without Columbus, could Spain have become a power in the New World?

Watson brings the discussion to a close with the issue still under debate. He wants to give the class the few minutes left before the lunch bell to choose partners and begin designing the dialogues.

Analysis

In this scene, the language arts are used, not "covered." Writing and speaking, as well as reading and listening, are exploited as the natural means by which these fifth-graders learn history, biography, astronomy, physics, economics, politics, geography, and literature. The written and spoken word flourish in this class because they are *not* separated from the rest of the curriculum for "special attention," but are allowed to be used for their best purposes: problem solving, group communication, and performance.

Moreover, they are used copiously and with variety, even in this one scene. The children present diaries within small groups, they orally analyze what they have heard, converse about new ideas, and revise their writing in response to the conversation. Within the large group, they perform the diaries, question and answer questions, and orally analyze the spoken diaries. They do group brainstorming of ideas, orally synthesize the data, create impromptu arguments to defend their choices, and debate opposing views.

Finally, in pairs, they discuss the new task, and begin to draft the dialogues. The summary points up a third essential quality of how writing and speaking are used in the class: they are interwoven, continually reinforcing one another in what might be called a unified "languaging" process. The writing is meant to be spoken and to be spoken about; the talk leads to writing and further talk. Note also that the communication is multidirectional: student to student, student to group, teacher to student, student to teacher, group to teacher, and so on. The languaging process here gives each person many roles within the classroom community and helps to bind it together. It also frees the teacher from having to dominate the classroom. Moreover, the complex interaction creates its own rules and, to a great extent, its own discipline. Recall that, although the voice level was high during the small-group phase, it was not so high as to interfere with any of the small groups.

By relying so much on small- and large-group talk, and by having students perform so often, Tom Watson achieves two learning essentials: (1) children identify themselves with what they are learning; and (2) important ideas get talked about and played with in many different ways. Consider, for example, the idea of the "Renaissance spirit." Another teacher might have culled a textbook definition and required students to memorize it for a test. The students would have no stake in the definition, and its terms would remain personally meaningless. However, by the time Watson asks students to suggest defining adjectives, they have already begun to define the Renaissance by having defined *themselves* through actual men and women of the time. Thus, the thirty or more adjectives that they suggest in the brainstorming session emerge from a rich store of their own experiences and reflections. When the teacher asks them to go the next mile—to synthesize the list down to three terms—they must use both their perceptions and those of classmates to achieve an idea that has meaning for the entire group. In short, they are doing history as professional historians and social philosophers do. Not only are they building up their treasuries of facts, they are developing complex modes of thought as well.

The interactions through talk and writing also give them a much better method of *testing* their knowledge than do usual school devices. The classroom give-and-take allows them easily to distinguish between a fact ("*Did* Galileo discover Uranus with his telescope?") and an opinion ("Give me an adjective that defines the Renaissance mind.")—a distinction that no fill-in-the-blank or multiple-choice tests can ever show. The methods used in this scene also give the student *instant* feedback, and of a most affecting kind. When Melody tells Jeff that he has forgotten to put a date on his Galileo diary, Jeff goes immediately to the classroom encyclopedia to check the facts. With the rest of the small group looking over his shoulder and chatting about the dates, Jeff discovers not only a suitable year, 1597, but also other facts about the mathematician/scientist that he will later incorporate into his dialogue.

More Ideas

Writing and speaking to learn can be explored in the elementary classroom in innumerable ways. Here are a few suggestions, all of which include large- and small-group interactions and performance. None requires purchasing expensive materials.

> The *Roman Times* and the *Knightly News*. Small committees can make history come alive by designing their own one-page, "pasteup" newspapers on butcher paper or posterboard. Committee members research and write news, sports, and feature pieces. Projects are presented in class, then displayed.

> At the town meeting. The class becomes a hypothetical town, with a mayor and council (perhaps elected after candidates give campaign speeches). Small groups of "townspeople" meet to prepare "budget requests" on behalf of special interests—the public library, the hospital, a new shopping mall. These are researched, drafted, revised after group consultation, and presented at a town meeting. The council votes on percentages of budget for each interest. The class discusses process.

> Great scientist's notebook. Each student takes on the role of a famous (or fictitious) scientist noted for his or her "great powers of observation." An unfamiliar object is brought in for each person to observe and describe (for "the Royal Society" perhaps). Each tries to name the object. Then, in small groups, the descriptions are read and compared; each person takes notes on the other descriptions. The project can continue indefinitely, with each scientist adding more observations of phenomena and presenting them to his or her small scientific society. Contributions from each group may be mounted and displayed.

"If a kid has twenty baseball cards and loses five . . ." Students can learn math principles and can write for outside audiences by creating booklets of verbal math problems for children in lower grades. This can be a class project, with small groups responsible for writing, discussion, and revising the problems. This project can be done from grade to grade throughout the school, with each "lower" grade writing "thank-you" letters to the grade above. A variation on this theme is:

Let's go metric. Here the class writes a guide for parents on converting to the metric system. Small groups can be assigned to explain various conversions: temperatures, measures, liquid weights, volumes. Other topics might include "Why Go Metric?" and "The History of Our Measuring Systems." This project could conclude with a metric fair, at which each group reports to parents, perhaps using charts and other displays.

Suggested Reading

Burgess, Tony, ed. *Understanding Children Writing*. Harmondsworth, England: Penguin, 1972; available in U.S. through Boynton/Cook.

Graves, Donald. *Writing: Teachers and Children at Work*. Exeter, N.H.: Heinemann, 1983.

Judy, Stephen N. *The ABC's of Literacy*. New York: Oxford University Press, 1980.

Martin, Nancy, et al., eds. *Understanding Children Talking*. Harmondsworth, England: Penguin, 1976.

Rubin, Donald, and Kantor, Kenneth. *Talking and Writing: Building Communication Competence*. Washington, D.C.: Basic Skills Improvement Program, U.S. Department of Education, 1983. (See chapter in this volume.)

Writing and Speaking to Learn in High School Science

One of Rich Gottfried's most successful assignments divides his earth science classes into "geological teams" employed by rival oil companies. Each group of four is given some geological survey maps, a hypothetical budget, and a challenge: "The chairman of the board wants you to decide if the company should drill for oil in this territory; if so, he wants to know where the wells should be and how deeply they'll have to be dug. Since this project will make or lose billions, you'd better be sure your conclusions are well supported. Your jobs are on the line."

Because the groups are working from data just as ambiguous as those facing actual field teams, this project is more than a test of whether students have assimilated textbook chapters and lecture notes. They must choose between viable alternatives, perhaps go out on a shaky limb. The group members must cooperate. Each group assigns smaller jobs according to the strengths of each person. One evaluates the topography, another the different strata of rocks, still another assesses the costs of drilling and production versus the expected oil supply. Sometimes, surprising jobs are created by a group. Once, Gottfried observed a student moving from group to group during a fifty-minute skull session. When Rich asked what he was doing, the student replied, "My company hired me as an industrial spy."

During the several days devoted to group meetings, Gottfried visits each team. Since the group reports will ultimately come to him as "chairman of the board," students take this opportunity to try their preliminary reports out on him. He responds with questions that they still need to answer, and comments on data not clearly explained.

When the final reports come in two weeks after the initial assignment, he evaluates them for thoroughness, accuracy, clarity, and strength of reasoning. Since there are no right answers, just plausible ones, no group can succeed in this project without having conscientiously weighed information and without having argued well. Besides Gottfried, the entire class assesses the reports.

When students in Gottfried's classes are tested, they write single-paragraph and multiparagraph responses, rather than fill in blanks or check printed choices. "After a two- or three-week unit, I might give a topic like, 'Write everything you know about rocks'; certainly, I'm looking for a good deal of information in their answers, but I think that even more, I'm hoping that the exercise will let them put the data into patterns, make connections between details. Also, I'm not looking for particular facts—you know, 'a, b, and c must be there'—students who write fewer details, but show a real grasp of how those connect, are just as successful as those who've memorized more data."

Gottfried also gives questions that demand a synthesis of different blocks of data: "I like comparative questions, such as, 'How are the properties of the halogens and the alkalines similar and dissimilar?' or 'Show the relationships among the contributions of four of the scientists we've studied.'"

In every writing students submit, he demands that they write in complete sentences. He complains that mere lists of data, which are acceptable in many science courses, encourage students to ignore the relationships between facts. "Writing sentences makes us think about the meaning of our observations. It's hard work. Students gripe about it at first, but once they see that they can do it—and how much it teaches them—they get to like it." On the other hand, he does not discourage them from lists or any other comfortable method for generating ideas on early drafts. "We talk from time to time about the problems people have getting started writing answers or labs. I draw a distinction between the writing people do to get their data and ideas onto paper and the writing they hand in."

As one would expect, Gottfried's lab reports differ from those in other classes, too. His students write what he terms "descriptive essays" (what theorists call "generalizations supported by instances"). Says Gottfried, "The traditional lab report includes statements of purpose, procedure, data, analysis, and conclusion. This would seem to ask the experimenter to achieve a synthesis based on data and then to organize the data to prove or disprove the hypothesis. But, in school practice, most of the analysis usually consists of math calculations, and the conclusion just restates the purpose. So, I tell my students that their conclusions have to *begin* with a thesis statement—the point the experiment has made—and then must go on to show how the data they've recorded supports the thesis."

To prepare classes for this format, he spends class time early in the year showing students how to come to a thesis based on experimental data. Students also practice the essay form. During the semester, he invites questions in class as students seek to learn the form. Much of his after-class conference time is devoted to helping individuals generate theses and organize data.

Does Gottfried sometimes feel that he is doing the English teacher's job by spending so much time on how students write? "Not really," he says. "I'm trying to help them learn science—and like it. They believe me when I say that 'doing science' is learning how to observe, how to make sense of the data, and how to express themselves. Even though many of the facts won't stay with them long after the course, they'll learn the important skills and be able to use them, no matter what fields they go into. So often, students leave science courses feeling that chemistry or physics or biology has nothing for them. I'm trying to change that view."

Analysis

Writing to learn is nothing new in training scientists, though it is rare in the secondary school classroom. Teaching scientists, many of whom might ask students to write only short, informational answers on tests—if they assign any writing at all—will speak fondly of the journals or logs that they kept in college and graduate school. Indeed, though much of the history of science is traced through the personal, speculative writings of such giants as Einstein (French, 1979), researchers have found that only a tiny fraction of the writing done by U.S. science students at the secondary level is in this form (Applebee, 1981).

Speech, of course, is also largely neglected in the secondary school science curriculum, where the usual student role is silent note-scribbler. The partner system within many labs does promote the functional use of spoken language, but, again, research—primarily British—has found that talk does not further scientific thinking as long as students are doing the imitative, unoriginal "experiments" of most high school and college freshman courses (Martin et al., 1977).

The same research has suggested that both talk and writing become powerful learning tools when the reigning idea of science within a given classroom is of a dynamic, venturesome, passionate human activity in which initiative and uniqueness are rewarded. In such projects as the "oil company drilling report," Rich Gottfried defines science as an exacting process of knowing—available to everyone—rather than as a text full of static "facts." The talk within Gottfried's groups sparks original solutions, reactions, and syntheses; this talk informs the writing, which in turn informs the talk. Gottfried's attitude toward lab reports—"I give more credit to a careful argument supporting the wrong results than to a hasty argument supporting the right ones"—also pushes the student to think, not parrot. A research atmosphere is created: the student whose solution fails to precipitate or whose culture fails to grow is free to consider carefully *why* the experiment turned out that way; he or she does not fudge data to pretend that everything went "perfectly."

As Stephen Judy (1980) has stated, "The science teacher need not know a great deal about English to teach science writing and reading." Nor does he or she need a background in speech theory to use talk profitably in the classroom. Gottfried's techniques come primarily out of his experience as a scientist and through years of teaching. He teaches them to other teachers through seminars. By the same token, these techniques and others are not so esoteric to professional scientists that they cannot be applied to any course in any discipline. Gottfried's point is that students emerge from his courses with skills that they can use anywhere.

In a way, Gottfried, and others like him, are doing what some might still call the English teacher's job only: they teach students to become better writers and speakers (and readers and listeners). The students develop these abilities because Gottfried, like the best elementary teachers, makes language modes indispensable to the student's learning. Students write and speak well because their desire is so strong both to understand and communicate.

More Ideas

The Think Book (developed by Anne Miller Wotring). Besides, or in lieu of, taking notes, students keep a regular journal in which they record observations, synthesize data, discover problems in understanding ideas, and try to solve them. Like the professional scientist's log, the think book teaches students to write for themselves. The book works best when the teacher encourages students to bring to class questions that have been sparked by the writing. These questions form the basis for conferences or class discussions. Teachers who have used this device report that student questions are more precise (thus more easily answered), and the entries in the book allow the teacher to see how the student has arrived at his or her quandary.

Thought experiments. These are based on Einstein's "gedankenexperimenten," which he credited for his, or any other scientist's, ability to do original research. The goal of these creative exercises is to have students attempt to explain phenomena in original ways, even if they at first seem implausible. Einstein felt that without such exercises his imagination could not have been agile enough to have conceived an alternative to Newtonian physics.

Thought experiments can be introduced to classes in innumerable ways. For example, before earth science students have been introduced to storms, the teacher might begin a class with the question, "What is hail and what causes it?" The teacher might then ask students to speculate an answer in writing, assuring them that this is a brainstorming session—all answers are acceptable. When everyone has written, each person (or several volunteers) reads the speculations aloud; the class compares alternatives in open discussion. This experiment engages the minds of students in the topic and gives each person a paradigm against which to test the data and concepts to be presented in the assigned reading.

Mental exercises. Another excellent way to stimulate this engaged flexibility is to do with students some of the mental gymnastics detailed by William Gordon's *The Metaphorical Way of Knowing* (1966) or Robert Ornstein's *The Psychology of Consciousness* (1972). In addition to mental exercises, Ornstein includes simple optical experiments which help to teach students how the brain processes information and controls attention.

Suggested Reading

Applebee, Arthur. *Writing in the Secondary School: English and the Content Areas.* Urbana, Ill.: National Council of Teachers of English, 1981.

French, A. P. *Einstein: A Centenary Volume.* Cambridge, Mass.: Harvard University Press, 1979.

Gordon, William. *The Metaphorical Way of Knowing.* New York: Harper and Row, 1966.

Gray, Philip. *Oral Communication Instruction in Middle and High School Classes.* Washington, D.C.: Basic Skills Improvement Program, U.S. Department of Education, 1983.

Judy, Stephen N. *The ABC's of Literacy.* New York: Oxford University Press, 1980.

Martin, Nancy C., et al. *Writing and Learning Across the Curriculum 11-16.* London: Ward Lock Educational, 1977.

Moffett, James. *Active Voice: A Writing Program Across the Curriculum.* Montclair, N.J.: Boynton/Cook Publishers, 1981.

Ornstein, Robert. *The Psychology of Consciousness.* (1972) Harmondsworth, England: Penguin Books, 1977, paperback edition.

Wotring, Anne Miller. *Writing to Think in Chemistry.* Fairfax, Va.: The Northern Virginia Writing Project, 1980. See also Wotring and Robert Tierney, *Writing to Learn in High School Science.* Berkeley, Calif.: Bay Area Writing Project, 1982.

Writing and Speaking to Learn in Mathematics

Observations: Geometry I, 8:45 a.m.

The class has just ended, and Ralph Smith has asked me if I want to review students' writing. So, while he teaches General Math, I sit at a table in the conference area and read. Nearby, a counselor lectures to a sleepy-looking bunch of juniors about taking the SAT.

Smith has asked his kids, mostly freshmen, to write during the last twelve minutes of class about their feelings—anything. The students expect him to read at least some of the pieces to the class the next day, because one note said, "Read aloud!" and several said, "Please don't read to the class."

I am impressed by their honesty—and ability to write. Few spelling errors, no clumsy sentences—obviously they are at ease with the assignment. What do they write about? Boyfriends, girlfriends, friends; but mostly, they write about why they do not want to take the test tomorrow— why it is unfair. Others write: "I'm tired," "I'm confused," "I'm in a daze," "I want to go home"—responding to the malaise of winter, end-of-quarter exams, and frequent snow delays. A few were very deeply unhappy. One said that she was unprepared, would get a low grade, and, consequently, suffer "child abuse" from her mother. She wanted this read to the class. One person said, "I find geometry keen, cool, refreshing."

9:30 a.m.

Smith says that he will ask for a more focused writing in the 9:45 Computer Science I class—mostly eleventh- and twelfth-graders. He wants them to relate their feelings about the subject, rather than about "anything and everything." He says that the mood in this class has been upbeat, not so overcome by weather and school pressures. Smith wants the writing to tell him about particular problems that they have with the material, which is much tougher than most of them expect. He adds that during the semester they have had practice with both types of personal writing.

9:45 a.m.

Students enter the classroom, alone, in pairs, and chatting. Some enter from the adjoining computer room, where they have already been working on the latest programs, or kibitzing while others program. In the few minutes before class officially begins, two or three ask the teacher to look over their program drafts; a few revisions are made.

The chatter ebbs when Smith begins talking about the next day's oral reports. Each student (some work in groups of two or three) will describe his or her latest computer project: how he or she has designed the program, what programming problems have been discovered. Though the class has known about the reports for several weeks, and most are prepared, the reminder is met with a few grumbles and several expressionless nods. Evidently, the mood takes Smith somewhat by surprise. The personal writing assignment that he gives the class next is quite similar to the open-ended one that he assigned earlier:

> I'd like us to relax for a few minutes and collect our thoughts.... When you feel you're ready, do some writing . . . about anything that's on your mind . . . something that's bothering you . . . something you feel good about. Then, if we have time, I'll read some to the class. (One student says, "Yes, read them!") Now some of you will say, "Wait a minute now—I don't want this read." I respect that. We'll read them aloud, unless you don't want to.

The class responds immediately. Some begin to write, one group of three decides to write together (smiling conspiratorially), others talk. Eventually, all are writing, glancing around for inspiration, writing again. One person looks up: "What if I don't have anything to write?" "Just write that down," says Smith. "Just say you don't."

One girl, head close to the paper, just writes and writes. Some finish, hand their papers to the teacher, then drift off to the computer room for a few minutes until all are done.

Smith reads each writing to the class. He carefully avoids those marked "Please don't read." The concerns of these somewhat older students differ from those of the earlier class:

> Dear Mr. Smith,
> The class is going fine. Only we need more time on the computer. We can't debug our programs.

Physics is giving me an ulcer and I'm frustrated about this class, but I was accepted to Tech yesterday. Now if only I'd hear from UVA!

Computer science really boggles my mind at times. Before I took this course I was considering going into a career involving computers—but now I'm not sure!

Three (the conspirators?) say, "Forget the reports—let's party!" Another quips, "There's $100 in it for you if you give me an 'A' for this quarter." (Laughter occurs when this is read.) And one, which draws bigger laughs, waxes proverbial:

Everytime I think I see the light at the end of the tunnel, it turns out to be an oncoming train. In the dog race of life I sometimes feel like a fire hydrant.

LYNCH'S LAW: When the going gets tough, everyone leaves.

During the rest of the period, teams of students take turns on the two computer terminals. Those groups waiting look over their programs, trying to "debug" (revise) them before testing them out on the machine. Some students remain in the classroom, working on programs or the upcoming reports. The teacher circulates, responding to requests for assistance.

One pair, at a terminal, puts in the program for an original battleship game. While Theresa works the keyboard, John watches for errors. When the machine rejects a command, they discuss how to revise the program. They ask for help from a nearby student; soon the program is clicking again. I glance at the pages still to be fed in. There must be at least five pages of closely written instructions, all numbers, letters, and punctuation. I ask John, "How long have you two been studying computers?" "Four months," he says. I'm dazzled. "How have you learned so much?" "Oh," he laughs, "I don't know anything!"

Analysis

"That's right," Smith says later. "Most of them will work hard for several months, learn a tremendous amount, and still not see any progress. That's one of the reasons I started having them do personal writing. I needed a way to know when they were feeling things like that, and I decided that maybe they'd put on paper—confidentially—what they might not *say* to me. And that's what's happened. When they write about their struggle with the subject—and these math courses are hard—I make it a point to boost them, show them how far they've come."

"But the writings are anonymous," I say. "Do they want you to respond?"

"That's interesting. I do keep the assignment anonymous, and to them that means I respect their privacy. But I know pretty much who's written what, and they know that I know. So, yes, they do appreciate the response."

"When did you start using the writings?"

"It was three years ago, in a geometry class. We'd had a test, and most of the students had done poorly. The day I told them the results, the tension was thicker in that room than in any other class I could remember. So I hit on the idea of the in-class writing as a fairly painless way in which they could express their frustrations about the course, the math, or my teaching.

"In fact, one of the students in this class today was there then. She was, and still is to some extent, one who would rarely speak in class or bring me a problem. But when I started asking for the writing, she opened up on the page, and still does." (This was the same student I'd seen writing so avidly before.)

"What was the result of the writing in that class?"

"Well, besides improving communication between them and me, I could see that after a while, it definitely improved the atmosphere. The writing seemed to relax the class, to make them more ready to do geometry. I guess you could say it removed a block to their learning."

"Have you changed the assignment since then?"

"I don't think I read the pieces aloud at first. But I started soon thereafter —you can see how much they like it. Some of the students write for the whole group—'Let's party,' for example—because they really want to lift everyone's spirits, lighten the mood. But I think that everyone wants to *hear* what's been written, because they really need the assurance that others are feeling what they're feeling. This is a pretty lonely time for many of them."

"Have you tried any other variations of personal writing—learning journals, for example?"

"I haven't yet, but I'm planning to, next semester. I think that regular entries in a journal would be an even better way of showing students that they come a long way in a semester, even in a day, sometimes. It would also keep me in pretty constant touch with the specific problems they're having with the material."

"How often do you have the students do the personal writing now?"

"I've been doing it about once a week, usually on Fridays. We spend about twenty minutes of the period, but its usefulness is much greater than the time spent. You can tell how good it is for the class just by observing the mood. For me, well, it's helped bring me closer to the students, to an understanding of what they *don't* understand, so in that way I'm a better teacher."

Analysis II

According to the comprehensive study by Applebee (1981), personal, expressive writing in secondary math classes is rare in this country. Nevertheless, its value is acclaimed not only by practitioners such as Ralph Smith, but also by researchers (e.g., Britton, 1970, and Emig, 1971) who see this type of writing as absolutely essential to the growth of language and learning.

Equally rare, but equally noteworthy, is the kind of oral interaction that attends this writing. That Smith reads the writings to the class influences *what* and *how* many of the students write. The students who worked together on "Let's party"—and the girl who wanted Smith to read about child abuse—were striving for an effect much different from, though just as important as, the goal being sought by those who wrote, "Please don't read aloud." Moreover, Smith encourages this dramatic use of the writing by allowing time for laughter or chatter that follows his reading of individual pieces. These interactions help achieve one of Smith's (and the class's) main goals: recreating a positive, cohesive spirit.

Without giving undue credit to Smith's handling of the personal writing, one can observe how this spirit pervades other activities of the computer science class. The mood is relaxed, respectful, full of purpose. No one resents anyone's time on the (only) two terminals, or feels imposed on by kibitzers or by a request for assistance from another group. I felt completely at ease, with several students asking me about my research—and being keenly interested in what I said—just as I talked with several of them about their programs.

More Ideas

Response, revision, and editing groups. Just as these have been boosts to learning in writing, social studies, and science classes, so can they be in mathematics, whenever creative problem solving is required. Such groups, well described by Hawkins (1976) and Elbow (1973, 1981), benefit the individual by providing multiple, constructive views on his or her work. These groups can reinforce the idea that math is a creative tool because the group process emphasizes the different methods by which problems may be solved, rather than the errors in a particular technique.

Two-step in-class response (Paik, 1981). When a difficult concept is being introduced (e.g., standard deviation in statistics), the teacher begins by asking the students to solve a practical problem that requires knowledge of the concept (e.g., "Is it valid for a cereal company to say, 'This box contains 10 percent more raisins'?"). After students attempt to solve the problem based on their prior knowledge, the teacher explains the concept and solves the problem. *Then,* the students write once more, *explaining the concept in their own words and why it has solved the problem.* If students discover that difficulty remains, they ask questions in class, encouraged by the teacher.

Suggested Reading

Britton, James. *Language and Learning.* Harmondsworth, England: Pelican Books, 1970.
Elbow, Peter. *Writing Without Teachers.* New York: Oxford University Press, 1973.
Elbow, Peter. *Writing With Power.* New York: Oxford University Press, 1981.
Emig, Janet. *The Composing Process of Twelfth Graders* (Research Report No. 13). Urbana, Ill.: National Council of Teachers of English, 1971.
Hawkins, Thom. *Group Inquiry Techniques for Teaching Writing.* Urbana, Ill.: ERIC Clearinghouse on Reading and Communication Skills and the National Council of Teachers of English, 1976.
King, Barbara. "Using Writing in the Mathematics Class: Theory and Practice." In *Teaching Writing in the Disciplines.* No. 12 in New Directions for Teaching and Learning. San Francisco: Jossey-Bass, 1982.
Paik, Minja K. "Writing to Learn in Statistics." In *Writing to Learn: Essays and Reflections on Writing Across the Curriculum.* Dubuque, Iowa: Kendall/Hunt, 1983.

Writing and Speaking to Learn in Social Studies

Gail's Log (December 10, 1981):

Today's class was confusing! Jerry and Mrs. Yalen role-played about a partner and another kid whispering over the partner's third interim. The partner was very scared of facing his parents with all the interims, so he wanted his friend to forge the signatures at lunch. You, as the labber student counselor, overhear the conversation and know that something must be done. Thinking to myself (when Mrs. Y and Jerry asked how we would have handled it) I would have come right out and said, "Now, Billy (or whoever), do you really think that's honest? Your parents are probably very concerned as to how you're doing in school." It turned out that when they asked Martha to role-play as the labber giving her thoughts to the partner, she started out a totally different way. Not even letting her partner know that she overheard the whispering. Am I wrong? Gosh, I'm getting so confused! I'm taking this lab program like it's right from a book—telling you exactly what to do without experiencing and learning from action. I *know* I have to let these things work out and develop a technique.

At Lake Braddock (Va.) Secondary School, teachers Tina Yalen and Alice Marsala have given behavioral science students the chance to learn not only from books, but also through action. Every year for the past seven, each of the 140 students in the ten-month introductory course has spent December to June working in one of three unique programs that develop courage and creativity by challenging both.

One program, the largest, is class-based. A typical project for these students is "Adolescent Issues: Course Design," in which groups of four devote two weeks to planning, evaluating, and revising a hypothetical new junior/senior course in behavioral science. Consulting frequently with the instructor, each group prepares drafts and a "finished product" that includes:

> an organized, structured outline of some form, revealing the syllabus content, in sequence and with lengths of units clearly indicated ... each unit should have its issues clearly stated. ...

> a detailed description of five lessons for any of the units ... the objective and the process for each lesson should be clear. ...

Another project uses the novel, *The Catcher in the Rye*. The class discusses the question, "Is this novel accurate to adolescent experience?" Yalen and Marsala challenge the students to justify their assertions by comparing Holden Caulfield's words and views to their own. Sometimes the topic produces unforeseen results: this year, the class has become so incensed over the inaccuracies of a filmstrip based on the novel that they have decided to produce their own for future classes. Parts in the "play" have been assigned, a script is being written, and scenes "on location" in Washington, D.C., are being chosen.

The second of the three programs, one for which students are carefully selected and trained, takes them off campus four mornings a week to work with the handicapped at the nearby Northern Virginia Training Center. Marsala heads this program, which also includes a biweekly seminar at which the students discuss their work and its attendant joys and problems. Biweekly, Marsala responds to the copious journals the students keep to describe and reflect.

The third program, like the second in that care is taken to choose and train participants, sends twenty-four students into seventh- and eighth-grade classes as "partners" of individual boys and girls. Yalen, who directs this phase of behavioral science, coordinates the pairing with classroom teachers who have identified students who could profit from, and are receptive to, a "Big Sister or Brother" relationship with an older student. For four mornings a week, one period per day, each "labber" (student participating in this program) attends class with his or her partner. For a few minutes before and after class, the pair converses about the younger student's schoolwork, which is usually suffering because of problems within school and out. The program has lasted seven years because the older students have succeeded in raising the confidence—and often the grades —of their younger partners. Moreover, the students gain tremendous insight into themselves and those that they work with—far more than they could gain in a conventional course.

Crucial to the success of this third program is the month of training which precedes it. Yalen and guidance counselor Jerry Newberry lead each of two groups of twelve in various role-playing exercises (such as that reported by Gail in her log that began this section). They also lead seminar discussions of typical situations the labbers will face. During training, students begin four-day-a-week logs, one key to their leaps in insight *and* their best means of keeping in contact with Yalen during the ensuing four months. Some training time is spent talking about how to keep a log. One instruction that always stays with the students is Yalen's warning to avoid "glop": sentences like, "It was okay," or "He's nice," that hinder careful analysis.

Every two weeks throughout the program, Yalen comments on the logs in writing, briefly and positively, entry by entry: "Don't be so hard on yourself! You're making progress"; "I feel the same way myself"; "That's quite a breakthrough! How's she doing in science?" Augmenting this written dialogue are the biweekly one-hour seminars which give the labbers a chance to compare notes and solve common problems. Kelly writes about one of these—and much more—in a log entry:

> Today we had only 20 minutes to work with. I love these meetings because I like to hear how everyone else is doing with their partners. David sounds like he has it made in the shade—he should be very proud of himself as well as his kid! When Jerry asked if anyone was bored, saying someone must be, I spoke up. Wow, whenever I talk out in the open about Lana, I always say "she never talks." Why do I say that? It's not really true—Lana does have her days when she seems really comfortable and more open to talk. Why do I expect so much? I seem to be waiting for her to make the move to "let out her guts to me." Since Lana is a rather quiet girl (LIKE ME WHEN I WAS HER AGE), she is obviously not gonna start the talking! Kelly, it's your job to start things off and get her talking a bit. Part of the key to do that is to open up your feelings—showing her you trust her.

By June, every student has recorded more than 100 descriptive-introspective entries, received twelve sets of written comments, and taken part in more than twelve seminars—in addition to the four meetings per week with the partner. They are ready to undertake Yalen's final exam: a multipage, multifocused assessment of their work. More than a test, this last, take-home project is meant to synthesize months of experience, to define the great growth that has occurred:

A. Identify the physical, mental, emotional, and social characteristics of an early adolescent, based on your observations. . . .

B. . . . describe your responses, feelings, attitudes, and behavior as it relates to being with young adolescents. . . .

C. . . . discuss any evidence of change in *yourself* since lab began. . . .

D. . . . discuss any evidence of change in your lab partner. . . .

E. Describe your accomplishments. Be a good lawyer in your own defense.

F. Describe your disappointments and/or failures . . . in yourself . . . in your partner . . . in your situation. . . .

G. From among several "critical or crucial" days . . . select the one which may well have been the turning point in the relationship and discuss why it was so crucial. . . .

H. Compare/contrast the first 2-3 weeks with the last 2-3 weeks.

Elizabeth, a participant in 1980-81, summarized her experience in part H of her exam:

> The first two weeks and the last two weeks of Lab are so different, it's difficult to believe there's only five months difference between the two. The first two weeks I was extremely paranoid about wanting to be the perfect Labber. My biggest concerns were Tom's grades and what I was supposed to talk about. I had my teacher and mother records on all the time. I also had some serious doubts about whether I was doing the right thing. I expected miracles, and fast miracles at that. And I was devastated by every little disappointment.
>
> The last two weeks of Lab, I was mainly concerned with strengthening our friendship and using every second of our final days in a constructive way. I quit worrying about his schoolwork and put all my attention and concern on Tom, the person. Instead of wondering what to say, I wondered how I was going to say everything in two weeks. All doubts were gone, only the fear of Lab ending. There was no time left for miracles, just friendship, and love, and communication. I left the disappointments, such as bad grades, behind, and grabbed at every bit of encouragement Tom gave me. And in the end it all paid off. I started out doubtful and fearful, and ended up confident, ecstatic, and fulfilled.

Analysis

Within the high school, Yalen's, Marsala's, and Newberry's programs are as close to being a "functional communication program" as an actual curriculum can be. Besides meeting many literacy objectives in all four language modes, the program does them all with no artificiality. Certainly, the training period, with its discussion, role-plays, and active listening exercises, contains nothing that the labbers do not need. Yalen has revised it over the seven years to eliminate from this all-too-short period anything not absolutely essential. The logs, too, are entirely functional: the students need them to keep records, to communicate with the teacher, and perhaps most importantly, to maintain detachment from their emotions. Yalen needs to comment on the logs for similar reasons—communication, emotional support, and her own objectivity.

The oral exchange within the seminar is also crucial. Kelly's entry (quoted previously), asserts this; my own participation in one of the seminars has reinforced the conviction. On the day that I sat in, we talked about how the students kept logs and how they had learned from them. What impressed me most about the talk within the circle was how each response acknowledged what the previous speaker had said. The seminar was obviously one of those rare situations in which ideas were carefully tested *and* everyone's self-esteem was protected.

Just as noteworthy for its functional communicating is the in-class program. Aware that these students might perceive themselves as "rejects" from the two more glamorous programs, Yalen and Marsala have established the class as a lab in its own right. Its purpose is to help teachers redefine behavioral science, as subject and course, for future students. Such interactive projects as "Adolescent Issues: Course Design" and the filmstrip, "The Catcher in the Rye," contribute to meeting this goal. At the same time, the students become more aware of their personalities and actions, as these projects expose them to a wide range of human behavior patterns.

More Ideas

Teachers inspired to assign logs, such as those used by Yalen and Marsala, might adapt the conditions which the students with whom I talked defined as best for getting the most out of the writing:

> Logs work best when kept frequently, at least every other day; from the logs I read, I noted that when days were missed, the students felt the loss.

> Most students write best after school, having put time and space between themselves and the events that they write about.

Students write best when relaxed—whenever that time is for each person. "Relaxed" means "not thinking about how you write." The opposite of relaxed is "schooly," which means "worried about things like topic sentences and semicolons." These factors, agreed the students, hinder memory and the ability to analyze.

Suggested Reading

On Functional Communication:

Allen, Ronald, and Kellner, Robert. *Putting Humpty Dumpty Together Again: Integrating the Language Arts.* Washington, D.C.: Basic Skills Improvement Program, U.S. Department of Education, 1983. (See chapter in this volume.)

Cooper, Pamela, and Galvin, Kathleen. *Improving Classroom Communication.* Washington, D.C.: Basic Skills Improvement Program, U.S. Department of Education, 1983.

On Responding to Ideas in Student Journals:

Staton, Jana. *Thinking Together: Language Interaction in Children's Reasoning.* Washington, D.C.: Basic Skills Improvement Program, U.S. Department of Education, 1983. (See chapter in this volume.)

On Writing in the Social Sciences:

Thaiss, Christopher J., ed. *Writing to Learn: Essays and Reflections on Writing Across the Curriculum.* Dubuque, Iowa: Kendall/Hunt, 1983.

Stopping Place (Not a Conclusion)

This collection of scenes and opinions, and dialogues and suggestions has run out of room; we leave off here, but do not conclude. We hope that as you have read, you have been saying to yourself, "They (the authors) need to know about [a project] or teachers (or parents) as inventive and sensible as these." Please see this chapter as an introduction (or a further contribution) to the use of writing and speaking as tools of learning in the home and the school. There are teachers at every grade level in every part of the country who have discovered the values of writing and speaking to learn, and who realize these values in remarkably various ways—we have worked with some of these teachers. And, of course, there are hundreds of thousands of parents whose learning adventures with their children are as exciting as those described here.

The point of this chapter has not been to "cover the field." What we have tried to show—more than tell—is how easy, really how natural, it is for people to learn through writing and speaking. We have focused on five distinct environments in which this learning happens enjoyably and quite intensely. We merely suggest the range of environments in which it does happen, and the many more in which it could.

Talking and Writing: Building Communication Competence

Donald L. Rubin, University of Georgia

Kenneth J. Kantor, University of Georgia

This chapter focuses on the ordinary extraordinariness of children and young adults making meaning in speech and in writing, how it happens, and how we, as teachers, can encourage this communication development.

Toby, a tenth-grader, writes and speaks about jobs. Her teacher first asks her to "free-write" about an ideal occupation.

> An ideal job for me would be a career. I would be working in the morning to the late afternoon. I'm not sure yet of what type of work but I would want to be active. I would want to be moving around and doing interesting things. I would rather like to work with my hands than other people.

Later, Toby participates in a simulated job interview for a position at a pancake house. The interviewer is a volunteer parent. Before beginning the interview, Toby has filled out a job application form.

Interviewer: Now, it says here that you would like to work as a cashier. Any particular reason why?

Toby: Well, because when I would be working . . . Well, see, the reason I didn't say cook is because I don't know how to cook and I don't like to cook. And, ah, the reason I didn't say hostess is because I would be, you know, talking with people a lot and everything. And so I'd rather be a cashier, just doing something with my hands and figuring up and things like that.

Interviewer: Good. Ah, let me see. Now, you haven't had a job before, so why don't you tell me a little bit about yourself as a student.

Toby: You mean how I like school and stuff?

Interviewer: Yeah. That kind of thing.

Toby: Well, school is alright. I don't like school that much, though. But it's OK. I want to, you know, get as much education in as I can before I have to graduate. And then, there are some teachers that I like. I get along with most of my teachers. There's . . . there's only been a few that I haven't liked.

At first glance, Toby's language seems quite unremarkable. Since many of us are trained in a pathology model of education (we are the knowledge doctors, and students and patients come to us with conditions which we must remediate), we notice certain weaknesses first. The last sentence of Toby's free-writing is ambiguous. Does she prefer working with her hands more than working with other people, or is she more partial to manual work than other people are? Her first response in the interview begins with a false start, and vacuous expressions like "you know" and "things like that" appear throughout the speech sample.

But observe, instead, Toby's strengths. In both passages, she shows an ability to use language conditionally, objectify her feelings, and examine them from a number of angles without rushing to an overly simple conclusion. "I'm not sure yet what type of work," she writes. She explains to the interviewer that she recognizes both good and bad aspects of school. Toby can do this because her speech and writing permit her to generalize from feelings and experiences. The power of abstraction enables Toby to put thoughts into perspective.

Toby also shows an ability to organize written and oral discourse so as to develop and modify statements. To be sure, there are points that need clarifying. The concept of "career" apparently has some special meaning for her which she fails to reveal to her readers. But Toby does explain what she means by "active" work in the two final sentences of the free-writing. In the interview, Toby's false start seems to reflect a change in course. She has discovered a better way to organize her reasoning. What follows is a process of eliminating the more undesirable job options, leaving Toby with a choice that she can tolerate. Similarly, Toby demonstrates that she can use a variety of stylistic devices to contrast and qualify. Notice the counter-point of her final reply in the interview: ". . . alright . . . though . . . but . . . there are some . . . most . . . only been a few . . ."

By using these logical devices and by elaborating meanings, Toby shows regard for the needs of her audiences. She is aware that writing and speaking are social transactions. Even her free-writing, for which Toby, herself, was the primary audience, follows the conventions of legibility and standard usage which aid readers. Furthermore, Toby indicates through her request for clarification in the interview that she is an active listener. She is trying to understand the interviewer's viewpoint so that she can respond appro-priately.

In short, Toby shows in these two brief passages that she is indeed a sophisticated communicator. In speaking and writing, she can transform her experiences and feelings so that they can be examined and understood. She uses her communication resources to unpack and modify her meanings. And she takes into account the needs and characteristics of her audiences.

Communication competence has no end point. It is a matter of lifelong development toward increasingly effective expression and understanding. Surely, Toby can refine her speaking and writing skills in a number of respects. And just as surely, her formal schooling has a vital role to play in fostering those skills. But that is not to detract from the fact that Toby, like all students, communicates in ways that should inspire respect from us, her teachers.

Characterizing Communication Competence

A student's spoken or written language can be described from a number of viewpoints. We could, for example, take a prescriptive approach and describe it as being either correct or incorrect. Thus, if a child says, "Chicago ain't the capital of Illinois, Springfield is where the capital is at," we might say this language is incorrect since it violates the prescriptive attitude. What is obviously ignored is that this child has successfully communicated accurate information. Another problem involves the issue of what standard should be used to judge correctness. Language is as much a growing, changing organism as is a human being. Many people use the word *ain't,* or end sentences with prepositions. Finally, there are some circumstances in which "correct" language simply does not work as well as more casual forms. In an auto repair shop, for example, you may risk your credibility if you ask, "To which contact is this wire supposed to lead?"

We acknowledge that a concern for linguistic propriety can be well motivated in the sense that "errors" often call attention to themselves, detract from the effect of a message on an audience, or convey a tone which a writer or speaker does not intend. The word *ain't,* for example, conveys meaning adequately. But it also waves a red flag for some listeners, signaling that the speaker may be unsophisticated or ignorant. By the same token, *ain't* signals solidarity and familiarity to other listeners. Speakers may wish to avoid *ain't* in some situations and use it in others. A focus on communication competence is not inconsistent with the responsibility to teach patterns of formal communication. But the framework of communication competence encourages teachers to judge messages according to their *effectiveness* in achieving writers' and speakers' purposes within specific situations. Instead of labeling a student's work as correct or incorrect, teachers note whether it is appropriate or inappropriate to the context.

The notion of *communication* competence can be better understood by contrasting it with *linguistic* competence. Linguists and psychologists claim that native speakers of a language possess rich knowledge about the structure of their language, knowledge that goes far beyond those speakers' abilities to articulate any principles of grammar or semantics. For example, one can understand, and even produce, sentences that have never before been uttered; determine when two sentences express the same meaning; and tell when a single sentence can be interpreted in two ways. To explain these kinds of insights about language, we view linguistic competence as a set of abstract mental rules of which we are not normally aware. Although factors like limited memory, aroused emotions, or limited vocabulary sometimes affect our performance, we are for the most part capable of applying these rules in producing and understanding an unlimited number of sentences.

Children acquire linguistic competence not as a result of any direct instruction, but simply because of innate capacities as humans. Parents do not reward children for linguistically well-formed sentences or punish them for incorrect ones. Instead, they praise children for the accuracy of their statements. When baby points to a picture and says, "That a armadillo," we do not respond, "No, Emmy, that *is an* armadillo." At the same time children do not merely imitate the language that they hear around them. Children regularly produce forms like "wented" and "tooked" which they have never heard from adults. These "errors" show that children are creating linguistic generalizations (rules). In these cases, they have overgeneralized regular verb endings to irregular verbs. Finally, children acquire linguistic competence at an age when their other intellectual abilities are not nearly as sophisticated. They enter public school already knowing virtually all the grammatical resources of their language.

This may be an impressive picture of linguistic competence, but it far underestimates our language abilities. Not only do we know about the structure of our language, but more importantly, we know a great deal about how to use our communication codes in real situations. The notion of communicative competence was first proposed by Dell Hymes, the anthropologist/folklorist/linguist/educator. In his monograph, *On Communicative Competence,* Hymes reminds us:

> We have to account for the fact that a normal child acquires knowledge of sentences, not only as grammatical, but also as appropriate. A child acquires a repertoire of speech acts, is able to take part in speech acts and to evaluate the speech acts of others. . . . The engagement of language in social life has a positive, productive aspect. There are rules of use without which the rules of grammar would be useless.

Teachers can readily help students see that they have internalized rules for language use by asking them to think of all the ways that they might address someone. Ask them also to think of situations in which they might use these terms. For example, "What would you call your boss if she was not much older than you and acted kind of chummy?" Or, "What would you call a friend of your father's you barely know?" One class developed a chart like this:

Terms of Address	Example	Situation
first name	Richard, Yolanda	casual, equals, not much age difference
nickname	Ricky, Beads	close friends, younger
cutesy name	Sweety Pie, Poochie	very close, much younger (baby)
Mr. + last name	Mr. Weitz	male, somewhat formal to very formal, he has authority over you
Miss + last name	Miss Farley	female, unmarried, somewhat formal to very formal, keeps distance between you, she has authority
Mrs. + last name	Mrs. Nitos	female, married, somewhat formal to very formal, she has authority
Ms. + last name	Ms. Frye	female, marriage status not important to her here, somewhat formal to very formal, she has authority

Ma'am	Yes, Ma'am	female, shows respect
Sir	Yes, Sir	male, shows respect
title + last name	Dr. Malcolm President Reagan	shows respect for position
last name alone	Jones, Devries	you have authority or power
family relation + first name	Aunt Esther	family, probably older or unfamiliar or family position is important to the person
nothing	Hey!	unsure of relationship, lack of respect

Although we do not often deliberate about what to call someone, we do operate according to a system much like this. As adults, for example, we become aware of the system mostly when we make a mistake ("Hello, Jacky." "That's *Dr.* Dintler if you please.") or when we face an ill-defined interpersonal situation. (What do you call your school principal when she is younger than you and you literally bump into each other at a disco?) Nor are these just matters of politeness and good manners. Relationships are defined in part through these terms of address. Can you remember what it meant the first time you called your father's friend by his first name?

Choosing the appropriate term of address shows sensitivity to the context in which we are speaking, its formality, and the characteristics and values of our listeners. We must be flexible in the sense that we need to control a wide range of terms of address. We must perform the communication act, actually utter the words, in an appropriate tone of voice. And we must be receptive to audience feedback to discover if the listener is offended or accepts the definition of our relationship that we have conveyed. Communication competence can be analyzed according to these very four principles: sensitivity, flexibility, performance, and feedback.

Sensitivity

To express themselves in appropriate ways, communicatively competent individuals must be sensitive to a number of situational features. With respect to the example of terms of address, I must sense whether my listener perceives me as an equal or a subordinate. I must recognize when I am in a setting that demands a particular form of address. For example, I may refer to my principal as "Ms. Lopez" in front of my students, but as "Phyllis" when she comes to my home for dinner. In general, situationally appropriate expression requires attention to six aspects of communicative context.

1. Medium of communication. Although both writing and speaking are forms of communication, written language is not the same as spoken language. Their similarities and differences are discussed later in this chapter. For now, we want to make it clear that just like speech, writing skill is part and parcel of communication competence, and conforms to the same basic principles of situational appropriateness. We can also regard in similar ways all the nonverbal media that accompany oral language—gestures, facial expressions, touch, how people arrange themselves spatially, voice tone and volume, and even our clothes.

2. Audience. In choosing what to call someone, we have shown that speakers are sensitive to listeners' age, status, degree of familiarity with the speaker, and so on. In this chapter, we are constantly trying to keep you, our reader, in mind. We must make guesses about what interests you, what experiences we can assume you have shared, and with what ideas you have already come into contact. Our job is especially difficult because we do not really have much information about you. So we attempt to create in our minds a representation of the audience. This process of mentally constructing one's audience is called "social perspective-taking." As we write, we try to view our message from your viewpoint.

   Effective communication is very much dependent on social perspective-taking. Imagine that you want to persuade your friend to go to a movie with you. He or she wants to stay home alone and read. Whatever you decide to say to him or her will depend on your knowledge of his or her attitudes and values. You might choose to capitalize on the individual's reading interest and say, "I hear the movie is pretty much true to the book. You said you liked that story, didn't you?" And you might add the universal appeal to thrift: "C'mon, it'll be my treat."

   We do not suggest that audience awareness or any other aspect of communication competence is necessarily deliberate; in fact, many of these decisions probably occur intuitively. Our sense of audience is often more a vague feeling that we acquire from many reading and listening experiences than a specific catalog of audience types. The means for coaxing a friend to go to a movie generally comes to us instinctively rather than by conscious design. At the same time, audience awareness is goal-directed, and even sometimes deliberately so, as we seek to achieve certain ends through our communication.

3. Function. That communication is purposeful is an obvious point, but we nevertheless lose sight of it often. For example, if we ask students to give an oral report about what they do in their spare time, or to

write a paper about summer vacations, we have really assigned them a very difficult task. They cannot begin to speak or write until they can create some purpose for their discourse. For example, a student might decide to relate an amusing incident, and thus entertain the reader. Another student might decide to write a persuasive paper to convince readers to use summer vacations in volunteer work. The two students will each draw on very different styles and strategies as a result of their differing purposes.

Much of what children learn during communication development pertains not only to the structure of language, but also to its uses. They learn, for example, that a sentence—"Do you know what time it is?"—functions as an order to go to bed, despite its question form. They learn how to get a turn in a conversation, and how to recognize the turn-taking demands of others. They learn to use "If . . . then" constructions to convince someone to act. They learn that if they want to describe an object to Grandpa over the telephone, they must use explicit language and avoid egocentric expressions such as, "It looks like that thing over there."

There is no one exhaustive list of communication functions. In fact, an interesting class exercise asks students to "Brainstorm all the things we can do with words." Most of us are familiar with the four traditional modes of discourse: narrating, describing, persuading, and explaining. The Speech Communication Association National Competencies Project, described in a series of booklets edited by Barbara Wood, lists five functions: expressing feelings, controlling others, imagining, describing, and performing social rituals. James Britton and his colleagues in the British Schools Council divide language functions into three categories: expressive, and branching from it, transactional, and poetic. Still another way of thinking about functions lists the numerous speech acts that we can perform just by using language: promising, pleading, betting, reporting, christening, theorizing, and so on.

4. Setting. Leaving the classroom at change of the periods, some students undergo a change as dramatic as Clark Kent's transformation to Superman. We wonder why we cannot coax two successive words from them in class discussion when we know that they are hallway talk-show celebrities. Physical and institutional settings noticeably affect our patterns of communication. We speak differently in the classroom than in the teachers' lounge, and differently again at home. We have distinct styles suitable for banks, for saloons, for professional meetings, and for places of worship. Conversations vary depending on whether we sit next to our partner on a couch, or face him or her

across a massive desk. Classroom talk also varies when seats are arranged in rows as opposed to a circle. Students write differently when they are required to sit in wooden desks for thirty minutes of uninterrupted writing compared to when they are permitted to move about with freer time limits.

5. Topic. Sportscasters have a special love affair with the English verb. Teams rarely "win" or "lose," they "vanquish," "pulverize," "mow down," "yield," "evaporate," or "wither." The subject of sports seems to engender this vivid vocabulary. Similarly, other kinds of topics affect communication style. A different tone is used to discuss current events than to describe great dining experiences. We talk about family differently than we talk about movie stars. In some bilingual communities, one language may be used to speak about school and another to speak about home.

6. Discourse process. Finally, regard a talk or a piece of writing as a dynamic, growing organism. Think about the stages of a typical telephone conversation, say, in which you want to ask someone for a ride to work. The conversation begins with greetings; you do not state immediately your purpose for calling, but instead make small talk to build rapport and a feeling of good will. Then, you say, "Well I did have a specific reason for calling. . . ." The other person responds to your request. You express gratitude and offer your friend another chance to back out of the obligation. After the other person confirms the arrangement, you say, "Gee, that's great. By the way did you hear . . . ," and introduce more small talk. You end by restating the arrangement, offering thanks again, and saying goodbye. Communicatively competent speakers know how such conversations progress and speak appropriately at each stage.

They are likewise adept at creating the setting for a story at the beginning, and resolving it at the end. In writing an essay, they know how to develop each point in turn and tie things together at the end. Some types of speaking and writing convey strong expectations about what goes where. For example, an after-dinner speech begins with an obligatory joke. An Italian sonnet has fourteen lines, the last six of which resolve a conflict.

We have described these six features of communication context in some detail for several reasons. First, we can recognize that communication competence represents an organized system of knowledge, not just a collection of arbitrary norms for acceptable speaking and writing. Identifying the features can also help us to understand in what areas our students need more varied practice. For example, we may recognize that almost all our speech work takes the form of oral reports to the class. We might decide to have students conduct interviews with older members of the community. Or, we might realize that we have been neglecting the expressive function in our class writing. Perhaps most important, identifying the features of communication contexts can help us construct learning experiences that provide for authentic communication. Is there an audience for our students' expression? Can they see some genuine purpose? Is the setting conducive to this task? Have we allowed the discourse process to run full cycle?

Flexibility

Can you recall a time when you were at your desk, perhaps writing a chatty letter to a friend or relative, and you remembered that your lesson plans were due the next day? You swept aside the pleasant writing activity, with its "Oh, by the way" and "Did I mention to you . . ." Instead, you began work on the more dreary task, filling in the space for learner objectives with "The students will . . ." and completing the list of learner activities with "Rd pp. 7–13 if time permits."

We all control a variety of communication styles and switch among them as the situation requires. Some people have very extensive repertoires of communication acts. They can write flowing narratives such as might appear in popular magazines. They can speak assertively when their rights are being challenged. Perhaps, they are also skilled at drawing out strangers, and can be counted upon to do a good job with the PTO meeting minutes. Communicatively competent individuals do not speak or write according to any single standard. Instead, they adapt to situations by intuitively selecting from their broad repertoires of stylistic options and strategies.

The most dramatic instances of this kind of flexibility occur among bilinguals. Bilingual speakers may begin a conversation with a stranger in their second language. But when they warm to their new acquaintance and discover a common cultural bond, they may signal the strengthening of the relationship by switching to their first language.

Each of us speaks a particular dialect of our language (or languages). The dialect conveys our social identity, our membership in a speech community —Bostonian, Appalachian, New Yorker, or Iowan; black, Norwegian-American, Chicano, or Puerto Rican; working class, middle class, or upper class. Some dialects are considered standard because they are historically associated with sources of economic and political power. Nonstandard dialects, however, are not inferior in any respect to standard varieties. They are equally pleasant sounding to an outsider's ear. They are capable of sustaining all the functions of communication. Nor does any evidence support the idea that nonstandard dialects interfere with learning to read or write. Their grammars are different from the standard, but fully as systematic. But because nonstandard dialects are linked to less powerful and prestigious segments of society, nonstandard speech may trigger negative stereotypes. For example, when a job applicant's speech contains many Mexican-American dialect features, the speaker's chances of being considered for a supervisory position may be lessened.

Unfortunately, many teachers also hold negative stereotypes of nonstandard dialect speakers. It is possible that one of the reasons why children who speak nonstandard dialects often do poorly in reading is that their teachers misinterpret dialect features in the children's oral reading as mistakes. It is frustrating and defeating for these children to be constantly corrected when they have, in fact, accurately comprehended the texts. It is also possible that many teachers expect nonstandard dialect speakers to be poor students. We communicate our expectations of students in subtle ways, like withholding eye contact, cutting off their answers, or standing further away from them—behaviors of which we are rarely aware. These expectations, then, can become self-fulfilling. The students achieve less than they would if our expectations were higher. These are unpleasant portraits to paint of ourselves, but we are all subject to stereotyping of one kind or another. We can reduce the effects of our stereotypes on our teaching behaviors, but not if we refuse to face them.

Despite the frequently negative consequences of nonstandard speech, people tend to hold fast to dialects because speech patterns are deeply enmeshed in their sense of self. Few educators now believe that we should try to eradicate nonstandard dialects, not only because of the immorality of such a policy, but also because it is fruitless to make the attempt. Instead, some school systems try to promote bidialectism among speakers of nonstandard dialects. Bidialectal speakers control both a standard and nonstandard dialect, using each in appropriate circumstances. Methods for teaching a second dialect most often involve frequent drill and techniques for highlighting the contrasts between the two systems.

We believe that the emphasis in bidialectal education is misplaced. Speakers of nonstandard dialects, like speakers of all dialects, can be flexible in their language styles. Inner-city teenagers who speak a dialect known as Black English Vernacular may use a great many dialect features when they wish to signal membership in peer groups, when they wish to avoid the image of being "lame." In other circumstances, though, they use fewer nonstandard features. Some teachers have observed groups of young Black English Vernacular speakers, normally reticent in class discussion, noisily playing school during recess. In their play, the students spoke in Standard English. We believe, therefore, that most nonstandard dialect speakers possess resources for using a standard-like style of speech, even without classroom drill. They will gain flexibility in using Standard English only to the degree that they perceive the appropriateness of the standard in a wider variety of situations. We can help if we can create classroom contexts for speaking in Standard English which are authentic and non-threatening to the students' sense of identity.

Of course, speakers of all dialects exhibit flexibility in speech. Caretakers speak differently to infants than to other adults. Children quickly learn to direct different sorts of arguments to friends ("I'll be your best friend.") than they use with parents ("It'll get me out of your hair for a while."). When mature communicators address audiences who come from unfamiliar backgrounds, they speak more formally—enunciate carefully, avoid slang words, use complex syntax, elaborate.

We tend to think of written style as being more uniform than speech, as conforming to rigid conventions. To begin with, there is some question about how rigid those writing conventions are. Professional writers do not always include topic sentences in paragraphs. The English minor sentence, lambasted as a "sentence fragment" in composition textbooks, is also fairly common. But more to the point, contexts also exert influence over stylistic variation in writing. Complex syntax is characteristic of persuasive writing, but less so of narrative. We take more care to include explicit transition statements when writing for the general public than when we write for friends. Business writing is different from school writing, which is different from technical writing.

In learning to write, children have a hard time differentiating between spoken and written codes. Speech is appropriately context-dependent. We rely on the physical context which face-to-face participants share. "Take the one that's on the left," can be a perfectly adequate instruction when individuals are looking into the same cupboard. Writing, on the other hand, must be context-independent. A written text must be autonomous in the sense that all the information a reader requires to interpret its meaning needs to be stated explicitly. If we leave a note behind with the baby-sitter, we write, "When Nicky needs a bottle, look on the top shelf of the refrigerator. Take the Yogi Bear bottle on the far left since that's his favorite." Many of the errors in beginning writers' compositions can be traced to failure to differentiate writing contexts from speaking contexts. This perspective on error is generally more useful than to whittle away at students' ignorance of the conventions of writing.

In fact, the notion of context dependence and independence (though probably not the terminology) can help beginning writers breach the scary feeling that writing is something utterly foreboding and unfamiliar. Some kinds of writing are quite similar to forms of speech with which students are comfortable. They are speech-like kinds of writing because they depend on shared context between writer and reader. By the same token, some kinds of speech are writing-like because they presume little shared context between speaker and listener. Borrowing from the work of Martin Joos, we can array both speech and writing along the same dimension of "intimate" to "frozen" styles. (See Figure 1.)

Performance

To communicate competently, then, it is necessary to read a situation and to respond to it appropriately by drawing from a repertoire of stylistic and strategic options. Yet a ball player who knows all the rules of the game, but keeps dropping the ball, will be sent back to the farm team. Similarly, competent communicators must be able to carry out their plans. Writing and speaking are, after all, forms of behavior. To be an effective speaker, you must open your mouth and talk; to be an effective writer, you must take pencil in hand and write.

Though it may seem foolish to make such obvious statements, there is an important point to be made about classroom instruction. Many students spend more time learning *about* speaking and writing than they spend in speaking and writing. There are several reasons for this, not the least of which is the burden usually placed on teachers to evaluate student performances. In neglecting performance (which after all does not *always* need to be evaluated), however, fluency in speaking and writing suffers. A pianist who does not practice will not be nimble at the keyboard. A speaker or writer who does not practice will not produce very much language.

When we speak of "practice" in speaking and writing, however, we are not talking about something divorced from a context—isolated from an audience, purpose, or setting. Communication competence is not acquired by reciting for the sake of reciting or transcribing for the sake of transcribing. British educator James Britton says:

> What children use language for in school must be "operations" not "dummy runs." They must continue to use it to make sense of the world: they must *practice* language in the sense in which a doctor "practices" medicine and a lawyer "practices" law, and not in the sense in which a juggler "practices" a new trick before he performs it.

Performance, then, pertains to the mechanics of communicating: finding the right words, pronouncing them intelligibly, or spelling them legibly, projecting loudly enough for the audience to hear without straining, and using punctuation marks so that readers can locate boundaries between ideas.

These things, too, are a vital part of communication competence, and are learned most effectively, however, not through isolated drill, but through the acts of communicating in speech and in writing.

speech:	whispering sweet nothings; joking about old times	family conversation; party talk	business talk; teacher talk	keynote speeches; public lectures	parliamentary debate; diplomatic policy statements
style:	INTIMATE ⟶	CASUAL ⟶	CONSULTATIVE ⟶	FORMAL ⟶	FROZEN
writing:	journal writing; passing notes in class	friendly letters; some contemporary fiction (e.g., Richard Brautigan)	business memos; journalistic writing	academic essays; technical manuals	legal documents; scientific reports

Students can profit from experiences spanning the full range of speaking and writing styles.

Figure 1.

Feedback

Communication is circular. Fully realized, all forms of communication involve feedback. Feedback is a crucial component of communication processes because it allows us to readjust and fine-tune our behaviors. In face-to-face conversation, we receive a continuous flow of both verbal and nonverbal feedback. When our partner says, "Yeah . . . Yeah . . . That's what I heard," accompanied by vigorous nodding, we know that we can skip background details and get on with new information. But if the listener knits a brow and frowns, we know that we should elaborate further. Even in more formal, less interactive speaking situations, we are aware of the audience's facial expressions, of shifting in seats, and rustling of papers. We have no difficulty interpreting feedback when audience members start filing out before we have finished speaking.

Although feedback is less immediate in written communication, most types of writing do allow for interaction. Personal letters elicit replies. Letters of complaint remedy or do not remedy the problem. Printed meeting announcements attract a large or small crowd. Manuscripts are accepted for publication, or not; become best-sellers or publishers' overstock. Classroom writing assignments are graded, perhaps commented on, or even hung on the bulletin board.

Writers, however, work isolated from their audiences. They must, therefore, second-guess readers' reactions. Speakers, on the other hand, are directed by listeners, spurred on in one direction or diverted to another. For beginning writers, some valuable instructional practices provide a bridge between the immediacy of face-to-face feedback and the delayed and indirect nature of feedback to writing. (In the final section of this chapter, we discuss how teachers and peers can enter into students' writing processes before the final stages, offering feedback and guidance throughout the act of writing.)

Writing, however, does offer one advantage over speech with respect to feedback. Not only can writers ultimately obtain feedback from readers, but they can also learn to "listen" to their own text-in-progress. Because writing is permanent, it affords authors the leisure to reflect on their compositions during the course of writing. Expert writers pause often, reformulate goals, and discover new lines of thought by examining what they have already written. This kind of revision occurs not only after the final punctuation mark is put in place, but repeatedly and on an ongoing basis. It is this aspect of writing—feedback between text and author—that allows writing to be especially helpful as a means for inventing new insights, and not just as a vehicle for conveying thoughts already thought.

We have discussed communication competence in terms of sensitivity, flexibility, performance, and feedback—not as a list of skills, rules, or minimal objectives in speaking and writing. Many such lists have been compiled, and they no doubt serve an important purpose in planning for instruction. But in the day-to-day challenge of actually working with students, it is most important to remember that communication competence cannot be reduced to atomistic components apart from meaningful expression. When we seek to foster communication skills, we are working with matters of judgment, sense of purpose, sense of community, and sense of self.

It is hoped, above all else, that this notion of communication competence is emancipatory. In speaking and writing, individuals actively engage the environment. They make choices, exert influence, and make value judgments. Communicatively competent individuals are free to move beyond the most familiar circumstances, expanding their worlds to encompass a broad range of possibilities. For such individuals, communication serves instrumental functions—influencing others to achieve extrinsic goals. Equally as important, such individuals find that communication, itself, offers intrinsic rewards—self-awareness, participation in a community.

To understand communication competence, therefore, we take a holistic view of its several facets. To understand how children develop communication competence—and how schooling fits into that process—we examine the broad intellectual foundations that support growth in speaking and writing.

The School as Communication Context: An Interlude

The following scenario illustrates some of the speaking and writing resources children may use within a classroom language community:

> Annie is a ten-year-old girl in the fifth grade. Her school is located in a middle-class neighborhood, but has a diverse population. It includes students of lower income and minority backgrounds; among them are black, Chicano, and Asian-American children. Annie performs above average in her schoolwork, although she tends to do better in science and mathematics than in social studies or language arts. She especially likes to work on "brain-teasers," and often gets the answer first. A sociable child, she likes to talk and work on school projects with friends. She has had some trouble with writing, but is becoming more fluent and confident as a result of recent classroom experiences.
>
> Annie's teacher this year is Ted Brockton, an intelligent and thoughtful young man who has been teaching in this school for six years. After serving in the Navy for two years, Brockton returned to the university to earn a teaching certificate. He sees his classroom as a place where students talk and write to learn both subject matter and social skills. He uses all available space, with learning centers and workplaces set up around the room, and children's writing and

artwork prominently displayed on bulletin boards. A visitor entering the classroom may find it actively noisy but not chaotic, as most students work on their own, with a partner, or in small groups. At times, Brockton will assemble the children for a lesson or activity; at other times, he will move about the room helping children individually with the work. His manner is friendly but direct and self-assured, and he truly seems to know and enjoy all the children.

Annie begins this particular day by finishing a library book that she had started reading the day before. The story is a science fantasy about a boy who lives in the year 2071, and Annie is fascinated by the computer technology described in it. After completing the story, she writes a paragraph in response to it, stating that she would especially like to have a computerized ice-cream maker like the one mentioned in the story. She checks the spelling of the word "computerized" in the book and then places her writing in a box labeled "Reading Responses." She knows that the teacher will read it later and return it to her with written comments, perhaps something like, "I'd like one of those machines myself—Do you think it could make Rocky Road?"

About a half hour into the day, Brockton claps his hands and calls the students together for a social studies discussion. He wants the students to become aware of democratic processes, and encourages this through talk about school issues. The topic is lunchtime. Some students have been complaining that they do not have enough time to finish the morning's work before the fifth-grade lunchtime of 11:44. One boy suggests that they write a letter to the principal asking her to allow time to go to lunch whenever they want, but others tell him that too much confusion would result. Annie asks the teacher if he can give them more time to finish their work in the afternoon. He says that he will, but also urges them to try to use time more productively in the morning.

After this discussion, Brockton reminds the class that they have history work to complete. This is Annie's least favorite subject, so she approaches it as an obstacle that she has to hurdle to go on to more interesting things. This day, she must fill out a worksheet with questions about Andrew Jackson. Most of the questions concern factual information, and she consults the history text for the answers. However, the last question asks for her reaction to the song, "The Battle of New Orleans," that Mr. Brockton had played for the class the day before. She writes that she liked it and mentions a part of it that she especially enjoyed. As she completes the worksheet, she feels relieved, and remembering the melody, hums the song to herself as she moves on to the next activity, a geography project.

Annie, Greg, Maria, and Jeff are constructing a large poster map of the school neighborhood. They are working on Annie's immediate neighborhood area, and the others defer to her in identifying the streets, stores, and other landmarks. Greg and Jeff joke some, and Maria sits back quietly while Annie sketches in the streets. But when Brockton comes to look at the project, they all turn their attention to making the map.

At lunch, Annie sits with Maria and two other friends, Cynthia and Susan. Their talk centers on a movie that they saw the past weekend—

with a few complaints mixed in about the tuna fish sandwiches and carrots on the menu. During the conversation, Susan also reminds the others that report cards will be issued next week, Maria talks excitedly about her cousin's visit, and Annie arranges with Cynthia to walk home with her after school.

After lunch, Annie returns quickly to the classroom because she is eager for the science lesson on the principles of magnetism. After discussing the concepts of attraction and repulsion, Brockton gives a set of magnets to each of six groups and asks them to experiment. Annie and the others in her group manipulate the magnets in several ways, and take delight in seeing them jump apart as the like poles are placed next to each other. They even devise an elaborate game, "magnet hockey," to see who can make the magnets repel the farthest. They write notes in their science journals describing what they have observed. The teacher engages them in a discussion, asking several to read from the journals. Jeff shares his entry, in which he has written that the magnets are like friends—sometimes they like each other and sometimes they do not. Another student extends the comparison by suggesting that friends sometimes have different interests but still can stick close together. Brockton says that those analogies might represent good ways to remember the scientific principles.

After the science lesson, Annie goes on to math work, which this day consists of multiplying fractions. Annie completes fifteen such problems quickly and confidently, but has difficulty with a story problem. The teacher notices this and offers help. As he explains to her, she suddenly understands what she had not and thanks him for assisting.

As Annie returns to her seat to complete the problem, the loudspeaker buzzes, signaling a fire drill. The students begin to scramble to get out the door, bumping into each other and knocking over books and papers. The teacher tries to gain their attention to have them file out orderly, but it is too late—most of them are on their way. Outside in the courtyard, the children are noisy and excited, some of them run around, making it difficult for teachers to establish much control.

After ten minutes, another signal sounds, and the students clatter in disorganized fashion back to class. Brockton attempts to move students back into math work, but soon gives up, seeing that they are still distracted by the fire drill interruption. (Annie never does finish the math problem that day.)

He decides to gather them together for music, one of his stronger interests. (He is a talented guitar player, and often accompanies the children as they sing.) The class sings American folk songs and spirituals, "Swing Low, Sweet Chariot," and "Michael Row the Boat Ashore." One boy asks to sing "Let's Boogie," and everyone laughs. Brockton then leads them in exuberant off-key renditions of the songs that they have requested. Except for a brief altercation in which one student tells another that he sings like a frog, everyone seems to have a good time, and even the quieter children join in. This activity clearly helps to create a strong group spirit.

For the day's final activity, Brockton has the class play a softball game. Susan and Greg are the captains, and they take turns choosing players. Brockton is the umpire, and arbitrates in disputes. Going into the last half-inning, the game is tied. Annie comes to bat with players on second and third and two outs. But before she steps to the plate, Maria whispers to her that Greg is playing away from third base. Seeing this, Annie turns her body slightly at the plate and on the first pitch, hits a ground ball over third base. The winning run scores, and Annie's teammates gather around to congratulate her. Greg walks off the field disgustedly, and Annie hopes he is not angry at her.

On the way home, Annie tells Cynthia about these feelings. Cynthia tells her not to worry, that Greg will probably have forgotten the whole incident by the next day.

As seen in the scenario, Annie and her classmates speak and write to serve a great variety of purposes: to respond to literature, engage in dialogue with the teacher, explore social issues, identify problems and pose solutions, participate in democratic processes, make requests, express appreciation, identify specific likes and dislikes, use their knowledge and expertise, share common experience, anticipate future events, discover ideas and concepts, create meanings, record observations, ask for assistance, entertain each other, contribute to group spirit, argue, provide information, share feelings, and offer reassurance. Success in school and other contexts depends to a great extent on children's ability to communicate in diverse ways, and the successful teacher provides opportunities for them to do so.

It should be noted also that reading and listening are not neglected in Brockton's classroom; in fact, they are reinforced and enhanced by speaking and writing activities. Unlike many classrooms in which students read and listen passively, Brockton's is a place where they respond actively to what they read, and listen attentively and interestedly to what others have to say. Although less visible to the outside observer, reading and listening represent the resources from which children draw for speaking and writing. In sum, the children have an investment in reading and listening, as these provide the stimuli for sharing, exploring, questioning, imagining, inventing, and working collaboratively toward common ends.

Especially important in this classroom is the peer group. Children serve as audiences for each other's expressions, as partners in common enterprises, as fellow discoverers, as friendly adversaries in arguing opinions and interpretations, and as sympathetic and helpful friends. Talk and writing help children deal with matters on their social agendas as well as the subject matter agenda. Indeed, at times social awareness *becomes* the subject matter, as in the discussion of the lunchtime problem. And children also interact with others from different cultural backgrounds, discovering ways in which individuals bring experiences and values to bear on learning tasks. Finally, and essentially, children use their communication abilities to deal with challenges associated with peer group belonging and approval.

A Model of Development

Planting a seed, say, for an apple tree is a supreme act of faith and optimism. The seed contains a blueprint for what the tree will ultimately develop into. The blueprint determines that roots will sprout before the stem, that leaves will emerge to nourish the tree, and that the tree will bear apples and not asparagus or onions. Still, the tree's growth will be affected by how much moisture it receives and how fertile the soil is in which it roots. It is hoped that rabbits will not munch on the young seedling, and that bees will track its fragrance to pollinate the blossoms. Perhaps we also learn about fruit tree cultivation, and when and how to prune back the branches to maximize the tree's production. Above all, we learn to be patient, realizing that it may be a decade before we can harvest enough apples to make a dozen pies.

We can talk about developing speaking and writing skills with the same mix of mysticism and pragmatism. Learners develop according to their own schedules and inner dynamics. But they do so interacting with the environment and with us, their cultivators. It is a mistake to assume that speech is a naturally developing ability and, therefore, requires no deliberate instruction. Students' sensitivity and repertoires grow as a function of their experiences. They refine their competence as a result of performance and feedback. Many people, for example, do very poorly interacting with health care professionals. They feel abused, do not understand medical orders, and are not motivated to comply with them. They simply lack knowledge of the appropriate speech behaviors in this difficult, but crucial, communication setting.

It is also a mistake if we assume that learning to write is wholly a matter of formal schooling, if we fail to regard the internal maturation of the learners. Careful research shows that most children know something about writing before they ever enter public school. Moreover, children's writing development is a clear reflection of their overall intellectual and emotional development. Some of the writing instruction offered in early years is motivated by a *logical* analysis of the composing task, but runs contrary to a *psychological* analysis of learners' capabilities. For example, some researchers strongly urge that teachers not expose elementary students to grammatical terminology (if, indeed, students need exposure to grammatical terminology at any age). Others suggest that too great an emphasis is often placed in the early primary years on writing as spelling out sounds.

Thus, in looking at the development of both writing and speaking skills, we refer to an interaction between minds unfolding and environments in and out of school that affect that unfolding in various ways. We have repeatedly stressed the point that communication is situated in specific contexts; context cannot be avoided when describing processes of growth.

When communicating, we are operating in three dimensions simultaneously: social awareness, coding, and reconstruction of experience. Growth in one dimension enhances development in the others. Conversely, when students become bogged down in one of these operations, they tend to be limited in the others.

Social Awareness

Humans are social animals, and the drive to participate in community dwells as deeply in us as any basic instinct for survival. Even young infants appear to be impelled to affect and be affected by others, and the roots of language acquisition lie in the primitive nonverbal routines involving eye gaze between infant and caretaker. As we mature, our abilities to understand the thoughts and feelings of others support our development as communicators.

Young children are egocentric (though not absolutely so). They are so impressed with the immediate ways of seeing that they cannot conceive of anyone else having different perceptions. Thus, there is the familiar picture of the young child substituting gestures for words in a telephone conversation. Or the familiar interaction: "I want a cookie!" "It's too close to dinner." "But I want it now, so give it to me!"

With age and experience, we decenter—that is, we become more adept at recognizing that others' perceptions of a situation can be different than ours. A child may have a pressing need to satisfy a cookie craving, but, at the same time, recognize that the parents' need is to see that he or she eats the nutritious food that they have prepared. So the child alters his or her persuasive strategy to adapt to the audience: "Dad, I promise to eat all my dinner if you let me have a cookie." It is worth a try, anyway.

Social awareness is an essential ingredient of reader-adapted prose as well as listener-adapted speech. The audience in written communication, of course, is much more abstract than in oral communication. Writers must mentally represent audiences to themselves. Also writers lack access to an ongoing flow of feedback that might help them adjust messages as they compose. These factors, in combination with the mechanical difficulty of writing, pose added burdens which hamper audience awareness in writing, as compared to speaking. One type of audience, the "general reader," creates particular difficulty in maintaining social awareness, even for older students.

Despite the challenge of sustaining a sense of audience in writing, competent writers do adapt to readers. Mature writers use more complex syntax when writing for older, sophisticated readers than for a younger audience; they use more transition cues in writing for unfamiliar audiences

than to friends. Similarly, mature writers take care to include background
information in compositions which will be read by an unknown and diverse
audience.

A classroom activity which highlights social awareness skills asks students to role-play a situation in which they deliver a persuasive message to
several audiences. When the topic of persuasion is held constant, the
students' attention is naturally directed to differences among audiences. In
this case, a ninth-grade class practices how they might go about selling
subscriptions to a school newspaper. As one student addresses his best
friend, note that their longstanding relationship allows him to reveal his
self-serving motivation (to win a prize) and that the speaker does not
bother with civilities like requesting or thanking:

> Hey Doug, gonna buy a newspaper subscription? You can find out
> what's happening in school and read the gossip section and stuff. Find
> out what's going on in the editorials and stuff. And it's only a dollar so
> it's a pretty good thing. And you'll get it the whole year. Buy it from me
> and help me out 'cause if I'm gonna get this prize I have to sell the most.

But when the speaker addresses an unfamiliar peer, he avoids mentioning
the prize, and is careful to thank his audience:

> Okay Steve, how'd you like to buy a newspaper subscription to our
> school paper? You can find out what's going on. And you can read
> about what's happening. It's only a dollar and you get it for the whole
> year. And it's a pretty good deal. You can find out what's happening in
> school and what's new and what dates are important and if there's any
> concerts or something you like to go to or dances or something. And
> I'd really appreciate it if you could buy it from me. And it's only a
> dollar, so you should try it.

In contrast with this message to Steve, more formal diction and a
deferential form of request are used when the student attempts to sell a
subscription to a teacher at his school:

> Hi, Mr. Swenson. I'd like to know if you'd be interested in buying a
> school newspaper we're trying to sell for our English class to try to get
> money to raise funds for materials and stuff. And it's only a dollar and
> you get subscriptions all year. And it's a pretty good deal considering
> what you get. I'd like to know if you'd like to buy one.

Another ninth-grade student makes direct appeals to her audience's
values. Speaking to a school teacher, she says:

> ... And I think you'd like it 'cause these are some of the students that
> you have and you can see how much you've taught them because the
> newspaper is part of an English class. And you can see how well they're
> doing. And it would be interesting to see how a young mind thinks ...

She is no less astute in reading her mother's sources of motivation:

> Mom, we're having a school newspaper in our grade. And maybe my work will be in it. And won't you be proud of me! And lots of your friends' sons and daughters would be in it, too . . .

While most students are able to tailor messages to their audience's perspective, there is a great deal of variation in the sophistication that they display. As this last example demonstrates, some students need considerable work in developing social awareness in communication. Here is another ninth-grader speaking to her best friend:

> Oh, do you want to subscribe to a ninth-grade newspaper? See, 'cause if I sell the most subscriptions I get a $5 prize. Well, it would tell a lot of stuff that's going on in ninth grade and the kind of stuff you like to read. It's only a dollar and you'd get it all year.

Her message to a peer stranger is virtually identical and shows an inability to distinguish between audiences:

> Hi. Do you wanna subscribe to our new magazine for the ninth grade? It tells a lot about what's going on in ninth grade. And it's only a dollar. 'Cause if I get the most subscriptions, I get a $5 prize.

We can also see varying degrees of audience awareness in persuasive writings of children. Our illustrations come from a sample of the National Assessment of Educational Progress in Writing (NAEP), *The Third Assessment of Writing, 1978-79 Released Exercise Set.* The persuasive tasks in this sample specify an audience and point the writer toward convincing that audience of a particular viewpoint. Nine-year-olds were presented with the following task:

> Pretend that your family is moving to a new apartment. The landlord has refused to let your puppy live there. Write the landlord a letter, trying to convince him to let you keep your puppy in the new apartment. . . . Sign your letter "Chris Smith."

Some writings reveal difficulty with this task:

> *about that puppy*
> *it has ben with me*
> *for six years and I*
> *hope to have him*
> *longer Chris Smith*

In addition to basic problems of fluency, qualities of egocentrism can be identified in these writings. In the first case, the writer seems unsure as to how to approach the reader—should he appeal, threaten, or simply give up? While he does consider alternatives, he does so impulsively, rather than thoughtfully. The writing also lacks politeness, which may not be the most important feature of audience awareness, but it often exerts a major impact on readers. The second writing simply assumes that the landlord knows what puppy is being referred to, suggesting that the writer is unable to take the role of his reader with respect to what information is required.

Another writing, although not much more elaborated, does show an emerging ability to consider an audience:

> *Please wood you*
> *let my puppy*
> *live here please.*
> *I will let*
> *my puppy outside*
> *I will sleep*
> *outside please.*
> *I will give*
> *my puppy a*
> *bath outside. Please*
> *from Chris*
> *To Chris Smith*
> *Please*

The repeated use of the word *please* and the promise to keep the puppy outside indicate a sense for appealing to the reader's sympathy. As an even more dramatic example, consider the following writing:

> I can understand why you won't let animals in your apartment house. But my puppy is very nice and I am sure he won't neck up the apartment. I will be sure to watch him and take him out alot. Please let me keep him.
>
> Sincerely,
> Chris Smith

This is a strong example of role-taking, as the writer bolsters his argument by explicitly acknowledging the reader's viewpoint.

Note, too, how this writer accomplishes her persuasive purpose:

> Aloy me to interduce my self My name is Chris Smith. My family will be moving into your Building soon, We have a puppy And I would like to know why you won't let us keep our puppy in the apartment. My puppy is very tender and somtimes he scard of someone. His name is Ginger. The reson why I'm writing this is because if you don't let us bring him in the apartment we will have to get rid of him. I hate to see

> that happen please let
> us keep him
>
> Your Truely
> Chris Smith
>
> P.S. I like it very much, if
> you would let us bring him
> PlEASE!

Not only does the writer show deference toward the landlord, as in the polite introduction, but also orients him toward the problem, and enlists sympathy by describing the puppy. She brings a number of arguments to bear on the issue, while remaining considerate of the reader.

Further aspects of social awareness are reflected in persuasive writings of thirteen-year-olds who were asked to write a letter to the principal suggesting an improvement for the school. As with the nine-year-olds, some students wrote brief, perfunctory letters:

> Mark Hopkins
> Have more activies like more clubs
> more space for the playground better
> food and bigger rooms. That might
> help a little. You should have sales
> to raise more money for school.
> More field trips. Have a school metings.
> Sign,
> Chris Johnson

Even though the writer does identify problems and makes suggestions, the clipped, imperative statements suggest egocentrism and lack of investment in the topic. (It is entirely possible that the same writer might have more to say about a topic that he *is* genuinely interested in.)

Here is a more "impelled" writing, as it focuses on a single issue:

> Dear Mary,
>   I think one thing that would help our school alot is to have more classrooms built onto the school, Because there are so many students in just one classroom that you don't have enough room to do hardly anything. That might be the reason that some students don't learn as much, because the teacher doesn't have time to work with everyone just a few people. I really think it would help us and our school a hole lot.
>   Sincerely yours,
>   Chris Johnson
>   333 West Street
>   Soden, Ohio 99999
>   September 5, 1978

While not an extended argument, it does define the problem in terms that a principal would recognize as important—the effects of overcrowded classrooms on student learning. Another writer uses a similar appeal in arguing for career education:

> Dear Mr. Hopkins,
>   I think Martin Intermediate School could be improved greatly by more career education. It

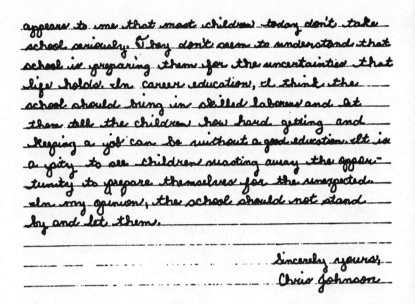

While the writer adopts a condescending "adult" view of students, she also shows a singleness of purpose and ability to reinforce the main point (preparing students for the unexpected).

In both speaking and writing, then, students demonstrate increasing social awareness as they mature. They make distinctions among types of audiences and anticipate the dispositions of listeners and readers. They bring a greater number of appeals and arguments to bear on the topic and balance respect for the audience with a strong personal voice.

Coding

We choose the term *coding* advisedly, because we see it as a broader notion than what is commonly referred to as "language." Certainly, competent communicators must have strong language skills—a rich vocabulary, the ability to form sentences, a sense for conventional usage. But speech communication also includes nonverbal coding through tone of voice, its rate and volume, through gestures, eye contact, touching, and through physical space, clothing, and time. Moreover, we are concerned with communicators' control of chunks of discourse larger than sentences. Coding skill includes abilities to maintain cohesiveness across sentences, organize entire talks or compositions, establish emphasis as appropriate, and create an aesthetic effect through imagery, rhythm, and sense of sound. Finally, coding also encompasses the pragmatics of language, how language is used to express an attitude toward a subject or toward an audience, and how people can accomplish various communication functions with different language structures. For example, I might meet a coworker in the hall and say, "My car is in the shop. I'm afraid I need to impose on you for a ride home." Or I might say, "Okay if I hitch a ride home with you today?" Even though one appears as a statement and the other as a question, the intent of both these utterances is to request help with transportation. In addition, one clearly expresses a less formal attitude toward the relationship.

In speaking and writing instruction, most efforts have been a direct assault on children's coding skills. Typically, the mode of instruction is atomistic. We assume that small units must be introduced (sounds, words, sentences, and paragraphs) before larger ones (entire talks or compositions). We assume that students must learn *about* these structures, in isolation, before they can learn to *use* them in context. The net result is too often a curriculum that is so busy with code that it has little time for communication. Students are so occupied with worksheets that they have little time for interacting with each other or with their environment.

We can only speculate about why this state of affairs has become so common. But we do know that the massive research literature on the subject strongly concludes that lessons about language structure do not improve students' communication skills in writing or speech. We know this by looking to our experience as well. Year after year, we review parts of speech, predicate nominatives, and gerunds. While some students (perhaps destined to be English teachers) enjoy this work for its intellectual challenge, most students learn rules of grammar and usage just long enough to pass a test, if they learn them at all. We perpetually ask tenth-graders, "Didn't your ninth-grade teacher cover this material?"

And why should it be otherwise? We learn to drive a car by driving with a trusted and experienced driver at our side, and do very well without ever understanding the organic chemistry of petroleum combustion. Except for the few of us who specialize in automobile repairs, we learn what little we know about engines out of some real need (e.g., to keep oil levels where they need to be, or to understand a repair bill). Indeed, we could barely make it out of our driveways if we had to constantly think about pistons and cams and distributor rotors. This is not to say that language mechanics are not important; only that students assimilate norms of standard language usage and structure when they perceive a need to do so during the course of authentic writing or speaking activities.

One of the characteristics of coding in the early school years—and one of the ways in which early writing is similar to speech—is the unsophisticated use of connectives for signaling relationships between ideas. Mature communicators use a variety of connectives to indicate how two ideas relate ("therefore," "whereas," "nevertheless," "although"). For youngsters, however, cohesion is accomplished by indiscriminately using three connectives: "and," "so," "then." This oral narrative was produced by a fourth-grader working with a desk-top stage and dolls.

> Let's see. Um, this one kid went um in this one room. Um, I mean this . . . Well, this kid's mother told him that he couldn't go outside *and* he wanted to go out real bad *so* he snuck out *and* his mother didn't know it *so* he went to this real old shack *and* he went inside looking around like *and* he found this gun like *and,* um, he wondered where it came from *so* he went upstairs *and* he looked around *and then* he saw this treasure like *and then* there was a lot of money and jewelry and stuff in it *and then,* um, this one guy he, he, um, yelled at him *so* the little boy he ran outside *and* the next day, um, um, he went back up there *and,* um, he went back upstairs again *and* he didn't see anybody *so* he went in this one, um, door, *and* he looked around *and* there was all this valuable stuff that the guy had stolen *and then* he went home *and* told his mom *and* his mom called the police *and* the police got him *then.*

This passage shows some ambiguous pronoun reference, typical of egocentric language: "This one guy he yelled at him," "The police got him then." While one can eventually figure out who the "guy" is and who all the "hims" refer to, it requires some effort on the part of the listener to do so. Mature speakers minimize this kind of listener effort through explicit reference.

As children learn about structures for linking two contiguous sentences, they also learn about the structure of entire pieces of discourse. Most children are immersed in the narrative form from an early age. Much of their informal instruction from caretakers comes packaged as stories, and most beginning readers are storybooks. Nevertheless, they do not master the "grammar" of storytelling until they acquire some maturity.

A first-grader tells a story in response to a colorful circus painting:

> OK, it's summertime and I went to a circus. And they were having a parade. And I saw some clowns, elephants, and some . . . two tigers in a cage, and some horses, and there are some clowns with flags, and there are some clowns on horses, and there's a clown in the middle waving. And there's some bears, lions, and tigers. . . . That's the end of the story.

The storyteller begins appropriately enough by creating a setting. She soon lapses from past tense reporting to present tense describing, however. She sustains few elements of action or plot.

The next story, told by a fourth-grader, does maintain a sense of action, but there is none of the conflict and resolution necessary for creating a real plot:

> Well at first that guy just got out of the wheel chair with the broken leg. And his friend brought him a present. And he's already well. The doctor is leaving. And he's saying he's all right. And this guy with the present is gonna sorta drive him home. And he says thanks to the doctor.

A fifth-grade student builds some rising action and even attains some minimal closure. She also begins with a more stylized story opener:

> One day a clown and a circus was riding along, going to a county fair. One day the tigers and the elephants and the clowns were riding along and the clowns were playing and the elephants were dancing and the horses were parading around. When they finally got to the circus fairgrounds the horse and the elephants in their cages and all the people gathered up and got the circus almost ready. All the people were ready and three days later they were finished so they went on and went to another fair.

The story conveys a feeling of potential climax through expressions like "finally got to the circus," "all the people gathered up," and "circus almost ready." However, no climactic event actually emerges. Eventually, this student will incorporate a sense of motivation, and perhaps also a sense of character development, as she develops greater control over story structures.

In writing, too, there are these developmental aspects of coding and narrative structure. These illustrations are drawn again from the NAEP sample, this time from writings of nine-year-olds in response to a picture of a girl trying to catch fireflies. Some students clearly had difficulties with mechanical skills:

> her hand is in the air
> I see light bug a she is
> haveing fun in summer
> and I know she is to
> if I dont know a till she
> is cath lightbug

> The girl is getten lighting bugs.
> When she get one she put it in a
> jar. Next she is going to put in a
> dark place.

The problems with handwriting, spelling, and punctuation are immediately noticeable. More crucial, though, is the lack of fluency and the inability to produce a greater number of words and sentences in the allotted time. It suggests that for children like these, writing is at best a chore, as they have yet to develop the motivation or confidence with writing that enables them to produce more discourse. Mechanical correctness is unlikely to emerge until that fluency is established.

In contrast, note what another nine-year-old does with the same topic:

One day when I looked out of my window I saw small lights flashing, I thought it was an invasion from outer space. I was very scared, so I went outside to see wat it was, I thought was it an invasion? No it wasn't, but I didn't know it, so I decided to try to catch whatever they where. I asked my mom if I could borrow a jar, she said "Yes." Then I went outside with the jar the lights started to move away so I tried going after them, but they where to fast. "whoosh!" my jar ffew to catch one, but I missed it. Then I put the jar down, and I tried catching them with my hands "Pow." I missed agian finaly one last try, I caugt one I really did! But it wasn't an invasion, it was only fireflies!

Here is an elaborated story written with expressiveness and enthusiasm—the use of sound effects, exclamations, varied punctuation, and personal voice reveals that the child has an investment in the writing. It appears that she enjoyed writing, as the next writer apparently did:

> One day Jan Thompson asked, "Why cant I ever go out In the woods at night." Her mother answerd, "Your to little". Jan whent to her room crying. That night she went outside in the wood to get fire flies. On the morning her mother came in to her room and siad, "You went outside". Jan could never go in the woods agen but she still had her fire flies.

Although the style is not as exuberant as in the previous writing, the use of dialogue (with nearly correct punctuation) suggests an involvement in the story, a concern for relationships, and what parents and children say to each other. In placing themselves inside their stories, these two writers have discovered a purpose for writing, and correspondingly a purpose for observing the structural and mechanical conventions of written discourse.

Skill in coding, then, includes more than just narrow sentence building: it comprises the ability to express logical relations among events. It encompasses the ability to structure whole pieces of discourse. Coding skill comes about not so much as a result of direct instruction in the "basics," but in response to real communication situations. In both speaking and writing, children develop coding abilities by producing discourse that will be listened to or read by others.

Reconstruction of Experience

Centuries ago, two astronomers lay on their backs, side by side, observing the starry skies. "Look over there to the north," said one. "There's a great bear, and across from it, there's a little bear." "I don't know what you're talking about," said the second astronomer. "But there's a big dipper and a little dipper, just as sure as the Sun revolves around the Earth."

The world does not present itself to us with prepackaged meanings. We learn to discern meaning in the world by fitting events and objects into sensible categories. Sometimes, we force the world into patterns that make sense, as when we see bears or dippers in the heavens, hear accusation in the voice of a parent who has come in for a conference about his child, or label politicians as either conservative or liberal. This view portrays humans as actively interpreting the world, rather than passively absorbing it.

Speaking and writing are vehicles for sharing knowledge with others. But they are also instruments for helping us to make sense of things. The notion that we think thoughts and then clothe them in words is too narrow a view of what happens when we use symbols. The processes of thinking and of "languaging" occur simultaneously, and are not altogether distinguishable. By searching for words to express ourselves, we discover what it is that we have to say. By linking those words in syntax, we discover relationships in the world.

Writing, in particular, is a powerful way of knowing. Many professional writers talk about their ideas "emerging" as they write. Many eschew preliminary outlines because they reject the idea that they can know where they are heading before they begin to write. The novelist E. M. Forster is quoted as saying, "How can I know what I think until I see what I say?" Even those who do use outlines alter their plans as new avenues of thought reveal themselves. In writing this chapter, too, we began with certain concepts of what constitutes communication competence, although we had only vague ideas of what we would include in the work. We talked between ourselves, and that helped us clarify our approach. We wrote a brief prospectus, then talked some more (and listened to the reactions of friends and colleagues). Finally, we reached the point when we knew we simply had to begin writing in earnest to fully understand what we thought about the subject. During the course of writing, we changed some old ideas and obtained some altogether new insights. We cycled through the processes of talking, writing, and revising several times, refining ideas at each stage.

People crave certainty and predictability, but when facing a blank page, they must make a leap of faith that they will find the ideas to fill it. They may feel less anxious knowing that the act of writing, by its very nature, promotes thought. Because writing permits the writer to review ideas, it extends the capacities of the mind. The writer can stretch out thought over time, reflect, reconsider, and allow previous ideas to launch new associations. James Britton and his associates suggest a simple experiment that will allow you to see this. Think of a topic which is abstract, but not unfamiliar: "Why do people feel lonely," for example. If you were to begin writing about the topic, you would, no doubt, create some very interesting insights. But try writing about it with a stylus on carbon-backed paper. You lose writing's potential for permitting revision, and you will likely discover that you are able to write but little on the subject.

The advice, "think before you speak or write," as it turns out, is not entirely good counsel. Countless promising ideas have withered on the vine as a result. If we wish to promote speaking and writing as agents of thought, then we must often respect the tentativeness of students' messages. We must give them ample time to finish assignments, and encourage revision. And we must avoid a wolf-pack classroom climate which pounces on errors of form and thus smothers a spirit of risk-taking and discovery.

Communication competence, itself, is one aspect of children's experience about which they rarely reflect. But children do show increasing abilities to generalize about the topic. A group of students was asked to explain why some persuasive strategies work better than others. Given a choice between pleading ("Give it to me, c'mon, c'mon, give it to me.") and offering an incentive ("If you give me the ball, I'll let you play with my game."), most students said that the bargaining strategy would be most effective. But a fourth-grader justified her choice rather egocentrically: "It's better because it just is." Her classmate offered a rule of politeness: "It's not nice to keep on saying, 'C'mon, c'mon.'"

One eighth-grader, in contrast, was able to justify the pleading strategy on the basis of fairly advanced, if narrowly pragmatic, social awareness: "I'd say, 'C'mon, c'mon' 'cause it would bug her a lot and then she'd give her the toy just to get her to stop." The beginnings of generalization can be seen in this fourth-grade youngster's reply: "I think that little kids whenever you say, 'Give me something,' I don't think they do, 'cause my mom's sister they just got a little baby and whenever his older brother says, 'Give me that,' he says, 'No.' But when he asks him nicely, he says, 'Yes.'"

The rationale's weakness is that it generalizes from a single case. An important advance in reconstructing experience is learning to use analogies. Here, a high school senior achieves considerable effect, as well as economy of expression, by means of an analogy:

People do what you want more when you're nicer. Even if ... They can even know that you're being nice just to get something for yourself. Like when they give something away at a store or something. They, They're just doing it because, so you'll go to their store. But at least it makes you feel like they want you to feel good or something. So say, "I'll give you the game."

Children's writings also reflect these signs of growing ability to reconstruct experience, and to generalize and create analogies. The following NAEP task, given to nine-year-olds, encouraged this kind of thinking:

Sometimes it is fun to think about what it would be like to be something besides a person. . . . What would it be like to be a goldfish? Or an airplane? Or a horse? Or a tree? Or any other thing? . . . Think about what you would like to be . . . Then write about what it is like to be that thing.

The task enabled children to relate what they already knew to a situation requiring an original response:

A Horse

You can roam through the hills. And you could play as long as you wanted. And you could eat as much grass and you could drink all of the water you wanted. You could let people ride you. And You could pull a cart or a wagon with someone in it. And maybe someday you would be a racing horse and win a race.

---

a cat

If I were a cat I would sit by a warm fire and lick my paws and drink warm milk. And in the early morning I would run outside and jump merely in the wind. I would run up a tree and down again. I would chase birds and mice and jump happily in the wind with the sun on my face. I think it would be nice to be a cat. Don't you think so to? I know I do! It would make me happy to do such things.

The End

In these pieces, the writers describe a variety of things that they could do if they were the animal, revealing an ability to generate original ideas and to provide concrete details. The second writing also contains a direct address to the audience, as the writer seeks to involve the reader in the imaginative experience.

Another writing on the same topic reveals an even more advanced thinking process:

If I Was A Mug

If I was a mug I would sit on the bathroom sink and wait for morning. When morning came, someone would come in and brush their teeth. Then they would fill me up with water and take a drink from me. It might feel like someone sucking my blood, but I wouldn't care. It would be fun to have someone pour water into me and then drink from me. I probably wouldn't sleep in case someone wanted a drink of water in the middle of the night. But I wouldn't get tired because

mugs don't get tired. The only
problem would be if some one
dropped me and I broke. That
wouldn't be fun. But then
if that some one glued me back
together it would be okay. But it
wouldn't be the same.

THE END

Here the writer has not only identified pleasant things that might happen to
a mug, but also shows the other side of the story. The series of sentences
beginning with the word *but* indicates that the child is considering possible
alternatives as well as solutions to problems. This is an impressive performance for a nine-year-old.

Growth in speaking and writing, therefore, is closely intertwined with
intellectual development, as children learn to construct meanings for
themselves. While thinking ability certainly contributes to language performance, opportunities for reconstructing experience in talk and writing
can also contribute significantly to thinking ability.

Interdependence Among Social Awareness, Coding, and Reconstruction of Experience

We separate communication development into three dimensions, primarily
for analytic purposes. In operation, however, no dimension exists apart
from the others. In discussing reconstruction of experience, for example,
we have introduced the concept of coding as a problem-solving instrument
that allows us to make sense of the world. The opposite is also true. If we
cannot make sense of some event—if we cannot find a viewpoint—we talk
or write about it in strained and stilted language.

Consider also the interaction between social awareness and coding in
writing. As mentioned, written language is context independent. Reference
is explicit, meanings are elaborated. Unskilled writers often violate these
requirements, however. A common problem is ambiguous pronoun
reference in writing: "Jeff and Mike were walking to the skating rink. It was
nighttime and there were no lights. So then he tripped and twisted his ankle
so bad he couldn't walk any more." This type of error does not reflect ignorance of the rules for using pronouns; rather, the problem here is egocentrism. From the perspective of the writer, it is perfectly clear who fell. But

readers cannot get into the head of the author, except insofar as the explicit text allows them to do so. Skill in providing sufficient detail, organizing ideas, and indenting paragraphs to break up the flow of writing, all are dependent largely on social awareness. And sometimes, students, to the amazement of everyone, can produce clean, error-free language when they perform tasks which allow them to speak or write to real audiences for authentic purposes.

Similarly, there is an important relationship between social awareness and reconstruction of experience. Figuring out what to say often presents a major stumbling block to students in both formal speaking and writing assignments. Teachers offer students the advice, "Talk about something you're familiar with." But choosing a general topic area is only a fraction of the difficulty. After all, how would you begin to write a three-paragraph theme about teaching, something with which you are no doubt familiar? Unsuccessful at finding a way into a topic, students often turn to uninspired rehashes of encyclopedia and news magazine articles: "Brazil is a fortunate country. It has many natural resources. The natural resources make it a great country in South America." But when you can create for yourself a sense of audience, the ideas begin to flow more readily. Talk about teaching to a person who taught *you* twenty years ago. Talk about teaching to an audience of computer programmers. (Does it at least suggest a metaphor you can play off of?) Talk about teaching to a group of disgruntled tax-payers. One way in which we can help students exploit the relationship between social awareness and reconstruction of experience is to be an audience for them. If students know that there is a trusted adult at the receiving end of their messages—someone who seeks to understand their viewpoint—then it will do much to free up their process of creative thinking.

Sometimes, when children are called on to discuss a particularly abstract subject, they simplify the task by making it more concrete. Often, this coping strategy takes the form of redefining a general audience in more identifiable terms. Thus, children may construct a second-person "you" audience when they confront a difficult problem in reconstructing experience. Explaining the rules of a game is one such taxing communication task. In this passage, a fifth-grader tries to maintain an abstract, generalized tone, but slips back and forth into concrete second-person address:

> First of all, one person takes the two birds and hides them behind their back and switches them around. Then takes those birds out. The other person takes . . . picks a hand. And you either get a yellow bird or a blue bird. Then the person who chose one will take the blue and yellow chip and throw it. If it lands on the yellow side up . . . and the yellow . . . If you're yellow you go first. If you're blue and the blue side shows up you'll go first. To start the game you start at the color dot. You zoom

up the board on the black spot. And then um, then, um, if you got to go
first take the cup with the die in it and roll. And when you get a color
you move to that spot. The yellow bird is like on the yellow then the
blue moves up to the yellow line. He has to go back. He can't move up
there. So, so . . . And if you have to you have to move back.

There is a clear relationship between fluency and use of a concrete "you"
audience in this speech sample. We can predict when the speaker will revert
to the second person by noting her hesitations or repetitions. These are the
spots where she finds it difficult maintaining a generalized orientation, and
so she simplifies the task for herself by adopting an audience which is more
immediate and familiar.

All Together Now

It is pleasing and enlightening to discover pieces of discourse in which the
child has "gotten it all together," in the sense of interweaving social
awareness, coding, and reconstruction of experience in skillful and successful ways. Here is such a piece, written by a thirteen-year-old in response to
the "Letter to the Principal" task:

Dear Mr. Hopkins,
    Our school needs an air conditioner. It
is hard to concentrate on school work
with such heat. Sweat drips into
my eyes when I work, and my shirt
sticks to my back.
    I think we could ask the school
board for money. Donations could
make up for the remainder of the
money needed. To get these donations,
we could have a carnival, sell candy,
and ask each child and teacher to
bring a small donation.
    I think all students could work
much better if they were comfortable
and relaxed in a cool climate. I,
for one get aggrivated and disturbed

when I am hot. Therefore, I cannot do my best work. Please consider getting air conditioning for this school.

Sincerely,
Chris Johnson

The writing is fluent and follows accepted conventions of spelling, handwriting, usage, and sentence structure. It demonstrates a strong sense of audience, addressing the reader politely but also directly and succinctly. It presents a reasoned, cogent argument. Most importantly, though, the writer has not sacrificed his own voice for the sake of making a point. He both identifies and personalizes the problem (he cannot work well when it is too hot), and poses a solution for raising money to pay for the air-conditioner. The expressive elements, then, make the letter appealing and ultimately convincing.

Conclusion: Teaching for Communication Competence

For many teachers, coding may seem to present the greatest challenge to students. Problems with the mechanics and structure of language are often the first aspects of students' talk and writing that teachers notice, and many spend a great deal of time trying to help students overcome these problems. It is easy, though, to confuse symptoms with causes. At the heart of these problems is lack of fluency—difficulty with producing language confidently and spontaneously. Exercises designed to correct mechanical errors put the cart before the horse, and often take precious time away from actual speaking and writing experiences. What seems to be efficient turns out to be inefficient if the foundation for effective coding is not first established.

To accomplish that purpose, we would argue for an emphasis on expressive discourse, the free-flowing record of thought and feeling that helps students build fluency in communication. As seen in Ted Brockton's class, students discuss experiences, problems and observations, and record ideas and impressions in journals or other free-writing formats. Teachers respond to writing and guide discussions in such ways as to help students break through obstacles to expression. They encourage students to capture the conversational and expressive qualities of speech in their writing, as well as adapt the vocabulary, diversity, and planned qualities of writing to their talk.

Sentence combining is one instructional technique designed to improve students' coding skills at the level of sentences. Sentence-combining exercises present students with two or more shorter sentences and ask them to create a longer sentence without leaving out any information. Given the cue sentences, "Isaac sat under the apple tree," and "Isaac discovered the law of gravity," I might combine the two to read, "While sitting under the apple tree, Isaac discovered the law of gravity." Some sentence-combining exercises direct students to combine sentences into specific constructions. Others are wholly nondirective and permit students to explore all the syntactic options. (As an interesting diversion, see how many ways you can combine the two sentences about Isaac. Did you get this one: "The law of gravity was discovered by Isaac who sat under a tree which bore apples"?)

Regular practice in sentence combining encourages students to use more complex syntax, and also helps them improve compositions. But since there is no absolute link between complex syntax and quality of expression, we believe that the benefits of sentence combining come about because the exercises make students sensitive to the varied possibilities inherent in language. Students enjoy discussing the merits of different ways of phrasing the same ideas. ("It was an apple tree that Isaac sat under when he discovered the law of gravity"—a good promotion for apple growers.) Significantly, sentence-combining instruction is most powerful when it is accompanied with as *little* direct instruction in grammar as possible.

To promote social awareness, we see the need to take advantage of the various classroom audiences. Teachers can emphasize "relationship-making," viewing the classroom as a language community in which students interact and share with each other as well as the teacher. Communication reveals itself not only in dialogue between teacher and student, but also in a complicated network of relationships. As in Brockton's class, children share ideas, work collaboratively on projects, identify and solve problems (both academic and social), contend with each other (most often productively), and offer help and reassurance. They come to see each other as important resources for learning and support, and thus add to their social awareness.

This is not to diminish the importance of teachers' leadership, however. Most children look to teachers for direction, approval, and decisiveness. But teachers need not sacrifice those roles for the sake of building a strong communication environment. If anything, their leadership is enhanced, as children come to regard them as trusted adults and role models, rather than inflexible authority figures.

The role of leading a group enterprise is nowhere more apparent than in the ways teachers structure discussions or writing processes. In oral work, they should allow students to express ideas and opinions freely, but also control those who tend to dominate, draw out quieter ones, and guard against instances of children hurting each other's feelings. Role-playing of social dilemmas can be an especially effective technique. Similarly, in writing instruction, the teacher should set up opportunities for students to write to and receive response from a peer audience, but also take care to establish a supportive atmosphere for those interactions. Children need to be shown how to respond to each other's writing, and teachers need to step in at various points in the process to help students generate ideas, consider how they might make their writing better, and revise and edit accordingly.

The classroom as language community, then, creates a connection between the available audience in speaking and the unseen audience in writing. In particular, the peer audience serves as a transition from personal to public writing. And correspondingly, the sense of a reader gained through writing contributes to a stronger awareness of the listener in spoken discourse.

Finally, the successful classroom offers students many opportunities to reconstruct experience, to use language to discover and make sense of what might otherwise be chaotic impressions. Our concern here is the making of meanings; few media allow us to do that as well as speaking and writing. As teachers, we often assume that students can learn simply by the one-day transmission of our own knowledge to them, and we are frustrated when they do poorly on tests. In the classroom as language community, however, students talk and write as a means of coming to know things for themselves, in their own ways. Brockton's lesson on magnetism serves as a good example, as students created their own analogies for understanding attraction and repulsion.

In addition to those activities described in our scenario, many others offer possibilities for reconstructing experience. Teachers might have students role-play historical events; record the growth processes of plants or animals; interview older people or other community members; take sensory walks and write about their observations; respond to newspaper articles and editorials; write letters to friends or strangers; share reactions to magazine articles, books, movies, and TV shows; brainstorm ideas for writing; produce stories, poems, scripts, and a personal essay; help each other in revising, editing, and proofreading; and put together a classroom newspaper or literary magazine. What is important is that teachers provide these varied ways for students to make their own meanings and share those creations with each other.

Clearly, between speaking and writing abilities, certain gaps exist for most children. To bridge those gaps, we need to create (to borrow a term from physiology) *synapses*—spark-like connections resulting in release and transmission of energy. For coding, the synapse is expressive discourse, stressing fluency and personal voice as bridges to gaining control of form and conventions. For social awareness, the synapses are relationship-making and the building of language communities, as means toward corresponding successfully with various audiences. And for reconstruction of experience, the synapses are meaning-making and discovery, as ways of achieving the power to make sense of things through language. These synapses are represented in the following diagram:

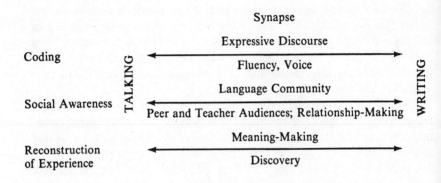

As teachers, we might ask ourselves some questions to see if these synapses occur within our classrooms. Do we give students opportunities for expression in conversation and journal writing? Do we encourage them to communicate in personal and honest ways? Do we create conditions in which students share and interact with classmates? Do we look for signs of growing social and linguistic development? Are we taking advantage of the peer audience for responding to writing, as well as responding ourselves in helpful ways? Do we allow students to experiment with speaking and writing in various forms and to various audiences? Are we encouraging them to forge expressions of meaning from the materials of their experience, thought, and language? And do we show them in as many ways possible that we value those expressions?

If we can answer "yes" to these questions, we will be supporting our students as they build communication competence in speaking and writing.

References

Britton, James. *Language and Learning.* Harmondsworth, England: Pelican Books, 1970.

Britton, James; Burgess, Tony; Martin, Nancy; McLeod, Alex; and Rosen, Harold. *The Development of Writing Abilities 11-18.* London: Macmillan Education, 1975.

Hymes, Del. *On Communicative Competence.* Revised as "Competence and Performance in Linguistics Theory." In *Language Acquisition: Models and Methods,* edited by R. Huxley and E. Ingram. New York: Academic Press, 1971.

Joos, Martin. *The Five Clocks.* New York: Harcourt Brace and World, 1961.

National Assessment of Educational Progress. *The Third Assessment of Writing, 1978-79 Released Exercise Set.* Denver: Education Commission of the States, 1981.

Wood, Barbara, ed. *Development of Functional Communication Competencies: PreK-Grade 6.* Also, *Development of Functional Communication Competencies: Grades 7-12.* Falls Church, Va.: Speech Communication Association and ERIC Clearinghouse on Reading and Communication Skills, 1977.

Additional Resources

Barr, Mary; D'Arcy, Pat; and Healy, Mary K., eds. *What's Going On? Language/ Learning Episodes in British and American Classrooms, Grades 4-13.* Montclair, N.J.: Boynton/Cook Publishers, 1982.

Dyson, Anne Haas. "Oral Language: The Rooting System for Learning to Write." *Language Arts* 58 (1981): 776-84.

Florio, Susan. "The Problem of Dead Letters: Social Perspectives on the Teaching of Writing." *The Elementary School Journal* 80 (September 1979): 1-7.

Graves, Donald H. *Writing: Teachers and Children at Work.* Exeter, N.H.: Heinemann, 1983.

Holdzkom, David; Porter, E. Jane; Reed, Linda; and Rubin, Donald. *Research Within Reach: Oral and Written Communication, A Research-Guided Response to the Concerns of Educators.* St. Louis: CEMREL, Inc., 1982.

Kroll, Barry M., and Vann, Roberta J., eds. *Exploring Speaking-Writing Relationships: Connections and Contrasts.* Urbana, Ill.: National Council of Teachers of English, 1981.

Lindfors, Judith Wells. *Children's Language and Learning.* Englewood Cliffs, N.J.: Prentice-Hall, 1980.

Mallett, Margaret, and Newsome, Bernard. *Talking, Writing and Learning 8-13.* London: Evans/Methuen, 1977.

Moffett, James, and Wagner, B. J. *Student-Centered Language Arts and Reading, K-13: A Handbook for Teachers.* 2nd ed. Boston: Houghton Mifflin, 1976.

Tough, Joan. *Talking and Learning: A Guide to Fostering Communication Skills in Nursery and Infant Schools.* London: Ward Lock Educational, 1977.

Thinking Visually about Writing: Three Models for Teaching Composition, K-12

Charles Suhor, National Council of Teachers of English

Why use visual models to understand the teaching of a written form? Did we not have our fill of visual doodads in the 60s and 70s, when systems analysts littered curriculum bulletins with their flow charts and quasi-scientific claims of precision? Were not those branching tree diagrams that filled up a chalkboard—one student called them "spidery"—enough to frighten many students (and teachers) away from visual models for years to come?

Let me admit from the outset that I have always been a compulsively visual teacher—a frustrated cartoonist, in fact. Yet I agree that many visual models are mainly educational graffiti. But some models *can* be illuminating, *can* make important theoretical and practical distinctions, *can* lead to better ideas about what to do on Monday morning. Those headachy tree diagrams, for instance, provided a theoretical basis for sentence-combining, a very practical classroom technique.

Actually, all of us have some kind of model underlying our teaching styles. The model might be eclectic, derived from and perhaps synthesizing various sources. The model might be followed consciously, or it might be implicit in our classroom activities and assignments. If there were no model operating as we teach, then teaching—if it could be called that—would be a random, disconnected activity. If a model were followed slavishly, teaching would be a pat, nonadaptive kind of behavior. What we *do* with a particular visual model seems to be crucial in determining whether it is a deadening academic exercise or a useful guide to teaching. What I will do with the three models of teaching composition presented in this chapter is: explain each model, relating it to important issues in English teaching, and discuss classroom applications. The models are the Content Area Model; the Mastery Model; and the Writing Process Model.

The models are not parallel in form, and each merits a different emphasis in analysis. To fill in some gaps, some sub-models are included along the way. I believe that the models are fictions that will ring true—at least partially—to your experience as a teacher. And if you find them to be useful ways of looking at the teaching of writing, then they'll certainly qualify as practical.

The Content Area Model

The starting point in the Content Area Model (Figure 1) is an *Abstraction* presented to the students—definitions of parts of speech, rules for subject-verb agreement, a description of paragraph structure, a list of elements in the short story, etc. The students move from these general ideas to more specific instances, as seen in *Models* or *Examples.* Sample paragraphs, model short stories, or similar illustrative materials flesh out the abstraction under study so that students have a clearer understanding of the concepts. Often, the students' understanding is further refined through *Exercises*— e.g., sentences that require underlining of subjects and verbs; scrambled sentences to be sequenced in paragraph form; incomplete short stories that require students to write an appropriate ending. Finally, the increasingly particularized activities are applied in a *Product* (A-B) created by the student—a well-formed paragraph, a five-paragraph theme, a short story containing the essential elements studied, etc. The movement from the abstraction to the models/examples and exercises is one of increasing specificity, usually involving subdivision of broader concepts into component parts. The ultimate intention, though, is for the product to reflect the

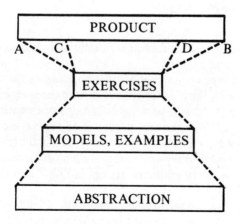

Figure 1. The Content Area Model.

richness of the abstraction—or at least, to embody the most important aspects of the models/examples. But no written product, even from a professional writer, is a perfect realization of its type. The dimensions of the student's product are likely to be considerably narrower, with C-D being a more likely (and certainly acceptable) result of the Content Area approach.

I used variations on the Content Area approach, as did most of my colleagues, in a comprehensive high school when I started teaching in 1957. The approach is still dominant, grades K–12, in innumerable textbooks, handbooks, and curriculum guides; and teachers I have met from all parts of the country speak frequently in terms of the approach. It would be incorrect, though, to identify the Content Area Model with "traditional content." The model represents a general approach to teaching writing, not specific course content. Abstraction-to-product approaches can be and often are used in teaching relatively new ideas such as transformational grammar and Christensen's (1966) sentence rhetoric. There is no concept, from Aristotelian logic to semiotic theory, that cannot be taught according to the Content Area Model. Take, for example, traditional sentence diagraming and transformational diagraming. A traditional diagram of the sentence "My son's coat is brown." might look like this:

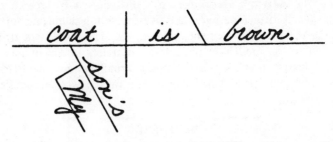

The same sentence, depicted in a transformational branching tree diagram, is shown on the next page.

Traditional or transformational, there is no escaping the teaching of abstractions along with the diagrams. In each case the teacher must explain the diagraming method and provide definitions of essential terms—e.g., possessive pronoun, linking verb, predicate adjectives, etc., in the traditional diagram; nodes, embedding, determiner, etc., in the transformational. (Admittedly, the transformational diagram is a more elegant description of the sentence; but as every graduate student in English knows, it is also far more abstract.)

The diagrams suggest a primary weakness of the Content Area approach. The teaching of heady abstractions *about* writing is unlikely to produce good writing. English teachers know this, I believe, through their collective

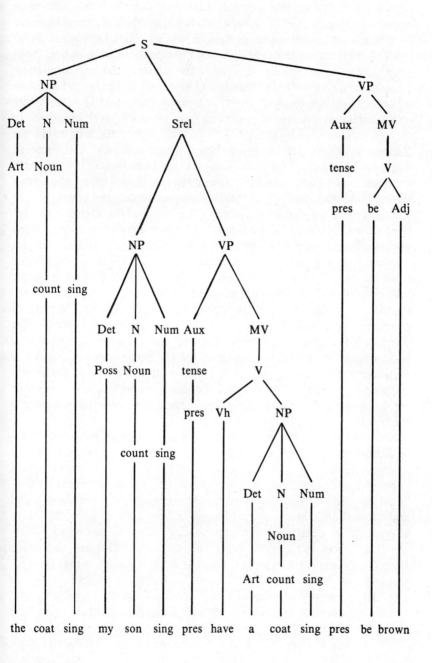

experience as well as from theory and research. Let me share a story from my own experience, one that has a parallel in the lives of many teachers I have talked to. As a tenth-grade English teacher in a senior high school, I would pretest my students each year on the most basic information about language: parts of speech. Invariably the students faltered somewhere between the definitions of pronouns and adverbs, and I knew that my work was cut out for me. I would have to go through the Grand Sequence in my own special and effective way, moving from parts of speech to phrases to clauses to sentences to paragraphs to essays. After all, how could my students write essays if they did not know what a verb was? And it seemed to me that the logic of my approach—moving from smaller units to more complex ones—was working, because at the end of the first semester, when the students started writing a lot, they seemed to do pretty well.

Then I noticed something strange. In the middle of the second semester I tried to use the terminologies that had been the building blocks of my program earlier in the year—and the students had *forgotten* the definitions. They were writing regularly, improving as they went along; yet most of the concepts they had mastered did not seem to be at their disposal when we talked about writing. It did not occur to me at the time that I might have started the students writing during the first week of school instead of commanding a forced march through grammatical terminology. The discussion, the writing, and the feedback of the second semester were what had worked, not the underlining of subjects once/verbs twice, labeling of prepositional phrases and adverb clauses, or taking notes on unity, coherence, and emphasis. My students did not start unifying, cohering, or emphasizing until they had things to talk and write about that were worth the trouble.

Nevertheless, I was satisfied that I was sending some fairly decent writers to Austin Wilson, my friend and colleague who taught English III. But when Austin pretested the students on the most basic information about parts of speech, he concluded that Suhor had not taught them a thing. What they really needed was the Grand Sequence, taught in his own special and effective way. With a few differences related to teaching style, Austin covered the same arsenal of abstractions, switched to real writing afterwards, and sent some pretty decent writers to Miss Taggart, the senior English teacher. You can guess what Miss Taggart thought about Wilson's students and his effectiveness as a teacher when she pretested them on essential knowledge of parts of speech. And so it goes.

The Content Area approach, whether focused on traditional or modern content, ultimately falters because it does not take into account how students learn. In terms of Piagetian theory and research, most students do not have sufficient skill in manipulating abstractions to understand, digest, and apply dense concepts like the absolute phrase, the gerund, and the participle.

In 1969 John Mellon did a review of twentieth-century research on the relationship between knowledge of formal grammar and writing skill. Steve Sherwin did a similar review, independently, in the same year. Usually such reviews are highly inconclusive, allowing the researcher and the reader to take whatever meaning from the data they like. The findings in the Mellon and Sherwin reviews, though, were remarkably consistent. Neither found a single study to support the notion that knowledge of definitions and rules will, in itself, improve student writing. True, the dozens of studies reviewed were vastly different in structure and focus; many of them were wildly inept in design. But logically, a potpourri of studies lumped together in a historical review should paint a dappled picture. Their very diversity should skew the collective results so that no conclusions can be drawn. Such is the case with research reviews in most controversial areas, such as phonics versus language experience instruction in reading. But this is not the case with research on formal grammar and composition. A message lies therein.

The message is *not* that teachers should avoid use of any formal terminology in discussing writing, although a sustained program of taxonomy is clearly not warranted. Students do not learn how to write by studying and mastering prescriptions any more than small children learn to talk by learning formal grammar. The Content Area approach is wrongly based: it directs attention to the structure of language, abstractly expressed, rather than to the student as a maker of language.

A final anecdote underlines the futility of dependence on the Content Area Model. Some sixth-grade students who had been through the rigors of Content Area instruction in grammar for several years were asked to give their own definitions of grammar. Here is what they came up with in a class-composed poem.

> Grrr—ammar
> Grammar is where words pop in and out of your head like floating
>   bubbles.
> Grammar is knowing what to say when the preacher comes to dinner.
> Grammar is when the teacher stands in front of the room and taps on
>   the blackboard and says we must never say ain't.
> Grammar is like coconut—I'm allergic to both.
> Grammar is parts of speech that talk in the right way.
> Grammar is when nouns are nouns and verbs are verbs until the time
>   comes and nouns become verbs, and verbs become nouns, and
>   only the teacher can say when the time is coming.

Grammar is learning one way and speaking another.
Grammar is asking permission to wash your hands when it's not your
hands you're worried about.
Grammar is wondering why it all matters to everyone but us.

Abstractions Made Easy

But what of simplified conceptual approaches, adapted carefully to
students' ability levels? Many teachers claim that certain highly structured
Content Area devices—like teaching the five-paragraph theme and basic
short story structure—do in fact result in coherent writing. Let us look at a
variation on the five-paragraph theme first. A bulletin from the Louisiana
State Department of Education, *Models for Writing, K-12,* contains an
extremely lucid treatment of teaching the essay through a simple format.
The bulletin describes a "basic sixteen-sentence pattern essay" that falls
into four paragraphs of four sentences each. The aim is to provide the
student with "an easily recognizable form which he or she can imitate."
Included are a visual model, teaching instructions, and credible testimony
that the methods have been used "extremely effectively with grades 7–12."
Several examples of the four-paragraph/sixteen-sentence pattern essay are
given, among them this one on "The Need for Exercise."

> 1. If given the opportunity, people have always endangered their
> health by eating too much and exercising too little. 2. The ancient
> Romans indulged themselves with large banquets. 3. Today many
> Americans have heart attacks because they are overweight and under
> exercised. 4. For good health every adult should follow a daily plan of
> exercise.
>
> 5. Many doctors recommend jogging as a particularly effective
> form of exercise. 6. Heart patients jog because they need bodily move-
> ment which will strengthen the heart. 7. Jogging also builds leg
> muscles. 8. It can help a person lose extra pounds.
>
> 9. Another effective form of exercise is swimming. 10. It stretches
> arm and leg muscles. 11. It even reduces bulging waistlines. 12. Some
> swimmers say that water sports improve a person's coordination.
>
> 13. Because many Americans work in offices, they neglect the
> exercise necessary for being in good physical condition. 14. As people
> become more concerned with their physical well-being, jogging and
> swimming will be joined by other forms of strenuous movement.
> 15. Some physical therapists predict a boom in the number of health
> spas and exercise clinics in the next few years. 16. Some day even
> grandmothers may be running the four minute mile!

The bulletin acknowledges that the approach is limiting and suggests that
students who master the form be permitted to move quickly to more
complex writing. Students with skill in organization, the bulletin says,
"would not benefit greatly from detailed attention to this model."

The caveats are well taken. It would be depressing in the extreme to think that the production of vacuous, formulaic essays is an important goal of the writing program. Yet I publicly confess that I taught essay-by-formula for several years in a comprehensive school, and I was successful in getting students to fill in numerous structural and rhetorical blanks that added up to well-organized trivialities. I went on to other things, of course; but the simplified, abstraction-to-product approach did give many students their first feeling of success in essay writing.

So I won a limited victory over compositional chaos. But those rickety little essays never told me whether or not my students could express themselves with honesty, courage, or even any basic feeling on a given topic. Genuine self-expression and communication emerged in class discussion, in one-to-one conferences, and in other writing—not in the essays written according to simple prescriptions.

For those interested in the visual model of the four-paragraph/sixteen-sentence theme, see Figure 2. Figure 3 gives approximately equal space to a satirical comment on the five-paragraph theme from Boynton and Cook. In the real world of classroom events, you get what you ask for. Formalistic teaching will yield formalistic results. An example from a short story unit, discovered by Yetta Goodman of the University of Arizona, illustrates this principle with a vengeance. After studying definitions and models of the basic elements in a narrative, fifth-graders were asked to write an original story. A student named Rachel apparently learned the lesson a little too well.

The Cat and the Rat
by Rachel

Once upon a time, there was an old house. There was nothing in the house but an old cat. This old cat was a antagonist. He hated mice he wontent let mice near the house. So one little mice came by the house, this mice was a protagonist. This takes place in California. The cat was asleep on some covers in the kitchen so the mouse was hungree so he decided to go see what was kitchen to eat. He jumped on the table then on the counter. The mice was eaten some old beans all of the sudden the cat woke up and saw that there was a mice in the house. So the cat and the mice had a climax and guess who won the mice did. And the mice lived in the old house all by himself.

Strengths of the Content Area Approach

Let us look at some of the benefits, on the other hand, of the Content Area Model. First, many traditional teachers reverse the first two elements, starting out with models and examples. Through Socratic questioning, the students come to understand the abstract qualities underlying the works under study. For example, students might be assigned simple interior

Number all sentences.
Underline the generalization in each paragraph once.
Underline the thesis statement (4) twice.

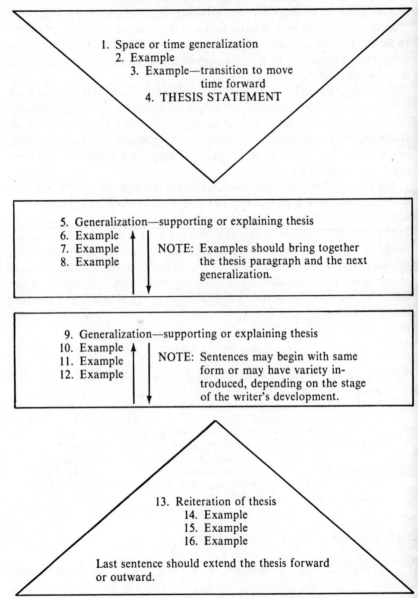

1. Space or time generalization
2. Example
   3. Example—transition to move
      time forward
   4. THESIS STATEMENT

5. Generalization—supporting or explaining thesis
6. Example
7. Example
8. Example

NOTE: Examples should bring together
the thesis paragraph and the next
generalization.

9. Generalization—supporting or explaining thesis
10. Example
11. Example
12. Example

NOTE: Sentences may begin with same
form or may have variety introduced, depending on the stage
of the writer's development.

13. Reiteration of thesis
14. Example
15. Example
16. Example

Last sentence should extend the thesis forward
or outward.

Figure 2. Four-Paragraph/Sixteen-Sentence method of essay writing.

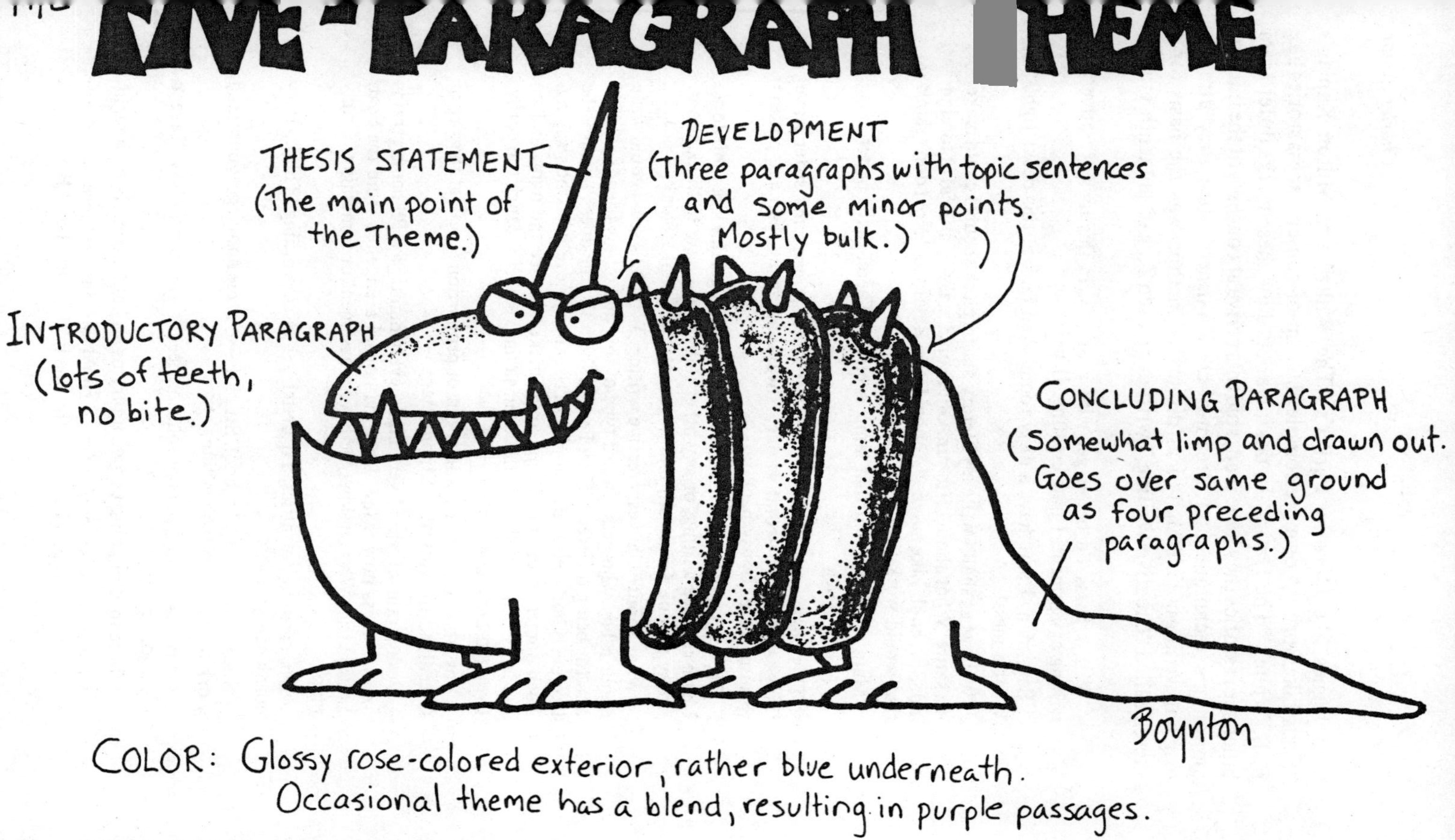

THE FIVE-PARAGRAPH THEME

THESIS STATEMENT — (The main point of the Theme.)

DEVELOPMENT (Three paragraphs with topic sentences and some minor points. Mostly bulk.)

CONCLUDING PARAGRAPH (Somewhat limp and drawn out. Goes over same ground as four preceding paragraphs.)

INTRODUCTORY PARAGRAPH (Lots of teeth, no bite.)

Boynton

COLOR: Glossy rose-colored exterior, rather blue underneath. Occasional theme has a blend, resulting in purple passages.

Figure 3. Sandra Boynton's model of the Five-Paragraph Theme.

monologues like Dorothy Parker's "The Waltz" and Milton Kaplan's "Feels Like Spring," or more complex stream-of-consciousness stories like E. B. White's "The Door." In talking about how these works differ from other short stories they have read, students arrive at concepts of the interior monologue technique and stream-of-consciousness; then they attempt original writings. This analytical/discursive method was the basis for a sketch called "Creative Writing," written by Fred Z., a bright tenth-grader.

Well, I guess I'd better get with it and begin this lousy creative writing assignment. I hate creating. It bugs me.

Say, man, I sure have a dirty room. And look at this desk! Ugh! What a mess!

Well, what shall I write my literary masterpiece about? I could make it a satire. What about? Hmmm. Oh! I could make it satirical of foreign aid. Say, cool. Like maybe "Animal Farm Revisited." No, I don't think that would work very well. Too complicated.

Man, the light from that lamp is bright. There, that's better.

I hate English.

This chair is uncomfortable. Drat it! Why can't my sister leave things as they are—comfortable. Always taking my chair and putting this one here. Lousy pack rat.

Oh, yeah, I better get back to work or I won't get this lousy job done. I hate creative writing, or any other thing that I have to think about. Lousy school. Come on, man, concentrate! Think! Think!

What about? Oh, yes, creative writing. Well, let's see. I could write about a boy who gets a weird type of toy, and all his friends ridicule him for being different. Then he tells them that he doesn't want to be like everybody else. But he doesn't really believe what he's saying. Then someone or something could make him see the light, and he suddenly believes what he has been saying. No! No! Much too corny. I've read fairy tales better than that.

Boy, that map on my wall is out of proportion. Look at the size of Greenland to Australia. Stupid map!

Pesky train whistle. Every night, every night. Say, I'll bet my trains are in a mess now. Man, I bet the houses are melted from the heat. Lousy attic. Why couldn't we have a basement or something? Grimy map.

Oh, speaking of attics, I'd better get mine working. Think! How corny can you get?

Stupid attic. Stupid school. Stupid! Aw, come on and get your mind working. Oil it, or something.

Oil it. Like man, I bet my Johnson needs oil in the gear box. Have to see about it.

Oh, man, I'm going to give up trying to hold a conscious thought.

Conscious. Like cool! Yes, I could do one of those stream-of-consciousness type stories like the one in class. But how? Hmmm. . . .

Oh, what a weird thought forming! Yes, I could start it like this:
"Well, I guess I'd better get with it and begin this lousy creative writing assignment. I hate creating. It bugs me. . . ."

As the example suggests, the use of models of literary types as the basis for student discussions is one of the strongest elements in Content Area instruction. Models are not sufficient for the teaching of composition, but they are probably necessary. Minimally, group discussion of others' work involves training in thinking skills and oral communication. I suspect that actual carryover from discussion to writing depends on a number of factors —the quality of the discussion (in terms of the students' interests, participation, and skill in developing points logically); the conscious attention given to compositional aspects of the model (style, logical structure, methods of achieving cohesion); note-taking skills; and the accessibility of the writers to the students.

The test of accessibility is whether or not the students, after discussing the writer's skills and flaws, believe that they can go and do likewise. Conventional textbooks were often packed with inaccessible models from Thoreau, Faulkner, or Henry James. In recent years textbook writers have taken the cue from good teachers, who instead go to the ditto machine with carefully selected models written by students or drawn from contemporary professional writers.

The greatest flaw in the use of writing models is that we expect too much of them. No amount of discussion of others' writings will substitute for the actual experience of writing. We have greatly overestimated the benefits of analysis of models. As Richard Barbieri of Milton Academy has said, "You cannot infer a pig from a sausage."

The Content Area approach has another virtue; it is often more efficient than other approaches. A content focus is well suited to teaching things that do not warrant a great deal of time—e.g., reviews of literary or rhetorical terms used earlier in the year. Metric forms in poetry, if taught at all, are probably taught less painfully through given prescriptions that allow students to move quickly into writing original haikus or limericks. Gifted students can often internalize abstract and formalistic guidelines rapidly, opening the way for in-depth treatment of more sophisticated aspects of writing. During my four years of teaching in a public school for gifted students, I noticed that teachers in many subject areas quickly brushed aside arbitrary "required" topics by asking students simply to read/listen and apply. The teacher of gifted students also knows that they often approach formulaic assignments playfully, satirizing the assignment even as they carry it out. Fred Z.'s "Creative Writing" sketch is one example. Another student executed a "How to . . ." assignment by writing a mock-serious guide to use of the telephone book. Another, late in submitting a cause-effect paper, wrote a wildly Gothic explanation of his tardiness.

Finally, it is hard to counter the argument that *some* rigid, formulaic writing is entrenched in both our educational system and our society for the foreseeable future. Maybe the five-paragraph theme, the self-advertising clincher sentence, and the ability to cultivate a certain amount of nauseating jargon are aspects of communicative competency—survival skills in the context of our educational system and society at large.

The Mastery Model

The Mastery Model for teaching composition (Figure 4) is a visual interpretation of Benjamin Bloom's ideas. The step-by-step image in the model is consistent with Bloom's belief that much school learning can be broken down into component parts, with each segment of a learning sequence carefully built upon the previous one. In a strict mastery sequence on proper use of the question mark, for example, Step A might make a distinction between questions and declarations, with a short exercise to be completed as a condition of proceeding to Step B. That step might involve an understanding of differences between questions and queries in the form of statements ("I wonder whether . . ."); and Step C might describe tag-end

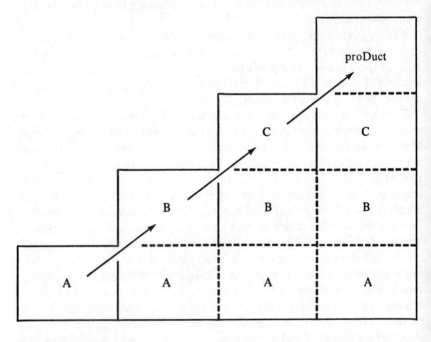

Figure 4. The Mastery Model.

questions, which appear at the ends of statements (. . . , don't they?). Brief exercises at the end of Steps B and C would demonstrate partial mastery. The final step, implicitly or explicitly embracing all the others, might ask the student: to distinguish questions from non-questions in a series of unpunctuated sentences; to label regular questions, tag-end questions, and query statements; and to produce original, end-punctuated sentences that exemplify the concepts included in Steps A to C. Similar mastery sequences could be developed for other punctuation marks and for many (but not all) composition concepts and activities.

Mastery learning can and often does move from abstraction to practice, similar to Content Area instruction. And many teachers who use the Content Area approach are careful to arrange their units of instruction in a logical manner, as in the phrase/clause/sentence/paragraph/essay sequence described earlier. But mastery instruction is far more rigorous in its specification of objectives and its sequencing of component parts. Moreover, the Mastery Model builds in evaluation at each important step, and it always allows for varying rates of progress among students.

Mastery learning is consistent with three important influences on education: Skinner's behaviorist psychology; Mager's specification of learning objectives; and the use of programmed materials in textbooks, computers, and other instructional materials. The idea of behavioral objectives, first popularized in the 1960s, reflects a Skinnerian view of teaching—viz., teaching as the systematic inducement of observable behaviors. The behaviorists' emphasis on that which is observable and measurable was in part a legitimate reaction to fuzzy, overgeneralized, traditional goals such as "appreciation of great literature" and "ability to write with verve and imagination."

The behaviorist would argue that such vague goals must be recast in ways that are useful to the teacher, the learner, and supervisory education agencies. Hence, a mastery-based learning sequence on "Clear Sentences" would provide several steps for distinguishing clear sentences from those with various kinds of ambiguity (improper modification, faulty pronoun reference, etc.). The abstract notion of "clarity" would thereby be "operationalized" in the materials, which specify the kinds of ambiguity to be avoided and the kinds of clarity to be sought.

Programmed materials can be (and often have been) put together in loose, non-mastery sequences, but they are especially adaptable to mastery learning. Textbooks can be carefully programmed, as in Blumenthal's *English 2200, English 2600,* and *English 3200* series. But mastery-based programmed materials are most suited to teaching machines, especially computerized instruction units. The definition of "teaching machine" in the AECT (Association for Educational Communication and Technology)

Glossary of Terms (1979) underlines the strong relationships among machinery, programmed instruction, and behaviorist theory.

> Teaching machine (programmed instruction)
>
> A device which presents programmed materials and provides for reinforcement. Such devices usually include: storage for programmed materials (ranging from printed pages to a roll of paper or a computerized information bank); a display panel for items (ranging from a written paragraph to a visual projection screen); a student response device (which may be a space in which to write, buttons to push, or a typewriter keyboard); and a feedback mechanism from which the student determines the correctness of the response (ranging from a page in a book to an answer revealed by a sliding door or a computerized print-out). Teaching machines may also record student responses permanently and some select subsequent steps on the basis of the student's response. (p. 185)

Programmed materials on computers can permit a high degree of individualization insofar as students with different problems in mastering a skill can be taken along different "branches" that deal with their particular problems. Computer programs allow students to advance at their own rate of speed, since a one-on-one relationship exists between the student and the computer. Many mastery-based computer materials on grammar and punctuation are already on the courseware market and in use in PLATO and other systems. (Of course, computer-assisted instruction is not limited to mastery learning. See Standiford et al., *Computers in the English Classroom*.)

The Mastery Model is appealing because it looks so orderly and reasonable—and even "innovative," given the emergence of computers as a sign of the future in our schools. Mastery-based programs look good to the PTA, the education reporter for the local gazette, and legislators who want desperately to be assured that something is happening in the schools. Surely, they reason, such a program cannot fail to promote learning. Does mastery not start from the beginning with "entry behaviors" then take students logically—and on an individualized basis—through the steps that lead to a product? What is more, mastery is demonstrated during the various steps in the process and at the end point as well. Here, at last, is proof that learning is taking place in the schools.

Flaws in the Mastery Approach

The apparent common-sense benefits of mastery learning ultimately do not square either with research or with the insights of practicing teachers. Benjamin Bloom, the father of mastery learning, points out in *Human*

Characteristics and School Learning (1976) that mastery works best in subject areas that can be "chopped up" into neat sequences. Most mastery research has been in teaching the sciences, and applications have been mainly in subject areas that lend themselves to the step-by-step approach. In the Army, I learned most things by a mastery method, from disassembling, cleaning, and reassembling a rifle to cleaning mess trays by-the-numbers. But on maneuvers we were led through situations that called for hypothesis-making, improvisation, and quick intuitive action—none of which could be "mastered" through mastery.

Bloom acknowledges that certain cognitive skills are learned in an erratic manner, according to developmental patterns that are not consistent with the mastery design. He points out that further work is needed in "reasoning processes, language development, and writing competence . . . before one can clearly identify and measure . . . generalized entry behaviors as a basis for mastery learning" (p. 51). Every parent knows that Bloom is right. Language acquisition in young children—an incredibly complex process in which most grammatical structures in English are learned by age six—occurs in ways that bear no resemblance to the rigidities inherent in mastery learning. Moreover, research about the composing processes of children and adults suggests that writing involves a complicated set of interrelated activities, probably best taught initially through more flexible methods.

Like the Content Area Model, the Mastery Model is subject to earnest misapplication based on a belief in logical organization of teaching materials. Yes, it is "logical" to segment the composition program, starting with a study of words and proceeding to the study of sentences, phrases, clauses, etc. But this logical organization of *materials* does not mean that *students* normally process such instructional sequences in ways that lead to more effective writing. In other words, the psychology of the learner, not presuppositions about the structure of the discipline or a sequential mode of instruction, should be the first consideration in developing a composition program.

Mastery learning is truly practical only in certain areas of English instruction. If you think of class discussion or small group work as an important preparation for writing, you cannot subscribe to a Mastery Model of composition teaching, because the dynamic of discussion cannot be segmented into distinct steps. But if you want to teach proper use of quotation marks, mastery materials can be helpful. In fact, mastery-based programmed materials on computer can provide good support for the teaching of many aspects of mechanics in a composition program. I can even imagine a computerized mastery sequence based on Kenneth Pike's strategies for exploring a topic. But the present state of the art is that mastery learning can guarantee little more than one-shot mastery of a limited set of skills, often to the systematic exclusion of more global skills such as prewriting discussion. My inability to produce student writing samples resulting from the Mastery Model is based on the simple fact that mastery instruction yields small parts, not wholes. I have never heard a teacher claim that any student essay was written in connection with a strict Mastery Model lesson.

Allan Glatthorn's NCTE book *A Guide for Developing an English Curriculum for the 80s* (1980) does champion a mastery curriculum in English. But Glatthorn says that the mastery curriculum's "emphasis on specific objectives, frequent assessment, and error remediation makes it inappropriate for all organic learning and for any integrated thematic units which would emphasize discovery and inductive learning" (p. 27). He speaks of (but does not delineate) an entire non-mastery "organic curriculum" that deals with oral language competence, affective learning, and other components of English study.

Glatthorn's fine instincts as a teacher usually prevail over his dubious dichotomy of a mastery and organic curriculum. To his credit, he acknowledges that his is not a rigid mastery program in Bloom's sense. He sometimes deviates radically from mastery theory (as in his excellent suggestions for warmup activities for composition). But I fear that Glatthorn's quasi-mastery program will give mastery instruction in English an undeserved good name; and at its worst, Glatthorn's program supports the narrowness of the Mastery Model's behaviorist bias and its tendency to whittle English curricula down to the dimensions of the mastery approach. (Witness, for example, Glatthorn's idea that the mastery curriculum, not the organic curriculum, should determine the selection of textbooks.)

A comment on the political implications of mastery learning is in order. Teachers should know that many administrators see mastery materials—in the forms of individualized learning packets, programmed materials, and computer courseware—as "teacher-proof." Some of our worst fears about the teacher's diminishing power to determine everyday programs and practices might be realized through the imposition of rigid mastery materials. Curriculum developers and school administrators live in a politically charged climate. They must deal with public demands for concrete information (i.e., test results) about student learning, and with legislatively-mandated competency programs. Even though no hard research exists to show that writing can be taught effectively through mastery techniques, administrators might find it expedient to invoke mastery as an ordered, sequential, self-proving method for teaching anything and everything. Certainly, mastery is easier to explain to the public than the rationale for teaching composition in accordance with the developmental learning patterns of the child.

Variations on mastery curricula in English or reading have already been used in numerous school systems—Chicago, Louisville, New Orleans, Salt Lake City. In one city I asked several English teachers how they felt about the program. Their views ranged from enthusiastic endorsement to bitter complaints about cynicism and blindness at the central office. One English department head claimed that the program gave a unity to the English curriculum in her school for the first time. I knew from direct observation that this teacher conducts good classroom discussions and has a varied writing program. So I asked how she personally reconciled the prescribed program with the use of journals, small-group discussions, and other things she does so well. Her answer was that there is a point at which she simply closes the door and teaches, doing what she believes is good for students. I, for one, am thankful that mastery programs are not proof against this teacher's skills.

If Mastery Models are imposed on English programs in composition, I see at least four results: first, teachers who now teach virtually no composition at all will be forced to make a show of it, at least. Second, many teachers will be either sufficiently impressed or intimidated by the approach and will stop looking for other ways of teaching writing. Third, many will carry out the program minimally but will make time for other things. Finally, a few will actively oppose the program and become, in effect, agents for further curriculum change.

The Writing Process Model

The Writing Process Model (Figure 5) is a synthesis of ideas from Graves, Britton, Stanford, and others. The elements of purpose and audience permeate the model. Even though the process is student-centered, drawing on the experiences and ideas of students, all activities relate to the purpose of an assignment—e.g., to create an essay of comparison and contrast. A sense of audience also permeates the model. Students are not writing solely for the teacher. Rather, at numerous points they share ideas and react to each other's writing, and their final product is intended to be read by someone besides the teacher.

Prewriting

The prewriting stage is an important feature of the model. Prewriting activities can include teaching of appropriate *thinking skills*. A two-step brainstorming/language game involving comparison and contrast might include these questions placed on the chalkboard:

	Prewriting	Drafting	Revising	Proofreading =	Product
P	—Brainstorming	—With the benefit of previous thought, talk, notes, activities	—With feedback— peer reaction, teacher reaction, self-assessment	—Mechanics, spelling, etc.	
U	—Discussion (with peers and teachers)— refining and organizing ideas				A
R					U
P					D
O	—Note-taking during the above				I
S	—Sample essays				E
E					N
					C
					E

Figure 5. The Writing Process Model.

How is a _____ like a _____?
How are they different?

In the first step, the teacher can provide five to eight pairs of nouns, beginning perhaps with simple word pairs (like *oak tree, rabbit; tricycle, jet plane*) then going on to more complex ones (including some with potential for humor—like *zoo, schoolyard; TV advertisement, soap opera*); and others of a more abstract nature (like *jogging, studying; friendship, love*). The students' interests and level of sophistication should be taken into account in selecting word pairs. As in all brainstorming, the emphasis should be on quick-paced response without hard evaluation of the ideas presented.

In the second step, each student can be asked to write on a slip of paper a single noun—anything from *hamburger* to *generosity*. The slips of paper are folded and put into a grab bag, and a volunteer randomly picks out any two slips. The questions on the blackboard are then applied to the randomly selected pairs. Students are encouraged to use their imagination so that odd pairings like *circus* and *sausage pizza* will result in some ingenious, even bizarre, comparisons and contrasts.

From the warmup games, the students move to *discussion* of topics that interest them—again, with comparisons and contrasts built into the topics. The teacher might lead this discussion to provide a model of good interactive discussion. Students who are skilled in discussion might go directly into small groups according to topics of common interest. In any case, students should be encouraged to make notes on key ideas in the discussions.

Topics for discussion might be comparison/contrast of two cities, television shows, football teams, popular singers, cars, newspaper ads, etc. Academic topics need not be excluded from consideration. Joyce Kilmer's "Trees" can be compared to Edward Field's excellent modern poem of the same name; D.H. Lawrence and Emily Dickinson both wrote poems about bats; and so on.

Reading and discussion of *model essays* will give students a chance to examine how others have organized comparisons and contrasts. As noted in the section on Content Area instruction, accessibility is important. Cicero compared the contributions of the soldier to those of the statesman. Montaigne compared personal experience with testimony and institutional wisdom. Lamb compared two kinds of intellect—the "Caledonian" or compulsively orderly thinker, and the "anti-Caledonian" or intuitive thinker. Yet these essays would, at best, convince most students of Cicero's and Montaigne's and Lamb's brilliance without developing confidence in their own potential for producing insightful comparisons. The "Yes/

Queen" essay below, written by Greg S., a high school senior, is not a classic, but it is a good model, briskly written. It can help students to get a feeling for how to organize comparisons and a conviction that the process is within their range of capabilities.

Two rock groups of British origin, Yes and Queen, have won popularity among young audiences everywhere, each achieving a recognizable style in the music they produce. Both bands have attained the aura of royalty typical of superstars in the world of rock. But despite surface similarities, Yes and Queen are two different bands.

Queen can be looked upon as rock conservatives, sticking to the instrumental basics (piano, bass, guitar, drums) and getting novelty by throwing in outrageous vocalizations or varied musical structures (blues, ragtime, opera, gospel). These factors alone have given Queen a style hard to duplicate. Yes is musically liberal, using the latest equipment and basing their overlapping melodies on classical music. The group experiments more with instrumentation than Queen does, and the result is a more convincing style.

Vocalists are usually the focus of attention in a rock band, and this is true of Queen and Yes. Jon Anderson, the lead vocalist for Yes, contributes heavily to the band's popularity, writing nearly all of the lyrics and a majority of the melodies. He has a wide vocal range, sticking mostly to his falsetto, which is very well controlled—a quality that is generally lacking in rock vocalists.

Freddie Mercury, lead vocalist and pianist for Queen, is one of the band members most responsible for the group's popularity. Mercury wrote "Killer Queen" (their first hit) and "Bohemian Rhapsody," which gained them national popularity in 1975. Like Jon Anderson, he has a wide vocal range, and he brings together a variety of influences with unusual perception.

Yes's tendency to experiment makes their instrumental work more interesting. Keyboard player Rick Wakeman has a menagerie of keyboards and synthesizers that he plays very effectively. Screams and sirens, bombs and choirs, feedback and euphoria are all at his fingertips as he works his synthesizers. Like the rest of Yes, his runs are classically oriented, so he fits right in with the group's musical blueprint.

Queen's elemental style rarely calls for synthesizers, but lead guitarist Brian May produces an adequate synthesis of sounds with his guitar. Although May has a definite rock orientation, he can create reproductions of trumpets, flutes, and flowing harmonies that one would believe came from a synthesizer. Yes guitarist Steve Howe produces a variety of guitar noises also, but he is best at throwing out dashes of linking guitar runs, intense solos in alternating patterns, and bright, classically influenced melodies.

Chris Squire, bass guitarist for Yes, is undoubtedly one of the most gifted bass players in rock. He is free-styled yet very disciplined, and his timing is immaculate. He executes syncopated, bouncing riffs that complement Yes's unique and complex rhythms. John Deacon of Queen, Squire's bass-playing counterpart, is noticeably rock-based in style. Though his rhythms are simpler than Squire's, his timing and heavy rock sound are appropriate for the tunes that Queen grinds out.

Roger Taylor, the drummer for Queen, also supports their rock 'n' roll approach. He has no outstanding qualities as a rock drummer, other than that he is, in fact, a good rock drummer. He keeps a solid, driving beat and can do effective fill-ins from one phrase to another. Alan White, Yes's drummer, is more flexible, perhaps once again because the group's music permits him greater freedom. He uses not only conventional drums but also drum synthesizers, gongs, chimes, vibraphones, crotales—the widest variety of percussive sounds available.

Because of their landmark achievements in developing rock, it is impossible to state that Queen is better than Yes or that Yes is better than Queen. Each group's style is distinctive, and you could not rate one against the other any more than you could rate the Eiffel Tower against the Egyptian pyramids. I personally enjoy both of them to the point of fanaticism, and I can foresee new musical ideas emerging from the better qualities of both bands.

© 1980 Scholastic, Inc. Reprinted by permission.

Students should be invited to react to the substance of the essay, if they wish. The author's approaches to comparison/contrast can be discussed afterwards. That discussion could include form-related questions like these:

> In the first paragraph, what similarities between the two bands were mentioned?

> What differences were pointed out in the second paragraph?

> Going through the rest of the essay, identify the points that the writer selected for comparison and contrast. Tell whether the writer offered adequate examples, descriptions, or comments to back up his comparisons and contrasts.

> Find key words in the essay that link ideas for making comparisons (*also, similarly, like,* etc.) and contrasts (*but, although, yet,* etc.).

Drafting: Feedback for Revision

With good prewriting preparation, students should be prepared for the first draft of their own comparison/contrast essays. They can choose from topics already discussed in class or select another topic. This draft is not seen as the culminating activity, or as a test of skills and understandings from the prewriting sessions, or even necessarily as a solo flight. For some students, further discussion with the teacher or with other students about potential topics and approaches might be useful before beginning the draft.

Since students are encouraged to see the draft as an initial attempt rather than a *magnum opus* (the first draft might in fact resemble Ken Macrorie's "free writing" or James Britton's "expressive writing"), there is less anxiety

here than in traditional do-or-die writing situations. Students know that
there will be refinement and revision based on feedback from the teacher,
the entire class, or small student groups.

The three most common kinds of teacher feedback are individual *written
commentary, conferencing,* and *Writing Centers.* Historically, written
commentaries from the teacher have been the main source of feedback; but
as students write more frequently, teachers are finding it virtually impossible to respond in writing to every student paper. The National Council of
Teachers of English statement on class size points out:

> the language arts teacher must have a class size and student load that
> allow time to meet school and classroom responsibilities and to
> provide attention to individual student needs. For a teacher load of
> 100 students, a minimum of 20 minutes per week per student for the
> evaluation of writing involves 33.3 hours—the equivalent of four
> working days—in addition to the time required for the preparation
> and teaching of the other language arts skills.

Yet some written comments are essential. They establish rapport while
offering substantive advice to the student, and they strengthen the image of
the teacher as one who communicates through writing. Here, for example,
is the response to an early draft of Greg S.'s Yes/Queen paper:

> You're off to a good start. Some specifics for consideration in your
> next draft: I like your contrast of Yes and Queen as "liberal" and
> "conservative," respectively. Could you explain that more fully in
> terms of their basic styles?

> Your treatment of the vocalists is interesting but scattered. You're
> treating Anderson in paragraph two, then taking up Mercury in
> paragraph five. Why not get the comparisons side by side? Most of
> your comparisons would be sharper, I think, if you paired them up
> more clearly and used more connectives as "glue."

> The sentence that begins "Screams and sirens" has great energy, as do
> most of your sentences.

As teachers require more writing, the need for less time-consuming response
increases. Student-teacher conferencing during class time appears to be
growing as a method for teacher feedback. In the conference the teacher
simply converses with the student about strong and weak points in the draft
and suggests strategies for improvement. Proofreading concerns—correction of spelling and mechanics—are normally postponed until later.

Some schools have established Writing Centers where students can meet
with a teacher-conferencer at different times of the day for help in
developing an assignment. For a good Writing Center design, see the article
by Luban et al., in the November, 1978 *English Journal.*

Peer feedback—students giving each other advice on how to improve their writing—was once known by the name of "cheating." It is not that at all, of course. Nor is it just a way of dealing with the time contraints inherent in teacher feedback. The fact is, students attend to each other's comments very carefully. And when teachers train students to react intelligently to each other's work, they are training students in critical thinking, discussion skills, and tolerance of others' ideas and feelings.

In the section on prewriting I noted that good whole-class discussion should precede small-group work. The same applies to peer feedback. Students need to participate in pertinent, sensitive discussion of their peer's writing before they are set loose in small groups. One excellent resource on teacher evaluation, peer evaluation, and small-group work is NCTE's *How to Handle the Paper Load* (edited by Gene Stanford and the NCTE Committee on Classroom Practices). Five specific ideas for small-group evaluation of early drafts are:

> Circulate a list of discussion points to be raised in each group. The discussion points should deal with the most important characteristics —"primary traits," if you will—of the kind of composition assigned.
>
> As an alternative to discussion points, circulate a checklist of things to look for in each paper. Again, the checklist should not be a single, overgeneralized list of broad compositional qualities; it should focus on important aspects of the particular assignment.
>
> Use other discussion-inducing techniques with students who are either inexperienced with discussion or inclined to use peer feedback sessions as a display of intolerance or braggadocio. For example, the "PSQ Method" used in the Cedar Rapids, Iowa, Public Schools calls for a positive statement (P) first; a suggestion (S) for improvement second; and a question (Q) to the author third.
>
> Suggest different strategies for working within the groups. One group might prefer to have each paper read aloud by the author, while another might wish to have each paper passed around and read silently before group discussion begins.
>
> In the initial peer feedback session on a given assignment, encourage students to overlook mechanical aspects of the papers so they can focus on substantive aspects. But if poor spelling or mechanics render parts of the paper virtually unintelligible, this should be called to the attention of the student writer.

Proofreading

A specific focus on proofreading for accurate spelling, punctuation, Standard English usage, etc., can await the late stages of revision. The teacher has long-range responsibility for diagnosing the spelling, mechanics, and usage needs of the class as a whole and of individual students. Problems observed in most students' papers over a period of time might be met head-on with the entire class through appropriate exercises. But as suggested earlier, an all-out attack on a broad range of principles of mechanics and usage each year is totally unwarranted, not to mention devastatingly boring. In other words, handbooks on grammar and punctuation should never be used as textbooks. Rather, a handbook is a *resource* for identifying and defining the specific problems the teacher discovers in student writing.

When students' errors are at a low level of abstraction—e.g., lack of commas for items in a series—the Content Area Model of abstraction-to-product might best be employed. When an error is more sophisticated—e.g., lack of commas around nonrestrictive adjective clauses—most students will respond more readily to sentence-combining exercises that involve both manipulation of syntax and appropriate punctuation. Sentence-combining exercises can be created for almost all syntactic structures and the conventions of punctuation that go with them. (See existing materials by Combs, O'Hare, and McHugh noted in the Reference section.)

Special effort should be made to individualize instruction in mechanics and usage. Some students in a ninth-grade class might have problems with almost all uses of the comma. Others might need help only with commas in introductory adverb clauses and restrictive/nonrestrictive materials. Conferencing can help straighten out many problems on an individual basis. Exercises, whether in handbooks or on computers, are important resources for individualization. Research in the teaching of conventions of Edited American English is soft. But we do know from National Assessment data that students are generally better at mechanics and spelling than they are at more central composing skills like producing clear, well-connected discourse. This is ironic, since the business community has traditionally expressed worry about errors in spelling, mechanics, and usage. A Wisconsin study, for example, showed that business people valued correct spelling and other cosmetic aspects of writing above organization of ideas. Research also suggests that excessive attention to minutiae in feedback promotes an exaggerated sense of the importance of mechanics and creates a fear of writing. Fear of writing limits the individual's chances of success both in school and in career choices.

It is in the final *product,* ready for delivery to the audience, that the students should seek the most complete realization of mechanical "perfection"—or more realistically, mechanical *excellence* in writing. The product has been thought through, talked through, and shaped carefully in successive drafts, tailored to a particular audience. The audience is the student's peers when the product is placed in a class or school anthology; displayed on a bulletin board; submitted to a school newspaper; or read to another class. The audience might be in the adult world, as in letters to the editor; character sketches or interviews (given to the subject of the sketch or interview); or queries directed to industries, government agencies, or public officials. Students are gratified to learn that products developed through the Writing Process Model are not in fact the end of communication. People *respond* to audience-oriented writing, just as they do in the purposeful writing that adults carry out in the real world.

The Process Model and Other Models—Comparisons

The Writing Process Model is likely to seem overinflated to some teachers and overstructured to others. Despite considerable hoopla over its innovative nature, the Writing Process Model is recognizable as a rearrangement of good things that have been going on for a long time. The strength of the model probably lies in its selection and development of some of the most effective elements in the traditional repertoire. Certainly the idea that purpose should underlie writing activities is not a new one. Purpose is a fetish in the Mastery Model and a major element in the Content Area Model, being immediately linked with the product in those models.

The idea of audience, though important in classical rhetoric, was largely neglected in content area instruction and is practically invisible in mastery instruction. Owing largely to James Britton's research, the idea of real audiences has been revived as a powerful motivator of student writing. Britton found that students seldom write for audiences other than the teacher, and that the teacher's role is characteristically not that of helper and guide, but tester and error-finder. The new emphasis on real audiences is supported obliquely by research in writing apprehension (Smith, 1984) and by National Assessment tests. Both sources suggest that students and adults who write for testers and wielders of red pencils often end up not wanting to write at all.

Prewriting is not a new idea. Good teachers have always invited students to discuss their experiences and analyze sample essays in preparation for writing. But in recent research by Arthur Applebee (1981) only a small proportion of teachers were actually found to engage students in prewriting activities. Prewriting is built into the process model—although it excludes content area prewriting techniques like the outline, emphasizing instead the organization of notes taken during discussion. The process model adds new dimensions to prewriting, such as language games that relate to pertinent thought processes, and it links these games to subsequent discussion and writing. (See Reference section, *Designing and Sequencing Prewriting Activities* by Larry Johannessen et al.)

Drafting and revising have been around for centuries. But again the concepts are refined in the Writing Process Model, where special attention is given to teaching students to help each other revise. When I was a student in elementary and high school, I considered my first draft an all-but-finished product. Students were not allowed to help each other. "Revising" meant copying a paper over again in ink. The teacher, though, was usually of a perfectionist mentality, calling for continued revision (or recopying) until the product met innumerable criteria for quality. The criteria, as the behaviorists would say, were not clearly specified. But I had the feeling that they included everything from neat margins to righteous thinking.

Between the extremes of simple recopying and merciless badgering, the problem of adequate revision remains. According to the 1977 National Assessment of Educational Progress Revision Test, most students have a limited concept of revision. In the NAEP tests, students took little advantage of the opportunity to reconsider their work. But when revision through teacher and peer reaction is part of the writing process, students develop a relaxed "first draft mentality" and a healthy attitude towards revising.

The Writing Process Model has certain unique problems. Many teachers find it difficult to create series of activities that flesh out the model—especially language games that evoke appropriate mental processes to link with the desired product. Only a few textbook publishers and curriculum specialists have attempted process-oriented materials. (See, though, textbooks by Olson and by Suhor; videotapes by Cedar Rapids Public Schools, Media Five, and Grossberg.) Also, little attention has been given, other than in laudable efforts like the *Foxfire* books, to finding real audiences for school writing activities.

The Writing Process Model requires that the teacher lead discussions and organize students for group work. This is no easy task in many situations—for example, inner city junior high schools, where keeping small groups on task is difficult; in schools where the principal thinks that students talking in small groups are wasting time; in rural schools, where students must often be convinced that speaking up in the classroom is not disrespectful.

Although the Writing Process Model is not intended to be rigid and formulaic, it is subject to abuse. The model represents *one way* of adapting an artificial environment—the classroom—to the diverse needs of learners. But learners are a varied lot, and overapplication of the concepts in the Writing Process Model can blur individual differences.

Revision strategies, for example, are idiosyncratic among adults, and we should expect some variation among students. I write or dictate most of my first drafts from notes, then scribble changes over a typewritten copy, often adding handwritten paragraphs on separate sheets, cutting and pasting, massively deleting, etc. I have seen students use my style, but I have seen others who write an entire draft without notes, treating the draft as a meditation for another, more refined draft. One student I knew crumpled and tore early drafts, then reassembled them to create later revisions. I thought his method was hilarious, but he ended up with first-rate writing. (For an excellent treatment of student revision styles, see Kirby and Liner's *Inside Out.*)

Many teachers find their greatest trial in treating matters of punctuation, spelling, and usage as secondary to elements like organization of ideas and development of a personal style. They have become accustomed to the Content Area approach, which invites "coverage" of innumerable rules and prescriptions within our discipline. They are not at ease in more dynamic roles: motivator, discussion leader, advisor, and—with relation to mechanics and usage—diagnoser of specific problems and prescriber of needed solutions.

The sequence in the Writing Process Model, as flexible as it is, cannot be followed slavishly. The sequence is not a stairway progression like the Mastery Model. It should be thought of as "looped," not tightly linear, since certain aspects—discussion, conferencing, note-taking, revising, proofreading—may take place at several points, not just in the slots assigned on the visual model.

Finally, let us acknowledge that some aspects of writing instruction do not fall into any of the three models. Cued sentence-combining might plug into a Mastery Model, but uncued sentence-combining is a valuable technique that does not relate to the models in this chapter. Student journals can be thought of as first drafts for more refined writing, but they have historically been treated as self-expression activities that need not be refined, and perhaps should not even be read except at the student's request. All of which should keep us honest when we consider models for composition and instruction. There are two ways, it seems, in which educational models can be useful and important—by stimulating us to think about and discuss our teaching, and by reminding us of the old semantic principle that the map, after all, is not the territory.

Nevertheless, I will not hesitate to say that the Writing Process Model strikes me as the most useful of the three. Although subject to misuse, it is the most fluid and least confining of the models. It alone is classroom-oriented, guaranteeing an opportunity for students to exchange ideas; it alone provides training in thinking and discussion skills related to compositional goals. It alone reflects writing in the adult world—with a real audience, genuine purpose, and opportunities for reflection, sharing, and revision. It alone is based on observations of skilled classroom teachers and not on academicians' views of what the study of English is all about. At the same time, it alone is consistent with theory and research on how students learn to talk and write.

References

AECT Task Force on Definition and Terminology. *A Glossary of Terms.* Washington, D.C.: Association for Educational Communication and Technology, 1979.

Applebee, Arthur. *Writing in the Secondary School: English and the Content Areas.* Urbana, Ill.: National Council of Teachers of English, 1981.

Appleby, Bruce, ed. "Sixth Graders' Definitions of Grammar." *Post-a-Pal-a-Poem* packet. Urbana, Ill.: National Council of Teachers of English, 1981.

Bloom, Benjamin. *Human Characteristics and School Learning.* New York: McGraw-Hill, 1976.

Boynton, Sandra. "The Five-Paragraph Theme." Boston: Boynton/Cook Publishers, 1980.

Britton, James, et al. *The Development of Writing Abilities 11–18.* London: Macmillan Education, 1975.

Cedar Rapids Public Schools. "The Writing Process" (Videotape production with Leader's Guide). Cedar Rapids, Iowa: Cedar Rapids Public Schools, 1981.

Christensen, Frances. "A Generative Rhetoric of the Sentence" and "A Generative Rhetoric of the Paragraph." In *The Sentence and the Paragraph.* Urbana, Ill.: National Council of Teachers of English, 1966.

Combs, Warren, and Wilhelmsen, Kathy. *Sentence Building: Teaching Grammatical Patterns Inductively, Books I–III.* Clearwater, Fla.: Wylie-Padol Publishers, 1979.

Glatthorn, Allan. *A Guide for Developing an English Curriculum for the Eighties.* Urbana, Ill.: National Council of Teachers of English, 1980.

Grossberg, Fred. "The Teaching of Writing" (Videotape series with Teachers Guides). Washington, D.C.: National Endowment for the Humanities, 1979-1982.

Johannessen, Larry R., et al. *Designing and Sequencing Prewriting Activities.* Urbana, Ill.: ERIC Clearinghouse on Reading and Communication Skills and the National Council of Teachers of English, 1982.

Kirby, Dan, and Liner, Tom. *Inside Out: Developmental Strategies for Teaching Writing.* Boston: Boynton/Cook Publishers, 1981.

Lockhead, J., and Clement, John, eds. *Cognitive Process Instruction.* Philadelphia: Franklin Institute Press, 1979.

Louisiana State Department of Education. *Models for Writing, K-12* (Bulletin

1484; edited by Barbara Cicardo and Cornelia Barnes). Baton Rouge: Louisiana State Department of Education, 1977.

Luban, Nina, et al. "One-to-One to Write: Establishing an Individual Conference Writing Place in Your Secondary School." *English Journal* 67 (November 1978): 30–35.

Macrorie, Ken. *Writing to Be Read.* Rochelle Park, N.J.: Hayden Book Company, 1976.

McHugh, Nancy. Sentence-Combining Strand in *Scholastic Composition Series,* edited by Charles Suhor et al. New York: Scholastic Inc., 1980.

Media Five. "The Writing Process." (Videotape with Leader's Guide). Hollywood, Calif.: Media Five, 1981.

Mellon, John. *Transformational Sentence-Combining* (Research Report No. 10). Urbana, Ill.: National Council of Teachers of English, 1969.

National Assessment of Educational Progress. *Write/Rewrite: An Assessment of Revision Skills.* Denver: Education Commission of the States, July 1977.

National Assessment of Educational Progress. *Writing: National Results.* Report No. 3; 1969–1970. Denver: Education Commission of the States, 1970.

O'Hare, Frank. *Sentencecraft.* Lexington, Mass.: Xerox, 1975.

Olson, Miles. *The Writing Process, Grades 7–12.* Boston: Allyn and Bacon, 1981.

Pike, Kenneth. "A Linguistic Contribution to Composition." *College Composition and Communication* 15 (1964): 82–88.

Smith, Michael. *Reducing Writing Apprehension.* Urbana, Ill.: ERIC Clearinghouse on Reading and Communication Skills and the National Council of Teachers of English, 1984.

Standiford, Sally, et al. *Computers in the English Classroom.* Urbana, Ill.: ERIC Clearinghouse on Reading and Communication Skills and the National Council of Teachers of English, 1983.

Stanford, Gene, ed. *How to Handle the Paper Load.* Classroom Practices, 1979–80. Urbana, Ill.: National Council of Teachers of English, 1979.

Suhor, Charles. *Scholastic Composition, Levels 1–6.* New York: Scholastic Inc., 1980.

Oral Communication in the Elementary Classroom

Barbara S. Wood, University of Illinois, Chicago

Recently, I overheard a conversation that reminded me of an unfortunate generalization that schoolchildren learn about communication:

Jeffrey: How'd you do on your report card, Greg?

Gregory: OK—I got mostly "E's" and a couple of "G's." (E = excellent, G = good.)

Jeffrey: Well, I got mostly "E's" too, but I got an "S" in library! I talked. (S = satisfactory, not considered adequate by most students.)

Gregory: Yeah, you can't talk or you flunk library. The only kinds to get an "E" in library are those who don't dare open their mouths.

Jeffrey: You know, a lot of smart kids don't get good grades in library.

Children form a host of generalizations that associate negative consequences with oral communication. To bring about effective learning, we must insist upon some degree of classroom order. But when students conclude that grades or evaluations are directly proportionate to the amount of talking they do—regardless of its overall quality—something unfortunate is happening. Children are associating a high value with quiet learning, while we as teachers are associating positive teaching with the same behavior. This chapter does not suggest that we reject teaching practices that regulate classroom talk; rather, it presents a communication framework that regards a "talking child" as a desirable student, rather than a troublesome one. Further, oral communication is seen as an integral part of the elementary curriculum, so that academic competence in students is measured by their development of oral as well as written communication skills.

Teaching of oral communication has traditionally involved presentational speaking. The idea is to get students in front of a group and ask them to make formal presentations that accomplish a goal. Success is measured in terms of physical behavior ("better not shake," or "stand up straight") and handling content ("Was your speech organized?"). We even require kindergarten children to "show and tell": "Stand up in front of your classmates and tell us about the new toy or treasure you have." Some educators have challenged this traditional format, suggesting that other formats are superior. The "show and question" format encourages inquiry in kindergarten children, whereas the "show and tell" format does not (Manzo and Legenza, 1975). Many educators agree that "show and tell" is dying as a classroom activity for communication (Harris, 1982). But what activities can elementary school teachers use to develop oral communication skills in children?

Some authors suggest that oral communication instruction include more informal and interpersonal goals (Allen and Brown, 1976; Wood, 1981). They suggest that students, instead of doing "show and tell" and making formal classroom speeches, develop communication competencies in five functional areas important in everyday life. These functions are relevant to persons of all ages and cultures and apply to communication at home, work, or school. They are:

> Controlling: communication in which we seek to influence others or respond to controlling communication of others (e.g., bargaining, refusing)
>
> Sharing feelings: interaction that expresses our feelings or responds emotionally to others (e.g., getting angry, supporting)
>
> Informing-responding: messages we use to give information or respond to information given to us (e.g., explaining, questioning)
>
> Ritualizing: communication that seeks to initiate or maintain social contact (e.g., greeting, using small talk)
>
> Imagining: communication that deals creatively with reality through the use of language (e.g., storytelling, fantasizing)

A six-year-old trying to be included in games on the playground or a forty-year-old trying to influence teenagers must be able to use these functions effectively.

Because elementary teachers face a demanding schedule, oral communication instruction should be integrated into various subject areas such as science, social studies, mathematics, and, certainly, language arts. Teachers want guidelines for integrating communication into the subject areas because it does not just happen. In fact, teaching in the content areas improves as a result of integrating oral communication. Holistic learning is the goal. However, to accomplish this, we must reconsider traditional practices and add new ones to round out our teaching styles. The idea is not to start all over; rather, the goal is a "gentle reframing" of teaching strategies to promote holistic learning. This chapter considers oral communication in the classroom from four perspectives:

1. The major milestones in the development of the controlling function of oral communication in children and their implications for classroom practices.
2. Classroom practices as techniques that *promote* communication as compared to techniques that *restrict* communication.
3. Guidelines on the effective use of classroom groups.
4. Communication activities for developing the five communication functions as integrated in a science unit.

This chapter presents a holistic view of developing oral communication, specifically the functions of communication. The first section outlines developmental milestones in the controlling function as an illustration of the functional approach. Teachers can find materials for teaching all five functions (Allen and Brown, 1976; Wood, 1981) and then follow the integration practice in this chapter.

Milestones in Communication Development

Research in the past decade on children's communication development has dramatically changed our view of children as learners. For example, we have discovered that the newborn has the ability to copy specific gestures (Metzoff and Moore, 1977) and to sort stimuli and remember facts (Pines, 1982). The abilities of young children are far more complex than we used to think. We can demonstrate, for example, that six-year-olds are better conversationalists than five-year-olds because they show more empathy in the way they carry on a conversation. Specialists call this ability "conversational congruence" (Welkowitz et al., 1976). Traditional studies of children's language examined vocabulary, syntax, and meaning. Now, with the focus on communication, findings seem even more relevant to the classroom and more practical for teachers. The milestones in the development of controlling are illustrated with invented—but realistic—dialogues from classes in a social studies unit, "people in groups." All elementary teachers should be able to identify with these interactions.

Early Communication Milestones

Most first-graders know the basic structures (syntax) of their language (Wood, 1981, ch. 6). Further, the size of their vocabulary is close to the adult's (Wood, 1981, ch. 5). However, the ability of typical six-year-olds to control is very much in the formative stage. Consider this discussion of "the family" (adapted from materials in Grossman and Michaelis, 1976, pp. 55-57):

> *Teacher:* See these pictures? What are these families doing?
>
> *Billy:* They're going tobogganing . . . and this family, they're playing some music.
>
> *Sara:* These guys are riding horses, and this sister is helping this guy ride a horse.
>
> *Billy:* Lemme see that picture? Gimme it.
>
> *Sara:* Don't grab it from me. I'm lookin' at it.
>
> *Teacher:* We can all see. OK, what does your family like to do?
>
> *Ben:* I like to go to movies. That's my favorite thing. I also like my Dad to take me bike riding.
>
> *Teacher:* But what do you all do together, as a family?
>
> *Ben:* Well, we eat dinner together most of the time.

This discussion illustrates communication milestones for the controlling function in young children, pre-kindergarten through second grade.

1. Directives are important strategies of control for getting someone to do something for you. Young children, such as Billy and Sara, use direct forms of directives: "Lemme see," or "Don't grab it from me." The direct forms are framed in clear, precise, and often blunt language (Garvey, 1975). Indirect forms are mastered by older children.

2. The direct forms of the directives are effective in accomplishing children's goals with peers (and adults in some situations) when children communicate confidently. Direct forms are less successful for children who are not as sure of themselves (Wood and Gardner, 1980).

3. While young children may not use indirect forms in their own communication, they do understand indirect forms used by others. When the teacher says, "We can all see," an indirect message to cooperate has been given. Children will learn three types of indirect forms: (from easiest to most difficult) affirmative indirect—"Can you let me see the picture?"; negative indirect—"Can't you let me see that picture?"; and state-of-affairs (must type)—"Must you monopolize that picture?", and (should type)—"Should you hog that picture?" Leonard, Wilcox, Fulmer and Davis (1978) found that four- and five-

year-olds understood only the first two types, where required action is stated (e.g., "Share the picture" or "Let me see the picture"). The difficulty of type three is that the opposite action (monopolizing the picture) is stated but not appropriate. However, six-year-olds did fairly well with these forms. Though not up to adult standards, first- and second-graders understand more complex forms of controlling than kindergarteners.

Primary Milestones

In a third-grade social studies class, the topics seem more abstract. For example, topics include how to act in groups, outsiders in groups, and the role of leaders in groups. In one social studies program for the third grade (Quigley et al., 1980), the final unit is on voting for leaders and rules in groups.

> *Teacher:* Sometimes groups vote to decide what's right, or they can decide in other ways. See the picture of the teacher at the blackboard pointing to the problem without an answer? Would voting be a good way to choose the right answer here?
>
> *Mary:* No, you can't vote in math. There's just one answer and you can't argue for it.
>
> *Ned:* Yeah, there's only one answer for the problem, but like in voting for president, there could be more than one president—like Carter or Reagan.
>
> *Teacher:* Good. What other things could you decide by voting, besides president?
>
> *Mary:* Like whether we're allowed to chew gum in class. (Everyone giggles.)
>
> *Teacher:* But I've already made the rule that there is NO GUM CHEWING in class, so could we really vote on that?
>
> *Mary:* Maybe if we could get the principal to vote on our side, you'd be outvoted. (Students chuckle.)
>
> *Teacher:* Hmmm. Sounds like wishful thinking to me.
>
> *Ned:* Well, if we promised to do all of our homework, maybe you'd let us chew gum one day.
>
> *Mary:* Yeah, maybe just for a half hour or something.
>
> *Gail:* We'd promise not to make too much noise, really.

The controlling communication in the discussion with these third-graders is quite different from that of the younger children.

Children are mastering the subtle strategies of bargaining ("I'll do my homework if you let us . . ."), gentle reminder ("Remember, you said once we could chew gum."), and verbal threat ("If you don't let us, we might sneak it."). According to Ervin-Tripp (1977), children of this age have mastered some rather perceptive strategies of control.

The use of timing enters the picture for eight-year-olds, so that obvious and instant methods of gaining compliance are often discarded for subtle and delayed request (Ervin-Tripp, 1977). Ned, Mary, and Gail may have decided that now was just the perfect time to ask for this special favor in class, since, after all, the topic came up in a most appropriate classroom discussion on voting.

Finally, the children are demonstrating advanced persuasive tactics: making something seem like "less than it is" and forecasting the other's reasons for denial. Children of this age understand their listeners well enough to phrase requests in ways likely to be viewed more favorably. Notice Mary's minimizing of the time element (just thirty minutes) and Gail's forecast (we won't make much noise).

Middle-Grade Milestones

By the time children reach sixth grade, they have entered what many call "the middle grades," launching their early teenage period. Consider this hypothetical social studies discussion (Cooper, 1979, pp. 347–98; skills workbook, p. 101).

> *Teacher:* In our story about the Europeans in West Africa, we learned something about contacts between groups. Would you say that their contact made life better for them?
>
> *Betty:* In one way it did—they were able to fight disease more and have better health.
>
> *Bob:* But the slavery was bad—that wasn't good for the Africans.
>
> *Teacher:* Is it possible that the negative effects, like slavery, could be canceled out by the positive effects, such as improved health?
>
> *Gil:* Well, our book says it's impossible to get rid of any effects of contact between peoples. So no, you could not get rid of that problem.
>
> *Bob:* Yeah, it's like if you hurt someone pretty bad, they'll always remember it. The pain hangs around.
>
> *Gil:* You could try to get them to forgive you—like you could say, "I really know you hated slavery but it's gone now."
>
> *Betty:* Yeah, but they'd still be angry—like they'd say, "We can't forget something so bad as that."

Gil: You could try though. It never hurts to try something.

Twelve-year-olds are becoming more competent persuaders as they adapt to listeners.

> As children enter their teens, they are more capable of adapting messages to listeners. Clark and Delia (1977) show children's progression in adapting skills from grades two through nine. Gil and Betty are excellent users of controlling communication where they have adapted to the hypothetical listeners.
>
> At first, children in pleading show awareness for the listener; Gil did this when he said that he would have told them that he realized their feelings about slavery. Next, children recognize the possible counter-arguments of the listener, as did Betty when she reminded her listener that people do not often forget something as bad as slavery. The third and final stage of adaptation is *stating* the advantage of the plea's fulfillment to the listener. Children try these strategies in the middle grades and show real progress by ninth grade.

Children in the middle grades make complex assumptions about listeners when they adapt messages. According to Kerby Alvy (1973), younger children base assumptions on observable characteristics of listeners: for example, "Don't get mad now, but I want to ask you something." Children in the middle grades control with far less obvious cues and assumptions: for example, "You're going to like one of the ideas I have, but I want to ask you a favor, too."

Implications for Instruction

Some teachers may say that their third-graders sound more like the first-grade children in this chapter. Other teachers may claim that their sixth-graders do not use the perspective-taking skills as depicted in communication studies. To be sure, milestones are only guideposts in children's development. For example, individual variation among children may place some at the "primary milestones" one or two years later or earlier than the ages listed. Teachers will have to use care in framing expectations regarding the level of development for their students.

Next we will consider the implications of communication development for classroom practices. Basically, we must give children experience in using communication functions while we also serve as models of these communication skills. Considering the control function in the elementary classroom, many of us teach with these beliefs:

> I must retain the floor as much as possible.

> I have to insist upon complete quiet from my students to retain control.
>
> Students cannot gain access to the floor without first getting my invitation. (I call on them.)
>
> Students should not ask questions or make comments about the topic until the proper time. (Such time is rarely provided!)

Whether we like it or not, our teacher behaviors are rather like military forms of controlling. We find it natural to maintain control of children in the classroom. Heaven forbid that the principal or district superintendent should walk into our classroom when all the children are talking at once. The military hand of control that we use looks orderly to the observer. But it often invites the passive behaviors from children:

> I must remain quiet as much as possible. I know I am being very good when I remain quiet.
>
> Unless I am really lost with an assignment, it is better not to raise my hand and ask a question because the teacher will think I am stupid or get mad at me.
>
> Wait until the teacher asks if we have questions before I ask—otherwise I will get punished.

How can children gain experience in effective controlling if their efforts are limited in these ways?

Communication apprehension is tied into the controlling function. Communication apprehension is considered to be an overall fear or concern about expressing oneself to others. Researchers (Garrison and Garrison, 1979) studied communication apprehension (CA) in elementary school students and teachers and discovered a rather interesting relationship. While younger elementary schoolchildren had a lower degree of CA than older children, the teachers of K–4 had greater degrees of CA than teachers at other grade levels. Early grade teachers and their students are truly mismatched, according to this research. They exercise control tactics in a classroom of children most eager and ready to learn oral communication skills.

We have read many accounts—and know from experience—that when we play an active role in learning it is more exciting for us, as compared to learning in which we are just passive custodians. Further, research with shy and apprehensive children suggests that a classroom that promotes communication helps children function more effectively in the learning environment (McCroskey, 1980). Pamela Cooper and Kathleen Galvin (1983) offer teacher techniques that encourage the apprehensive child to contribute in a meaningful way. We must reconsider the communication climate of our classrooms and move from a restrictive climate to one that promotes communication. There are several advantages in doing this:

> Children feel more involved in the learning process, like learning better, and subsequently learn more.

> The pressure of performance is reduced for the teacher, and the demand for control is lessened.

> Because students are encouraged to respond freely to materials and ideas presented by teachers, feedback to teachers increases the chance that teaching is more effective.

It is not easy to revise classroom management procedures. With a climate that promotes communication, two questions arise: How will I deal with my feelings of loss of control when children have the freedom to talk? What can I do to avoid chaos and unproductive chatter? Think about the most terrible things that might happen if we give up some degree of control in the classroom:

> A student might ask a question that we are not prepared to answer. What will we do?

> A student may not like an activity and say so. How will we feel about his or her comments?

In most cases we can answer student questions. Occasionally, we need to check into the matter and report back to the class. Rarely will people judge a speaker/teacher negatively simply because that teacher was unable to answer questions. In fact, honestly responding, "I will get that answer" often produces favorable judgments.

Although we do not like to hear students' negative comments about our teaching activities, we can choose simply to acknowledge that we heard these comments. Consider two student responses that teachers hear as judgmental:

> "I don't understand why we're cutting these pictures from the magazines. What is this for again?"

> "I thought this part about different families doing different things was good, but I don't like the part about putting subtitles under these pictures."

There are ways of "hearing" such comments that allow us to tap into the feedback that we receive, and capitalize on it for our teaching.

One helpful reaction is to paraphrase student comments in a supportive way:

> *Student:* I didn't like that assignment.

Teacher: You didn't like the project of making subtitles—well I'm sorry you didn't find it as rewarding as I planned it for you, Ben.

Student: I don't get what we're supposed to do in these groups.

Teacher: Oh, you are unclear about your group task. Others may be in that situation, so I need to clarify it more.

Student: This activity is too difficult to do.

Teacher: You find that writing a poem about your family is a difficult assignment. I knew it would be challenging, Clare, but I'd like to see you give it a good chance.

In these examples, the teacher helps to create a climate that promotes controlling strategies that are effective and sensitive to the needs of others. The climate is created with these techniques:

Paraphrasing: The teacher paraphrases the child's reaction/response, showing understanding of the child's reaction.

Supportive response: The teacher comments on the acceptability of the reaction, reacts empathetically to the child's situation, or is generally encouraging.

Classroom Communication Practices

Many classroom techniques afford teachers a comfortable degree of control over students. Teachers, who probably learned them from their own teachers, use these techniques without much conscious effort. The following is a first-grade science discussion (based on Abruscato et al., 1980a) exposing how we teachers sound much of the time:

Teacher: Moving air is called wind. Wind can move things. Here is a picture of a . . .

Children: (in unison) . . . sailboat.

Teacher: Yes, a sailboat. The sailboat is moved by the wind pushing against its . . .

Children: . . . sail.

Teacher: Good. Now here's a picture of a . . .

Children: . . . fan.

Teacher: And a fan can make wind because the motor turns the . . .

Children: (The response is mixed, with children shouting different responses.)

The unison answering could go on forever and can be called, "fill in the blank." Teachers find the pattern relatively easy to master, and students easily understand what is required of them. While it is probably an effective technique for allowing students to perform in reciting meaningful material, the "fill in the blank" technique requires little thinking from either teacher or students. Consequently, the long term effects are doubtful.

Another favorite technique can be illustrated in this first-grade science program:

> *Teacher:* Air can help us, can't it? Tell me one way air can help us.
>
> *Child:* We dry our clothes sometimes in the air.
>
> *Teacher:* Good answer. Is there another way air can help us?
>
> *Child:* We breathe it. Air helps us live.
>
> *Teacher:* OK, now what else can you think of?
>
> *Child:* We can use it to blow up the tires on our bikes.
>
> *Teacher:* That's right. . . .

The "let's make a list" approach to teaching is used fervently; teachers somehow believe the longer the list, the more the students know about something. Teachers seldom ask students to go into detail about any one item. Rather, the aim is to create the longest list possible. While the list approach to learning is undoubtedly an indication of the general knowledge in a certain area (e.g., students' knowledge of air is a product of knowing more than one or two functions of air), this method of classroom interaction gives no more than an index of students' collective "breadth of knowledge."

A third technique is related to the basic lecture-discussion format, which follows a special form: the "easy-difficult question format." Consider a group of first-graders talking about water (adapted from questions and material in Abruscato et al., 1980a, pp. 75-78):

> *Teacher:* Water is all around us. We need water to live. We can make water into ice cubes, or we can turn on the water faucet and get water in a stream of liquid. Water does not have its own shape—it takes the shape of the container it's in, like a glass or a dish. If it's frozen into an ice cube though, it has its own shape. But what happens to an ice cube if you leave it on a plate?
>
> *Children:* (in unison) It melts.
>
> *Teacher:* Good, will it melt slowly or quickly?
>
> *Children:* Slowly.
>
> *Teacher:* Why does the ice cube melt?
>
> *Children:* (No one answers; no one raises a hand.)

The format goes something like this: the teacher gives a minilecture, then asks easy questions which the children answer (often in unison); then the teacher asks a difficult question. It is likely that we are not really interested in answers to the first, easy questions. We know that the children will provide these answers, but begin with them anyway. The answer that we want is for the more difficult question that we toss in, at the peak of the exchange. And mumbling, silence, or guessing are results of this approach. A more productive questioning technique leads students directly to the area of importance.

"Fill in the blank," "let's make a list," and "easy-difficult question format" are helpful in giving teachers a sense of confidence. They also give students—even the most quiet and slow-to-learn—a sense of belonging. But the benefits of these techniques must be weighed against their lack of power to stimulate productive thinking in the holistic development of the child. And in this sense, they are not as effective as they might be. The following section offers additional techniques that might produce a more well-rounded battery of communication techniques for teaching.

Techniques to Promote Communication

Much attention is given to classroom practices that promote holistic learning. The first chapter in this book, "Learning Better, Learning More: In the Home and Across the Curriculum" (Thaiss and Thaiss), offers innovative techniques that view children holistically rather than mechanically. Following are several techniques that encourage holistic learning in an environment of observations, questions, and comments from children.

The first is called "make an observation," and is shown in discussion in a first-grade science class (Abruscato et al., 1980a, pp. 79-81):

> *Teacher:* Water can help us. In this picture, the firemen are using water to put out the fire. Those hoses look heavy to me; look at that large spray of water coming out of the hoses.
>
> *Child:* I bet it's hard to hold one of those big hoses. That holds a lot of water. I couldn't hold it.
>
> *Teacher:* But we need a lot of water to put out that big fire, don't we? A little water won't help us, so we need big people and big hoses.
>
> *Child:* Once we tried to put out our campfire with a pail of water, and the fire started back up again.
>
> *Teacher:* Yes, that can happen. It probably wasn't enough water to counteract the force of the fire. Fire is very forceful.
>
> *Child:* My house burned once.

This discussion could continue fruitfully for some time, so long as the teacher is able to continue offering exciting, insightful, and relevant observations for the children to react to. We use the "make an observation" technique frequently when we talk to adults. The technique works extremely well for elementary school students, too. It shows students what level of observation we expect of them, and gives them a good indication of what they should be learning.

A second technique is a question-and-answer procedure, but it requires students to phrase the questions for discussion. The "student question" approach is illustrated in this science discussion (Abruscato et al., 1980a, pp. 85-89):

> *Teacher:* In some places our air and water are dirty. Dirty air and water are bad for people, plants, and animals. We can help clean up our air and water, right? What would you want to know about cleaning up our air and water, Karen?
>
> *Karen:* I know air smells sometimes. But I can't figure out how you get the smell out of smelly air. (Students giggle.)
>
> *Teacher:* Who has an idea for Karen?
>
> *Fred:* Sometimes a smokestack in a factory smells up the air. You could close up the smokestack.
>
> *Bill:* Or like when buses smell up the air with their fumes, you could keep them in the garage and not let them go out.
>
> *Teacher:* Both of your answers are excellent ways of stopping air pollution by closing down the operation of the machine that's causing the trouble. Another way of approaching air pollution is to repair or fix the machine that is polluting. What would you like to know about repairing to stop pollution?
>
> *Bill:* I can think of ways to repair a bus. But I'd like to know what you could do to repair a smokestack in a factory.
>
> *Fred:* You don't repair the smokestack, you repair the machine that uses the smokestack.

The advantage of this approach is that the fuel for the discussion comes directly from the learners themselves. We usually assume that a teacher's perspective is the most productive starting point for discussion. This approach begins quite simply from what the child wants to know, confident that this is a productive starting-point.

A third technique requires imagination on the part of both the children and the teacher. Students are asked to play the roles of persons, things, or concepts being discussed (Abruscato et al., 1980a, pp. 82-84):

Teacher: Plants and animals need air to live. They need water to live, too. Here's a picture of plants and animals under water. How would it be if you were this fish, swimming around in the water?

Child: I like to swim. I'd swim around real smooth if I was a fish. I'd swim around everywhere.

Teacher: And how would you feel if someone scooped you out of the water and put you on shore?

Child: I'd thrash around and flop around a lot. I've seen fish flop around a lot when they're pulled out of water.

Child: Yeah, it's like the fish is choking for air, but it's not—it really wants water, right?

Teacher: Yes, the fish needs water, not air. And you're right—it does seem like the little fish is choking for air, doesn't it?

Interesting and productive discussions can emerge from inviting the students to role-play subjects of study. While young children will have difficulty in taking the perspective of inanimate objects, and may struggle with perspective-taking of any type, they will try it when we encourage them.

A fourth technique—using groups—deserves a special section. In group work, students are more intensely involved in learning because their chances of oral participation are increased. The next section explores some techniques for using groups effectively in the elementary school classroom.

Using Student Groups in the Classroom

Teachers try different arrangements of students' desks to alter the learning environment. These arrangements, however, tend to keep children working quietly on projects. The small-group approach to student learning is frequently—and successfully—used on the high school and college level. The recent use of groups in the elementary school has met with predictable obstacles. Young children do not manage peer groups as effectively as teenagers. But it is worth the effort to have them try.

Children in Groups

The ability to work effectively in a group develops slowly in children. They have difficulties in many of the skills underlying effective group work: staying on the topic, reaching a cooperative goal, managing distractions, and making effective contributions. Until children learn these skills, student groups may seem chaotic and results may sometimes appear haphazard. If the task is trying a scientific experiment, as with the ice cube on the plate, all children may wish to touch the ice cube at the same time. The activity level is high, and the noise and pushing may be intolerable. Young children as a group get sidetracked very easily, and group members are not likely to remind their peers that they are getting off the track, a skill that older children do seem to have. The teacher cannot attend to the needs of each group simultaneously. If the teacher moves to one group, another may require the teacher's immediate attention. No wonder teachers feel drained after group work: it sometimes seems that all students need the teacher's help at the same time.

Teachers worry about using groups because they fear the loss of control and the lack of effective instruction. Inservice workshops can be used to teach critical skills in using groups, but students too can be taught the "group rules": dealing with disruptions, understanding misinterpreted assignments, coping with the troublemaker, and including the outsider.

Group Training Time

Both students and teachers need training in using groups. Teachers need assurances that groups can work without total confusion and extreme disorder. First attempts at group work can be limited to shorter time periods followed by a period of discussion for "how it worked." This training period might last two weeks. The success of groups depends on open communication between teacher and students about how interaction is working and what to do when problems arise.

In the training period, the following obstacles and difficulties might arise:

A group may become noisy and disruptive as they tackle the assignment.

A group may misinterpret the assignment and do the wrong thing.

A student may choose not to participate in a group and become an "outsider."

A student can be a "troublemaker."

The teacher can spot a group having trouble working together. They are usually noisy and often blaming each other for "doing it wrong." The first reaction to a disruptive group might be to reprimand group members. Instead, let children define the source of the problem, argument, or disagreement. Let them talk about it openly. They may have one or more explanations, and each can be considered in the group—with the teacher and students talking freely. Our best tactic is to agree that any one of their "problem statements" would be correct and difficult to deal with as a group member. Rather than taking sides or trying to settle on which reason explains why things failed, support each explanation. Then ask the children to come up with a solution to their problem(s). Each solution can be discussed, with the teacher serving as a moderator for that discussion. The discussion gets students back on the track so that they can then begin working effectively together.

A teacher has asked the groups to select pictures from magazines showing possible sources of air and water pollution. The groups were given thirty minutes to select three pictures, mount them onto construction paper, and then present them to the entire class for discussion. The teacher's initial observations indicated that all groups seemed to be working harmoniously. After thirty minutes, the teacher called everyone back into the classroom setting to discuss the pictures. The first group to present pictures has misinterpreted the assignment. They show pictures of polluted air and water, but neither their pictures nor their comments discussed the sources of the pollution.

Again, consider a child-centered approach to the problem. Just as the disruption problem was solved by asking the children to label the problem and possible solutions, the assignment problem can be solved by asking children to think about what went wrong. Assuming that other groups did not "misinterpret" the assignment (if they did, it would be very likely that the instructions were unclear), then discussion of why the group got off the track might be helpful. Another point of discussion can center on the group's feelings about being in the group that "misinterprets."

It is easy to spot outsiders in groups. Our inclination may be to approach the group, asking why the outsiders are not participating or why the others are not including them. However, this approach may not do much to change the situation. A more productive approach involves questions related to the learning process:

> "Do you feel you are getting something out of this group?" (Question given to "outsider.")
>
> "Do you think Jennifer (an "outsider") might have some ideas to add to your discussion?" (Question delivered to other group member.) "I bet she does if you just ask her."
>
> "What do you like best about what is going on in your group?" (Question directed at an "outsider.")

Our assumption, that "outsiders" are not learning anything from the group, can be wrong, and we can check that assumption with students.

The "troublemaker" is particularly difficult to deal with when the teacher has split the class into groups. As soon as we notice a child acting inappropriately, we can approach the group and ask some questions:

> "Something is not working here. What seems to be the problem?"
>
> "How is this problem affecting the work in your group?"

"How does it feel being in a group having this problem?"

"How does it feel, Alan, being the one everyone is blaming for the trouble?"

In talking about the "group problem," the "troublemaker" is treated in a more cooperative manner. Attention is given to the disruptive child, but fingers are not pointed in a way that will create defensiveness or cause further unhappiness. The problem becomes the group's problem and not the individual's.

Developing Communication Functions

Our goal is to achieve a holistic learning in which the child grows in all areas at once: reading, writing, oral communication, science, math, social studies. Learning in content areas can be enhanced by using techniques of classroom discussion in which children participate actively in the learning process. Children learn oral communication skills if the instruction climate is shifted from using techniques that restrict communication to those that promote communication ("making an observation" or group work).

We have already discussed four techniques which develop oral communication competencies in children: "make an observation"—informing/responding; the "student question" technique—informing/responding; "how would it be?"—imagining; and group work—serves all functions. The final section of this chapter suggests a classroom activity in science related to each of the communication functions. R. R. Allen and Robert Kellner's chapter, "Integrating the Language Arts," considers other approaches to integration. Explanation of the functional approach is also given in booklets I have edited (Wood, 1977a; 1977b).

Controlling Activities

Most discussion questions within or at the end of a science unit require students to use the informing/responding function. Rarely are there questions that develop oral communication competencies in any of the other functional areas. It is possible to transform questions and materials into activities that develop controlling communication skills. Consider the following questions in a third-grade science unit.

Where does the energy come from to cause each of these changes:

Wet clothes drying in a backyard.

Wet clothes drying in a dryer at the laundromat.

Coffee boiling.

Clouds forming in the atmosphere. (Brandwein et al., 1966, p. 116.)

Students' answers to such questions often contain more than one answer. (For example, wet clothes dry as a result of wind and heat.) Capitalize on the phenomenon of multiple explanations of scientific concepts. Teachers can phrase classroom science activities in terms of persuasive communication on "the one component most significant" in explaining a scientific process. In the case of the example, students can hear arguments for the action of heat versus wind in drying clothes on the clothesline, or the action of the tumbling motion of the dryer versus the heat in drying clothes in the dryer. This prompts children to think clearly about the scientific *and* personal factors of the experiment. This technique can also be applied to discussions in social studies and other subjects.

Sharing Feelings

How can we develop children's competencies in sharing feelings in a unit that deals with scientific concepts? Would it not be easier to integrate this function into discussions of social studies or health, since science seems non-emotional? The idea is to capitalize on those units and topics in the science program where sharing feelings is an appropriate focus of instruction. An example of this, illustrated with certain techniques, follows.

After the unit on changing water to water vapor (drying clothes on a clothesline and in a dryer), there is a unit on mixing liquids with air. In particular, perfume gases that escape from the perfume liquid reach our noses through the air (Brandwein et al., 1966, p. 119). A discussion of this rather complex scientific process can be combined with an exercise in sharing feelings. We can preface the discussion with a basic "human factor": that we will all smell the same gas in the air. However, since human beings react differently to different gases or smells, feelings and reactions to different smells may vary. Consider questions such as these:

Talk about your feeling when you smell this particular perfume. What does it remind you of? How do you feel when you smell this?

If we substituted mothballs for the perfume, how would you feel? How are the mothballs like the perfume? How do they differ?

Essentially, where human reactions enter the scientific picture, try to integrate sharing feelings into the discussion. An important goal of feelings discussions is the use of clear, vivid language.

Informing/Responding

The informing function is usually the focus of classroom activities. Questions in textbooks are most always based on the informing/responding function. Most exercises and questions have a narrow focus, and require a few words or a sentence to satisfy the task. Consider these rather unimaginative questions for students in a sixth-grade science unit (Abruscato et al., 1980b, p. 129):

> What is the name for the smallest particle of many substances that is still that substance?
>
> What determines whether something is gas, liquid, or solid?

Neither question would be good for a stimulating class discussion. If the goal is an interesting class discussion, rather than papers-to-be-graded, consider these:

> Look around this room and try to find at least five different types of molecules that you can "see." Tell us about these five molecules in a special order—from the one that moves the fastest to the one that moves the slowest. Let's draw a continuum of these molecules on the blackboard.
>
> Let's go inside our mouths for a minute and think about the molecules we have there. Are there gases, liquids, and solids? Let's talk about the molecules in our mouths.

Both sets of discussion probes elicit informing/responding communication that is likely to be more elaborated and complex than the one-word responses that textbook questions typically evoke.

Ritualizing

Ritualizing primarily serves a social function in human interaction and ties only indirectly to actual topics of communication. Again, the primary role of ritualizing communication (e.g., greeting, introducing, taking turns talking, engaging in small talk) is to initiate and maintain social contact with others. Social studies topics can be fertile areas for integrating social concepts and ritualizing skills (e.g., family dinner table rituals, cultural differences in communication rituals). But what about the less personal area of science?

One purpose of science teaching is to improve children's skills of verbally demonstrating a science experiment to others. First, the scientific experiment needs a brief, clear, and interesting introduction. The introduction must capture the attention of the listener. Each experiment must be segmented into its key steps by the student. Each step must be introduced, demonstrated, and then commented upon. Finally, the closing of the demonstration must be brief, clear, and interesting. The format in presenting the scientific information is almost as critical to the success of the experiment as the content of the demonstration. And this set of skills develops ritualizing communication.

Imagining

One interesting application of the imagining function in science is in the area of speculating. Here, we encourage children to master basic scientific concepts inductively. Consider the topic, changing water into water vapor. Children can be divided into groups and given a project or question and asked to speculate about "what would happen if?" The following are some speculative topics (questions) related to water and water vapor:

> Humidity is really water vapor in our air. Is there any way we can increase the humidity in our air at home? How can we do it right here in this room?

> What would happen if you were drying clothes on your backyard clothesline and the temperature in the air went from thirty-five degrees to twenty-three degrees? What would happen to the water vapor coming into the air from the clothes?

> Since water constantly changes to water vapor, why have our lakes and rivers not dried up much more than they have?

> Can you think of some reasons why air is usually drier (lower humidity) in the winter as compared to the summer?

Let students speculate. Encourage all speculation which is based on some scientific fact. The goal is not so much to scrutinize all aspects of children's speculations as it is to get them to use their imaginations.

Conclusions

In an environment that promotes communication, teachers and students participate actively in the learning process. While children are learning concepts in science, mathematics, or social studies, for example, they are developing critical skills in oral and written communication. The holistic view in oral communication development outlined in this chapter connects the five communication functions, and the content areas of elementary education.

The methods and techniques apply to instruction at all grade levels. By knowing the communication milestones for the functions like controlling, sharing feelings, and informing/responding, teachers can gear their instruction to the total development of the child. The five communication functions are relevant to children from Hispanic, Chinese, and other bilingual backgrounds. All children must develop a repertoire of communication skills in a variety of situations, and communication functions can be learned through teaching practices that promote communication.

We want to develop strong learners. It is not an easy task to manage a classroom filled with thirty to thirty-five children. And we are expected to manage well so that the children will learn basic skills, including effective oral communication. It takes a special person to pursue an elementary school teaching career. This chapter was written with that special person in mind.

References

Abruscato, Joseph; Fossacca, John Wade; Hassard, Jack; and Peck, Donald. *Holt Elementary Science.* New York: Holt, Rinehart and Winston, 1980a.

Abruscato, Joseph; Fossacca, John Wade; Hassard, Jack; and Peck, Donald. *Holt Elementary Science.* New York: Holt, Rinehart and Winston, 1980b.

Allen, Ronald R., and Brown, Kenneth. *Developing Communication Competencies in Children.* Skokie, Ill.: National Textbook Co., 1976.

Allen, R. R., and Kellner, Robert. *Putting Humpty Dumpty Together Again: Integrating the Language Arts.* Washington, D.C.: Basic Skills Improvement Program, U.S. Department of Education, 1983.(See chapter in this volume.)

Alvy, Kerby T. "The Development of Listener Adapted Communication in Grade-School Children from Different Social-Class Background." *Genetic Psychology Monographs* 8 (1973): 33–104.

Brandwein, Paul; Cooper, Elizabeth K.; Blackwood, Paul E.; and Hone, Elizabeth B. *Concepts in Science.* New York: Harcourt Brace and World, 1966.

Clark, Ruth Anne, and Delia, Jesse G. "Cognitive Complexity, Social Perspective-Taking, and Functional Persuasive Skills in Second- to Ninth-Grade Children." *Human Communication Research* 3 (Winter 1977): 128–34.

Cooper, Kenneth. *People in the Eastern Hemisphere.* Glenview, Ill.: Silver Burdett Social Studies Series, 1979 (Textbook and skills workbook).

Cooper, Pamela, and Galvin, Kathleen. *Improving Classroom Communication.* Washington, D.C.: Basic Skills Improvement Program, U.S. Department of Education, 1983.

Ervin-Tripp, Susan. "Wait for Me Roller Skate!" In *Child Discourse,* edited by Ervin-Tripp and Mitchell-Kernan. New York: Academic Press, 1977: 165–83.

Garrison, John, and Garrison, Karen. "Measurement of Oral Communication Apprehension among Children: A Factor in the Development of Basic Speech Skills." *Communication Education* 28 (May 1979): 119–28.

Garvey, Catherine. "Requests and Responses in Children's Speech." *Journal of Child Language* 2 (1975): 41–63.

Grossman, Ruth H., and Michaelis, John U. *Working, Playing, Learning.* Reading, Mass.: Addison-Wesley, 1976.

Harris, James A. "Death of Show and Tell." *Learning* (January 1982): 119.

Leonard, Laurence B.; Wilcox, M. Jeanne; Fulmer, Kathleen C.; and Davis, G. Albyn. "Understanding Indirect Requests: An Investigation of Children's Comprehension of Pragmatic Meanings." *Journal of Speech and Hearing Research* 21 (September 1978): 528–37.

Manzo, Anthony V., and Legenza, Alice. "Inquiry Training for Kindergarten 2 (April 1975): 479–83.

McCroskey, James C. "Quiet Children in the Classroom: On Helping Not Hurting." *Communication Education* 29 (July 1980): 239–44.

Metzoff, Andrew N., and Moore, M. Keith. "Imitation of Facial and Manual Gestures by Human Neonates." *Science* 198 (1977): 75–78.

Pines, Maya. "Baby, You're Incredible." *Psychology Today* (February 1982): 48–53.

Quigley, Charles N.; McKay, Susan Williams; Santill, Michael A.; and Sears, Thomas Gavin. *Exploring Our World: Groups*. Chicago, Ill.: Follett Publishing Co., 1980.

Thaiss, Christopher J. *Learning Better, Learning More: In the Home and Across the Curriculum*. Washington, D.C.: Basic Skills Improvement Program, U.S. Department of Education, 1983. (See chapter in this volume.)

Welkowitz, Joan; Cariffe, Gerald; and Feldstein, Stanley. "Conversational Congruence as a Criterion of Socialization in Children." *Child Development* 47 (March 1976): 269–72.

Wood, Barbara S. *Children and Communication: Verbal and Nonverbal Language Development*. 2nd ed. Englewood Cliffs, N.J.: Prentice-Hall, 1981.

Wood, Barbara S., ed. *Development of Functional Communication Competencies: Pre-K Through Grade Six*. Urbana, Ill.: ERIC Clearinghouse on Reading and Communication Skills and the National Council of Teachers of English, 1977a.

Wood, Barbara S., and Gardner, Royce. "How Children 'Get Their Way': Directives in Communication." *Communication Education* 29 (July 1980): 264–72.

Writing Growth in Young Children: What We Are Learning from Research

Marcia Farr, University of Illinois at Chicago Circle

"I'm glad this classroom has lots of paper," Andrea said as she spread four clean white sheets onto her desktop. The eight-year-old slid her chair closer to the desk. "I'm going to write on this page," she explained. "Then if it's not perfect, I'll use the other pages to make it better."

Andrea bent over her desk. Her dark pixie hair covered her eyes. She wrote, then pulled back to see what she had said. Her light-blue eyes scouted the page, turning each section over in her mind. Now, with pencil poised, she works her way slowly down the page. A phrase is underlined, a detail added. Soon her page is filled with jagged lines, starred sections, and scrunched-in additions.

Over the next week, one page grew into four. On separate bits of paper, Andrea tried different descriptive paragraphs, experimented with several endings, and listed possible titles.

Andrea's progress in learning to write, and that of fifteen other children, was closely observed and documented daily by researcher Donald Graves and his two research associates, Lucy Calkins and Susan Sowers. For two years, the researchers worked in several classrooms in a public elementary school in New Hampshire. The opening excerpt was used in an article by one of the researchers (Calkins, 1979) to illustrate that Andrea had learned, over the course of several months, crucial revising processes. That is, she had learned that her writing was changeable, something she had been unable to see a few months before. As a consequence, her writing abilities began to grow perceptibly and her final written products to improve.

I use the excerpt to show how readily accessible, and how relevant to real teaching concerns, much of the recent research on children's writing is. Andrea's behavior while writing was closely studied for patterns of writing development. Andrea's teacher's behavior also was closely studied, and her knowledge of teaching tapped, to identify patterns in effective teaching practices. The result is an abundance of information about the successful

126

teaching and learning of writing which can be made widely available to other interested teachers. Not only is the research information relevant to daily teaching, but the language is clear and understandable to researchers and nonresearchers alike.

The work of Graves and his associates defies the traditional stereotype of educational research as being distant from the classroom and quite removed from the daily concerns of most teachers. In fact, their research is one example of a growing number of genuinely collaborative studies by teacher-researcher teams. One reason for the increase in collaborative research is the recognition by many educational researchers that teacher knowledge and behavior is an abundant source of data which can be analyzed to provide significant findings. These findings, drawn from real-life classrooms, are readily applicable to other classroom situations.

In this chapter, I will describe a few such classroom-based studies which have been completed only recently, and attempt to synthesize what we are learning from them about children's writing. Let us first reconsider what the term *writing development* really means.

What Is Writing Development?

One of the findings from recent and ongoing efforts to learn about writing development in children is that we may have to redefine what we thought we were seeking. Our traditional notion of development rests on assumptions of relatively discrete stages. Piaget, for example, provided labels for stages of mental development that explained the behavior he was able to evoke from children. Typical, current instruction in both reading and writing seems to rest on assumptions that there are subskills that children must learn before they are able to comprehend or produce a whole language product; that is, there are definable stages which they must pass through to reach the ultimate goal of literacy. However, language is not learned or used in such discrete chunks, as other subject matter areas—math, for example—may be. Language is learned and used "all of a piece," so to speak, i.e., in a holistic fashion. It is true that toddlers do not speak like adults, that children cannot read and write texts that adults read and write. However, they are not using subcategories of adult models. As Harste, Burke, and Woodward (1982) have shown, they are *doing* what we do, but with different data. They learn language processes, then progressively feed more and more information into the processes.

Language processes can be defined simply as what people *do* with language. If we define language as the system of knowledge (with both individual and cultural variation) which speakers of a given language share, then we can say that language processes are what people do with that system. That is, they may speak it, they may listen to (and understand) it, they may read it, and they may write it. Of course, there are both similarities and differences between and among all four of these language processes. Their acquisition is similar in that learners seem to begin by trying out the processes, first. Then they use those processes to learn the appropriate forms of language. For example, babies begin acquiring English by acting like speakers of English: their first attempts to communicate meaning are not with exactly learned English words and fully formed sentences. With experience in the processes of speaking and listening, however, they learn increasingly sophisticated forms.

Competence in a language not only entails learning the forms of that language (e.g., sounds, words, sentences), but also encompasses learning appropriate *rules of use* for those forms. This is what sociolinguists refer to as *communicative competence*. For example, speakers must learn not only how to form interrogatives in English, but must also learn how to make requests (with varying degrees of politeness) to different audiences in various situations.

Language functions, such as request-making, are uses of language that we keep learning, often even through adulthood. Most people, we hope, eventually become skillful, through experience, in a variety of language functions. Unfortunately, however, some still need to learn, for example, the subtleties of making requests or offering condolences. These explanations of language competence (including both rules for forms and rules for using those forms) and of language processes are illustrated in the following model:

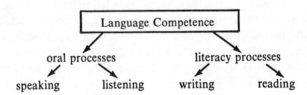

The model and its explanations are provided as a context in which we can begin to understand writing development. That is, writing should be seen as a *process,* and it should be seen as a natural part of *language,* and not as an artificial extension of "real" (i.e., oral) language.

This chapter does not cover in detail speaking, listening, or reading as language processes, although I do believe that the case that I will make for writing can also be made for them. Think for a moment how writing is taught (and unfortunately usually not learned well) in most elementary schools: first letters, then words, then sentences, then stories, then themes. On what information about writing development in children is this based?

As far as I can determine, none. It is, instead, apparently the result of an attempt to think through from an adult logical viewpoint what would be reasonable for children to learn first. Unfortunately, in all too many cases, this prevents children from learning the *processes* into which they could feed increasingly complex pieces of data, whether they be linguistic forms, cognitive structures, or social and cultural information about the world.

Assessment information about student writing abilities (e.g., NAEP 1981) tells us that the major problem is with processes beyond the sentence level, and yet we are not teaching students—some would say not allowing them—to practice writing elaborated texts. There are, of course, exceptional schools and classrooms, and some researchers are studying these exceptions to a typically dismal picture. This chapter details some findings from several of these studies. The findings are being confirmed across studies, and therefore seem to be highly significant. Because this information is emerging on a staggered and ongoing basis, I will confine my discussion to four key studies: those by Harste, Burke, and Woodward; King and Rentel; Graves; and Staton. Like language and literacy processes, my analysis will grow as I feed more research findings into my synthesis.

A key finding from Harste, Burke, and Woodward's work with three- to six-year-olds is that there seems to be *process universals* in literacy events. That is, the researchers began to see that three-year-old children were engaging in the same literacy processes that adults use. They are grateful that they videotaped the experiments with the children because toward the end of data collection, they began to see the raw data with new eyes. Thus, they were able to reanalyze the raw data. The process universals which the three- to six-year-olds used knowledgeably, and which are not outgrown but maintained and used in all literacy events, are textual intent, negotiability, using language to fine-tune language, and risk-taking. They comprise a model of literacy acquisition and use which acknowledges that meaning resides in context, and is negotiated in context.

Textual Intent

This strategy as defined by Harste, Burke, and Woodward entails "not only an expectation that written language makes sense, but also includes a 'shape' of what that sense is going to be like" (p. 49). That is, a literacy user expects both that print will carry meaning (sometimes this is referred to as "semantic intent") and that meaning will be carried in a particular form which one has learned to expect from previous experience. The expected form may include the kind of print, the semantic or syntactic structure of print, or the lexical form of print. The chart (Harste, Burke, and Woodward, 1982, p. 51) shows that children as young as three already have learned to expect meaning from print and also that different literacy activities follow different forms of structures.

As can be seen, children's responses in story dictation are different from their responses in reading a piece of environmental print. Their "textual shapes" are different. Although the responses are not as exact or fully formed as adult responses would be (e.g., the stories do not have a complete adult structure), it is not difficult to decide which set of responses occurred in story dictation. This shows that children as young as three can differentiate forms appropriate for various literacy activities.

Same Child Response to Environmental Print and Language Experience Story Tasks: The Shape of Things to Come (three-year-olds)	
Environmental Print Responses	Language Experience Story Responses
Don't know Eggs Ronald McDonald Coke Toothpaste Burger Chef	That tree. I'm going to fall down. Block. Boy. That a boy. Block. Tree.
A thing A cup Eggs A cup Toothbrush A Burger King Cup	A spoon. A spoon to eat. There's a string. You put it round your neck like this.
Don't know Eggs McDonalds Coke Toothpaste Burger Chef	This is a box. A car. A candle. A string.

Negotiability

This strategy seems to be a process universal in literacy use. Negotiation refers to the shifts made by literacy users (readers and writers) in interpreting or transmitting text. That is, in a *literacy event*—which involves both a writer and a reader—shifts are made by the participants that create the meaning in that context. For example, the children in the Harste, Burke, and Woodward study frequently moved across communication systems in an attempt to respond to a writing task assigned to them by the researchers. That is, they frequently used art, as well as what they knew of writing, to accomplish a task. They coped with a difficult task by renegotiating it to a level that made sense to them. This strategy not only allowed them to "keep going" with a particular task, but also to continue learning written language.

Using Language to Fine-Tune Language

This strategy often involves parallel uses of what one knows about language (oral *and* written) to produce new written language. For example, children learn how stories are typically organized (e.g., setting, initiating event, attempt, consequence, response) from hearing stories. The stories that they hear may be oral ones which are told to them, or they may be written ones which are read to them. Children use what they have learned about organizational structures of stories when they begin to write their own stories. The more they use language, the more they learn about language; and the more they learn about language, the more linguistic data they have to work with. With increasing amounts of linguistic data to use, and with experience in coordinating the data to produce new language, children become increasingly sophisticated language users. That is, they experience (oral and written) language growth.

Risk-Taking

This strategy is closely related to the other three. Risk-taking allows the language user to try out a new way of using written language to test whether or not the new way works in a particular context. Children use both what they already know about written language and also what they do not quite yet know, but suspect. In this way, they are able to test their most recent insights, often simply pretending to write, in order to learn more about literacy. Harste, Burke, and Woodward give the example of Dawn's doing precisely this:

> On a task assigned to solicit name writing on two occasions so that we might study the stability of the child's marking, Dawn used two different markings. In the first instance, she wrote her name quite clearly, DAWN, and in the second instance she wrote it in an English-like cursive script. When asked if she had put her name on the later paper she said, "Yes," pointing to the line where she had announced she was going to write it in the first place. Knowing how to simply write one's name isn't good enough. Dawn already knows that. She now must try it a new way showing us that she is aware of the different options available to her.

These four process universals help define a new conception of development. They negate the traditional notion of discrete stages, supporting, instead, the concept of "learning how to mean," in Halliday's (1977) phrase, first, and then incrementally refining one's language, or writing, through experience. Harste, Burke, and Woodward argue against confusing growth with experience. That is, one learns language through language experience, and writing through writing (and other language) experiences. There do not seem to be "natural" stages which unfold in the child apart from real-world experiences. Whereas we previously looked for age-correlated developmental stages, we now see that there is little evidence to support such an expectation. This may be why findings from all four of these key writing research projects stress that *individual variation* in learning to write is the rule, not the exception.

Like Harste, Burke, and Woodward, Graves and his research associates (Calkins and Sowers) define as one of their key findings the "unearthing of process ingredients." They, too, see the processes as universal ones for both children and adults. Children reveal them more easily because the processes are still overt in children, rather than covert, as they are in many adult writers. In Harste's words, they are "unfrozen" in children, and are therefore perhaps more accessible to investigation. The essential ingredients of writing which Graves et al. identified are topic choice, rehearsal (conscious or unconscious), composing, reading, and revising. Their data show no set order to these processes within the writing of a piece. They occur recursively and in differing orders from writer to writer, and within one writer writing different products. These findings underscore the theme of individual variation in both writing and learning to write which is echoed throughout all four writing research projects.

Graves et al. have identified what they call "general developmental sequences" which the children in their study seemed to go through as they learned to write. However, they caution that "great care must be taken to view them along several axes" rather than along the lines of any one behavior. As these children grew as writers, they did not "reach stages," mastering one aspect of writing at a time, then moving to a "higher level" aspect of writing. Rather, they began practicing the processes immediately at the beginning of first grade, gradually moving on a number of axes toward increasingly complex and elaborated pieces of writing. Graves, like Harste, Burke, and Woodward did not find age correlated with growth in these processes. Instead, growth seemed to occur as a result of experience with writing. There was such variation in ages at which various aspects of writing were learned that, again, it seems clear that we cannot expect biological "stages" to unfold.

Transition from Oral to Written Language

Many of the projects' key findings focus on the theme of a transition from oral to written language. This is not to say that writing develops solely from an oral language base. There are other significant sources from which writing can grow. The relationship of art, or drawing, and writing is one of these which is increasingly being investigated. Play behavior and the development of symbol systems in general are other sources. Certainly, reading (or being read to) and the exposure to environmental print is another significant source. Having acknowledged the multiple sources that contribute to development of writing, I would like to focus on what has been learned about the relationship of one of them, oral language, to growth in writing.

King and Rentel gathered language data in three modes of discourse: story retellings, dictated stories, and written stories. Children from grades K-2 in two different schools provided the data; one population was followed from kindergarten to first grade, and the other population from first grade to second grade. Thus, they were able to track the children's growth in the three modes of discourse over the first two years of school. One of their key findings confirmed that "learning to write has its roots deep in oral language development." As can be seen in the writing samples below from one child in their study, elements of the children's writing retraced elements of earlier growth. That is, patterns of growth evidenced in the oral retellings appeared later in dictated stories, and then in the children's writing. This was true mainly for both the researchers' analysis of cohesion and analysis of story structure in these oral and written texts. This remarkable information about writing development confirms what many have long sensed: their analysis provides concrete examples of particular features of language development (e.g., the use of conjunctions) which develop first in oral language, and then in writing.

Writing Samples from One Child (King and Rentel)

May of Kindergarten Year (Writing):

1. I like Hm He   (I like him
2. Day Maj   He did magic
3. He jagdo   He juggled)

May of Kindergarten Year (Speech-Dictated Story):

1. well once upon a time there was this chicken
2. and the chicken you know was going to the barnyard
3. and the chicken didn't know

 4. but a cat was looking at him
 5. and the cat jumped out from behind and ate the chicken up
 6. and then another chicken came
 7. and then the chicken was looking at the cat
 8. and he knew what to do
 9. he called the dog
10. and the dog came and chased the cat away

. . . .

16. and everybody went back to the barnyard
17. the farmer was waiting with dinner
18. and then it was time for bed
19. and then they went to bed
20. and the next morning they woke up
21. and they had breakfast
22. and they brushed their teeth and washed their face and hands
23. and they went out for a walk

. . . .

40. and they went to bed.

October of Grade One (Writing):

 1. once upon a time there was a little man and a little woman
 2. one day they went on a walk
 3. on their walk they met a giraffe!
 4. it was strange to meet a giraffe in the middle of the road
 5. so they went home

End of Grade One (Writing):

 1. once there was a bear that lived in the woods
 2. he was lonely
 3. he only had a few friends
 4. his friends were a squirrel a racoon and a deer
 5. one day the bear went to racoon's house
 6. they talked a while
 7. they had something to eat
 8. the bear liked to eat!

9. it was time for bear to go home

10. he was tired

11. he went to bed—the end.

Another interesting point is that their data—like the data of Harste, Burke, and Woodward, and Graves—show patterns of incremental growth, a gradual adding of information into processes already underway. Their data, like the others, also show extensive individual variation in development.

Staton and her associates also have provided information about the transition from oral to written language. Because the writing in the dialogue journals which comprise their data is *interactive* (i.e., it is a written year-long conversation between students and teacher), the journals may provide a useful pedagogical step between oral dialogues and written monologues. Also, there are strong parallels between the conditions for dialogue journal writing and natural conditions for first language acquisition. This may be particularly true in the apparent use of scaffolding by the teacher in dialogue journals and by the mother, or caretaker, in first language acquisition. (More detailed information about scaffolding is presented in the final section of this chapter, including the question of the relationship of written language growth to teaching.)

Another way in which dialogue journals parallel oral language development is the focus on "learning how to mean," first by immediately practicing *processes,* then refining those processes by incorporating increasingly detailed and complex pieces of information into the processes. Finally, as Shuy (1982) has pointed out, there are interesting relationships between the language functions used orally and the language functions used in dialogue journal writing. We do not know at this point whether or not there are developmental trends in oral language which are later retraced in dialogue journal writing (as in the King/Rentel data), but it would be interesting to pursue that line of analysis.

Graves et al., with their observational data of children *during* the writing process, have shown clear transitions from oral to written language. Graves has tentatively defined three stages that many young writers pass through when learning to write. Furthermore, he has linked some of the transition factors with what professional writers, appropriately enough, call "voice." His three stages are: (1) overt manifestations of speech while writing (sometimes these are verbal, sometimes they are "sound effects," and sometimes they are nonverbal kinesics); (2) page explicit transitions (e.g., heavy use of prosodics in writing—exclamation points, underlined or large words for stress); and (3) speech features implicit in text (e.g., information selected for the text is organized so that it flows like speech; also, heavy use of prosodics through punctuation, and capitalization drops off).

Although Graves has tentatively identified these processes as stages, he cautions against applying them too rigidly. In fact, he reports that "*individual exceptions* to the data increased in dominance as the study progressed." He underscores this theme by recommending against developing scope and sequence curricula for classroom writing instruction because there is simply too much variability between and within children to allow for this. In fact, he shows how this variability is linked to teaching through the use of context. Instead of developing writing curricula, his findings support providing teachers with information (such as these studies provide) so that they may use it to draw out of each child the curriculum, which he sees as being within the child. This concept leads to the final section of this chapter which focuses on the relationship of written language growth to teaching.

How Is Written Language Growth Related to Teaching?

There are three aspects of the relationship of growth in writing to teaching. The first is the overall instructional approach to literacy in a particular classroom or school, not a particular pedagogical technique. The second and third aspects of the relationship (scaffolding and text ownership) do involve specific pedagogical techniques within a broader instructional approach.

Overall Instructional Approach

King and Rentel and associates worked in two schools which at first appear to be quite similar. One is in a suburban upper-middle class setting; it is the "open learning" alternative school located next to its traditional elementary school counterpart. Parents in this section of the suburb have the choice of sending their children to the traditional elementary school or to the newer alternative school. The other school is an inner-city "magnet" school which is also organized according to "open learning" concepts. Parents from other parts of the city also have the opportunity to choose this school for their children, and enough middle-class parents have done so to provide King and Rentel with a middle-class population for their study.

Despite the apparent similarities between the two "open learning" schools, however, it became clear during the study that the overall instructional approaches to literacy teaching were different. The suburban school integrated reading and writing in almost all learning activities. Moreover, the school's classrooms were "literacy rich"; stories and books were constantly being used for reading and writing activities. The inner-city school, in contrast, relied heavily on workbooks and worksheets to teach "skills" (i.e., word recognition, handwriting, and spelling). Thus, reading and writing were treated as separate subject areas, rather than as integral parts of other content areas.

These different overall instructional approaches seem to have made distinct differences in writing growth in two populations of middle-class children. Predictably, those with more exposure to literature and more practice with the processes than the mechanical skills of writing led the way developmentally on a number of different measures (e.g., higher proportions of conjunction and lexical cohesion in their written tests).

The overall instructional approaches in the classrooms in which Graves and his associates worked match more closely the "literacy rich" classrooms than the "skills-based" classrooms of the King and Rentel study. In fact, the interaction between the Graves researchers and the teachers at this particular school produced not only a truly collaborative study, but also an evolution in the way writing was taught. According to Sowers (1982):

> The climate of experimentation allowed teachers to test their implicit theories of learning and new approaches to teaching. They articulated discoveries and reorganized classroom time and materials.

Although there was no uniformity in teaching styles among the classrooms, there were underlying similarities which allow us to generalize some conclusions from the study. First, the teachers created situations that permitted students to write without teacher assignments. For example, one teacher equipped a writing table with a variety of paper, pens, and pencils. Then she asked her first-grade students to write, and reorganized the classroom to allow each day for individual, small-group and whole-class responses to the writings. Soon, all the students were writing and reading other students' writing (Giacobbe, 1982). In fact, the teacher soon stopped using basal readers, and turned to the many "books" produced in her class.

Crucial to this "writing without teacher assignments" was the teacher's decision to allow what has been called "invented spelling" (Read, 1975). Expecting conventional, correct spelling from such beginning writers is unrealistic. And if the children wait until they are good spellers before they begin to write, they lose valuable time during which they could be learning writing *processes*. This particular teacher decided to encourage writing, without teacher assignments and with invented spelling, at the beginning of first grade. She learned three things by doing this: her students learned to read at least as well as they would have with basal readers (as evidenced by standardized tests at the end of the year); they learned to write better than they would have with her previous skills-based approach (as evidenced by the pieces of writing her children produced); and their learning of skills did not ultimately suffer. Skills were learned primarily in context; that is, as students wrote, they discovered needs for different kinds of punctuation, capitalization, and other mechanical aspects of writing.

On this last point, some discussion may be needed. Advocating a process approach to writing instruction does not mean eliminating skills instruction. It is not an either/or question: Should skills or processes be taught? Both. What the Graves study revealed, however, is that skills seem to be best taught in context—that is, during process instruction. Often, such skills instruction occurs during teacher-student conferences.

Scaffolding

Conferences are characteristic of the second aspect of the relationship of written language growth to teaching, called scaffolding. According to Cazden (1981):

> A scaffold is, literally, a temporary framework for construction in progress. Metaphorically, the term *scaffold* was first used by Jerome Bruner to refer to adult assistance to children's language development.

Sowers (1982) has taken the concept of instructional scaffolding and has applied it to the writing conferences that she observed during the two years she worked on the Graves study. Sowers observed that these conferences were the most significant instructional aspect of writing in the classrooms, and saw in them a model of internalization for learning writing. That is, because the children "heard their own and others' writing read and questioned," they were able "to internalize the qualities of good writing and the voice of an audience with high expectations." The conferences, in which writing was shared, included both formal and informal peer-peer and teacher-student conferences. Teacher-student conferences were of three types: one-to-one, teacher with a small group, or teacher with the entire class. As students became familiar with the predictable routines of these conferences, they seemed to internalize the model, asking themselves the questions that they had learned to expect in conferences. This internalization is captured in the following words of a second-grader named Hillary (Sowers, 1982):

> "I have an individual conference with myself," Hillary, a second-grader, explained. When Graves asked her to tell what she did in her solitary conferences, she told him she read the piece and thought of questions the other children would ask. She gave him an example from her current book, "On the Farm": 'Your horse's name is Misty. Well, do you ride it or feed it or what?' So I'm going to put, 'I ride her every day unless it is raining.'"

Hillary had learned to anticipate a reader's reaction to her writing, and to accommodate this anticipated reaction during the original drafting of the piece. She was able to do this because the conferences all followed a consistent pattern. In this consistency, and in other characteristics, conferences are similar to mother-infant interactions during first language acquisition. Sowers identified ten ways in which the principles underlying mother-infant interactions during language acquisition are characteristic of the writing conferences that she observed. Writing conferences worked to:

focus the child on the task;

reduce degrees of freedom (i.e., only a limited number of issues were dealt with in any one conference);

maintain the direction of the task (i.e., each conference served to move the writer along the global writing process toward completion of the piece);

mark critical features (i.e., the limited number of issues dealt with in each conference were chosen on the basis of their criticalness at that point in the writing process);

control frustration (e.g., the teacher provided help *during* the writing process, rather than after a piece was completed);

demonstrate solutions (e.g., teachers waited until a child presented a problem, and then modeled its solution);

limit and make familiar the semantic domain (e.g., since children chose their own topics, they wrote about content familiar to them, rather than about topics outside their own knowledge base);

offer a structure in which utterances can be inserted (i.e., a predictable interaction structure in which new content can be inserted);

provide reversible roles (e.g., just as mother and infant can exchange roles in the interaction, a child can become the "teacher" for another child, or for himself or herself); and

provide a playful atmosphere (i.e., one in which children feel free enough to innovate).

In these ways, the writing conferences described in the Graves study provide a model of learning which closely parallels oral language acquisition: both cases epitomize the concept of scaffolding. Another study by Staton (1982) yielded a similar model of internalization through scaffolding.

Staton and her associates identified clear patterns of instructional scaffolding in written interaction between students and teacher in the dialogue journals that they studied. Students in this sixth-grade class made nearly daily entries in dialogue journals during the entire academic year; the teacher responded in writing in the journal to each student entry. The result is a year-long, written conversation between student and teacher which represents what appears to be a very effective model for learning writing.

The teacher uses dialogue journals with her students (and has done so for twenty years) to develop a more personal relationship with each student. She hopes to "break down the communication barriers" between teacher and students so that she can then teach them. It is apparent, however, that she is accomplishing far more than "clearing the way" for teaching. Many learning patterns are evident to a careful reader of these journals, including a clear pattern of written language growth. This growth, or learning, seems to occur partly as a result of the scaffolding which the teacher provides in her responses. The responses often provide a model of reasoning about a student-identified problem which, by example, extends the student's competence, both in writing and in thinking. The example below, from an analysis by Farr (1982), shows how the teacher leads one student through such a model of reasoning. This student could virtually speak no English when she began the school year; by December or January, she was writing English fluently and effectively.

Example of Written Dialogue:

Student	*Teacher*
You kow Debora call me (B)	When someone calls you names or uses bad language you can move away. Ignore them, play like you did not hear them. They will not stop if they think they are making you angry.
You can tell Debbie the not sei bed worr	I've told Debbie not to use bad words. She says she doesn't use them. Around me she doesn't use them. Around you she uses them to show off.
Ms Reed Debbie use de but she sed no cas she sharr	Of course Debbie would say "No." She does not want to get into trouble.
Ms Reed I think Debbie af to not sei nothing like bad wors because is not good.	Debbie wants friends but she says bad words so she does not have many friends.

The patterns in such teacher responses during the year support the notion that the teacher, consciously or unconsciously, is providing scaffolding when it is most needed by the student. The teacher uses responses to get the student writing, reasoning, and elaborating on topics the student has initiated. When the student is doing these things, the teacher begins to reduce the number of responses, thus gradually dropping the scaffolding as it is less needed by the student.

I have discussed two aspects of the relationship of written language growth to teaching. The first was the overall instructional approach in a particular classroom or school (what has been called either "literacy-rich" or "skills-based"). The second aspect was scaffolding, first defined as a concept, and then in terms of how particular pedagogical techniques manifested the concept (e.g., writing conferences and dialogue journals). A third aspect of the relationship of written language growth to teaching is text ownership.

Text Ownership

This concept, first used by Harste, Burke, and Woodward (1982), essentially means that the meaning in any literacy event is created by the participants in that event. That is, a writer creates meaning when writing to a reader, and a reader creates meaning when reading the writer's work.

The four process universals which Harste, Burke, and Woodward have identified (and which have been explained above) support the concept of text ownership in both literacy use and in literacy acquisition. In other words, the strategies of textual intent, negotiability, using language to fine-tune language, and risk-taking all assume a kind of *control* on the part of the literacy user. The reader and the writer create and negotiate meaning; it does not reside purely within the written text. Pedagogically, this concept is manifested in the teaching approaches used in both the Graves and the Staton studies.

In the Graves study, the heart of the writing instruction program was in the conference process. Because teachers and students, together, worked their way through the writing of each piece by sharing the writing (in various stages) in conferences, the learning and teaching of writing was paced. This pacing allowed time for writers to field questions by readers, and to use these questions in considering revisions. In this way, both the particular piece of writing and, more importantly, the learning of writing processes were nurtured. Use of such conferences also resulted in a sense of ownership of the writing by the children. As one teacher said (Calkins, 1980):

> I used to try to shortcut things by assigning topics and correcting papers, but now I find that when children choose their own topics and

revise their papers based on their own decisions, they really care about their writing. It belongs to them.

Whereas teachers can help by carefully listening, questioning, and suggesting, the responsibility for selecting topics, creating drafts, and making revisions lies with the student. Previously, the teachers in this study, like many teachers, used up energy in doing many of these things. With the writing conference process, that use of energy was shifted to the child. When the child feels that kind of control, he or she has a sense of *text ownership* and, consequently, readily provides the energy and motivation needed to do the best writing.

A sense of text ownership is also manifested in the dialogue journals of the Staton study. The journals belong to the students; they are private, written conversations between each student and the teacher. (Students whose journals were studied, however, gave permission to the researchers to use them.) Students almost always initiated discussion of topics, and each student determined what and how much he or she would write about each topic. As in the Graves study, the teacher's role was to listen, ask questions, and make suggestions. Also, as in the Graves study, the student had responsibility for, and therefore control of, almost all aspects of the writing process. As a result, real growth, or learning, occurred. Students no longer felt compelled simply to "write something" on a topic chosen by someone else—a process which often results in both lackluster and poor writing. In contrast, the writing in these journals is what can be called "engaged" writing; it is full of voice and original meaning. That this kind of writing results from the fact that the writers feel a sense of ownership of the writing may be best summed up by a quote from one of the student dialogue journal writers (who was struggling not only to learn to write but also to learn English). After a particularly long and expressive entry in which she introduced twelve new topics, and elaborated on each of them, this student wrote:

> Today I like to write a lot I donth know way meaybi cos I got somenithing to write.

References

Calkins, Lucy McCormick. "Work in Progress: One School's Writing Program." *The National Elementary Principal* 59 (June 1980): 34–38.

Cazden, Courtney. "Peer Dialogues Across the Curriculum." Manuscript, 1981.

Farr, Marcia. "Learning to Write English: One Dialogue Journal Writer's Growth in Writing." AERA presentation (March 1982).

Giacobbe, Mary Ellen. "Kids Can Write the First Week of School." In *A Case*

Study of Observing the Development of Primary Children's Composing, Spelling, and Motor Behavior During the Writing Process, by Donald H. Graves. NIE final report (NIE-G-78-0174), 1982.

Graves, Donald H. *A Case Study of Observing the Development of Primary Children's Composing, Spelling, and Motor Behavior During the Writing Process.* NIE final report (NIE-G-78-0174), 1982.

Graves, Donald H. "Andrea Learns to Make Writing Hard." *Language Arts* 56 (May 1979): 569–76.

Halliday, M.A.K. *Learning How to Mean: Explorations in the Development of Language.* New York: Elsevier, 1977.

Harste, Jerome C.; Burke, Carolyn L.; and Woodward, Virginia. *Children, Their Language and World: Initial Encounters with Print.* NIE final report (NIE-G-79-0132), 1982.

King, Martha L., and Rentel, Victor M. *How Children Learn to Write: A Longitudinal Study.* NIE final report, Volume 1 (NIE-G-79-0137 and NIE-G-79-0039), 1981.

National Assessment of Educational Progress. "Writing Achievement 1969-79: Results from the Third National Writing Assessment," Volumes 1–3. Washington, D.C.: U.S. Government Printing Office, 1981.

Read, Charles. *Children's Categorization of Speech Sounds in English* (Research Report No. 17). Urbana, Ill.: ERIC Clearinghouse on Language and Linguistics, ERIC Clearinghouse on Reading and Communication Skills, and the National Council of Teachers of English, 1975.

Staton, Jana; Shuy, Roger; and Kreeft, Joy. *Analysis of Dialogue Journal Writing as a Communicative Event.* NIE final report, Volumes 1 and 2 (NIE-G-80-0122), 1982.

Shuy, Roger W. "A Comparison of Oral and Written Language Functions." AERA presentation (March 1982).

Sowers, Susan. "Writing Development in Context: The Atkinson Study." Manuscript, 1982.

Thinking Together: Interaction in Children's Reasoning

Jana Staton, Center for Applied Linguistics, Washington, D.C.

> The real voyage of discovery consists not in seeing new landscapes, but seeing old landscapes with new eyes.
>
> —Proust

This chapter is intended to help teachers see a very familiar "landscape" with new eyes. That landscape is the language interaction which occurs between teacher and student, and between student and student, whenever a genuine dialogue about an important event or problem occurs. The development of thinking for all children occurs through particular kinds of language interactions in which a child can work through a problem jointly with an adult or peer. These language interactions are so familiar and so hard to capture for observation that we may fail to see them for what they are: the most important encounters that a child can have in learning how to think.

Research on classroom teaching has found that in the very act of teaching, the teacher's way of *thinking out loud* (or thinking on paper in written dialogues) becomes a model for students (Green, 1983; McNamee, 1979; Staton, 1982a). For this "model" to be acquired and internalized, however, students must be active conversational partners *with* the teacher in situations in which they are thinking *together* about the same topic or problem.

Jerome Bruner has described this practice very succinctly in *Toward a Theory of Instruction:*

> ... what the teacher must be, to be an effective competence model, is a day-to-day working model with whom to interact. It is not so much that the teacher provides a model to imitate. Rather, it is that the teacher can become a part of the student's internal dialogue—somebody whose respect he wants, someone whose standards he wishes to make his own. It is like becoming a speaker of a language one shares

with somebody. The language of that interaction becomes a part of oneself, and the standards of style and clarity that one adopts for that interaction become a part of one's own standards. (1966, p. 124)

What Is the Connection between Dialogue and Thinking?

Learning to think is like learning a language: it simply is not enough to learn isolated strategies any more than it is enough to learn a vocabulary list. To be able to think in new situations—which is the real goal of all education—children need a lot of experience in thinking with someone who is good at it. Thinking is invisible until we use language to make it visible. However, a student, by just passively listening to someone else talk about an unfamiliar problem or topic cannot begin to learn how to think about his or her *own* tasks or problems. Just as we learn a language by talking with someone who is good at it in specific situations concerning tangible, shared experiences, so we learn to think by thinking *with* someone to solve a joint task or problem.

Following are some actual examples of dialogue—language used in interactive situations involving a teacher and one or more students—that serve to define the meaning of interactive mental processing or "thinking together."

Two Views of Classroom Dialogue

Some researchers, and perhaps some teachers, have thought of class discussions as simply ways to find out if students know the right answers. This elicitation approach sees a class discussion as only a series of teacher questions, student answers, and evaluative responses by the teacher:

> *Teacher:* John, what's the capital of the United States?
>
> *John:* Uh, New York?
>
> *Teacher:* No. Mary?
>
> *Mary:* Washington.
>
> *Teacher:* Right.

However, there is another kind of language interaction in which students and the teacher together share in a *conversational partnership* to jointly build a framework of knowledge. The teacher's comments and questions are substantially different. What the teacher says builds on and incorporates what students have said, so that the students' thinking becomes part of the teacher's framework.

Following is a transcript of a kindergarten classroom discussion about how plants grow from seeds (Lucas and Border-Simmons, 1982).

Teacher: I need to talk with you for a minute so you'll be able to watch back there on the science table to see what's going to happen to your plants. What do you suppose a plant needs, the seeds need, in order to grow?

Unidentified Student: Oh I know.

Charles: Plenty of sunshine.

Teacher: Now I'm not going to call on you until you stop yelling out.

Unidentified Student: In the ground.

Teacher: Someone says that you put the seeds in the ground, and then after the seeds are in the ground, then what's coming down on them?

Unidentified Student: Rain.

Teacher: It has to have water and someone has just said we have to have water on our plants.

Charles: And we have to have plenty of sunshine.

Teacher: And they have to get some sunlight.

Ken: So, so, so, so . . .

Teacher: So, Katrine, this is what the seeds have to get.

Ken: So the rain'll stick on, stay on.

Charles: And there, they're cracking open the plant.

Teacher: The plant that you planted yesterday will have to have water on it. You'll have to see that it gets some water today. And it'll have to have some sunlight. And after the seed begins to get some sunlight and rain, something happens to it right away.

Rachel: (Inaudible)

Teacher: Yes, it comes up. And Rachel says that there's a little plant inside of that seed. So the plant does something. Now let's look at (it). Look what happens. (Shows plant roots.)

Ken: And the roots come out.

Teacher: That's right. What do you suppose happens?

Ken: If they didn't have roots they wouldn't grow.

Tammy: And they would die.

Eve: They, they, they, they. You have to have. The reason why plants have to (have) roots to stay underground.

Eve: So they could stay up.

Teacher: Well, those are some good answers. But where else does the plant get its food, from what, children?

Eric: Plant food.

Teacher: Someone said that it keeps it standing up. That's a good answer. And also it gets its food through that root. And then something else will come out of that little plant, too.

Ken: The plant!

Teacher: As you see right here (holds up plant) something else will come out of that. What's coming out of here, children?

Ken: The plant!

Teacher: Yes, well the whole thing is the plant, here, but what is this part? (Points to stem)

Ken: The stems!

Teacher: All right. That's the stem part of it. And what else will come out of here?

Unidentified Student: The flower.

Teacher: Well before it gets to the flower.

Charles: The plant!

Teacher: What else? What's another part of the plant—anybody have an idea?

Teacher: What about the leaf? What about the leaf of a plant?

Eric: The leaf of the plant (inaudible) the leaf of plant starts growing. The plant just starts growing and then all the leaves comes out of the stem.

Teacher: All right. So the leaves come out from there. Now children, I want you to be some little plants for me. Who wants to, who wants to be a little seed for me?

Unidentified Student: I do! I do! (Eric, Derek, Joyce, Tammy, Donna have hands up.)

Unidentified Student: Me.

Teacher: All right. Get yourselves down and make yourself a seed. Now how do you suppose a seed is? (Children all curl up.)

The example illustrates what is meant by the claim that teaching and learning occur through a cooperative conversational partnership. It shows the teacher actively modeling a way of thinking about what a plant is and about the process of growth—at a level which students not only can understand, but can participate in actively. Instead of the teacher asking many questions and students giving one-word answers, each child thinks aloud about what he or she knows. The students feel free to build on each other's answers instead of always waiting for the teacher to speak.

A metaphor used to describe this process is "interactional scaffolding." The term means that the adult establishes a common goal with students and then actively engages them in finding out together how to reach it. The teacher builds a scaffold, or framework, to hold each child's contribution, along with the teacher's, as they converse. The children are actively constructing the knowledge with the teacher—which is the goal. It is more than just getting the "right answer"; it is a process of jointly building knowledge.

The goal, in this instance, is to understand how a seed grows into a plant. The teacher could have given a minilecture—a monologue—and simply told the children about seeds, roots, stems, and leaves, and how they absorb water. Instead, she engages in a dialogue, which has lots of openings for students to make contributions. You might want to review the transcript and mark the students' contributions.

Also, the teacher does not evaluate each answer immediately as to its "rightness" or "wrongness." Instead, she incorporates the best answers into the framework that she already has in mind. You can identify in the transcript where the teacher incorporates students' responses into her next statement. When Charles mentions sunshine too "early" to fit the framework that she is constructing, the teacher at that time does not respond to his idea, but lets him offer it again five turns later, when it fits, and then incorporates it.

An analysis of students' responses in the lesson shows that they understood it as a *mutual* conversation. As the lesson progresses, they stop raising hands to be "called on" and simply listen and then talk when they understand and have something to offer (Lucas, 1981).

The heart of the seeds lesson is that students become deeply engaged in thinking together with the teacher, and the teacher no longer needs to regulate turn-taking by having students raise hands and wait to be called on. The structure of the teacher's "thinking aloud" becomes the means of regulating turns in the dialogue.

When students fail to provide the most appropriate piece of knowledge, as in the case of identifying the stem, the teacher recycles questions and gives more precise instructions as to what part of the plant she means until Ken says "the stem." These strategies are ones that we use with friends in any mutual conversation.

This may seem very ordinary to many teachers because it is the way they teach. But what occurs is an excellent example of the *mutual* construction of world knowledge, in which no child feels that what he or she says is "wrong."

Discussion of another kind of student-teacher dialogue, this time in writing, follows. The point of using both oral and written dialogue examples is to show how complex and varied student-teacher interactions can be and to convince you—if you still need convincing—that classroom dialogues are rich instances of how children's thinking can be developed through language.

Written Conversations: Another Way of Thinking Together

Using "dialogue journals" is another way in which language interaction involves a teacher and student in thinking together. These journals are private written conversations between each student and the teacher, daily or weekly, about whatever topics and concerns that the student wants to discuss (Staton, Shuy, and Kreeft, 1982). In the seeds lesson, the teacher initiated the task and established the goal: "... so you'll be able to watch back there on the science table to see what's going to happen to your plants." By contrast, in using dialogue journals, students generally initiate topics, thus bringing up problems that they want to solve (the goal). The teacher's role in the dialogue becomes one of helping the student to see his or her experience from a different perspective, and to suggest how actions and outcomes are connected. Again, student and teacher are thinking together, and the student can observe and participate in the teacher's way of thinking.

The two excerpts are from dialogue journals of sixth-grade students in Los Angeles and their teacher, Leslee Reed. They concern two very different kinds of experiences—a science experiment and getting along with other students. In both cases, the student selected the topic, and then the teacher and student became involved in thinking together about how to accomplish a goal: "finding out what happened" in the science experiment, and "handling the problem of Dino and taking cuts" in the second example. (Note: These excerpts are from writing done in winter or spring periods of the school year, after the students have become comfortable and familiar with using this written conversation as a way of communicating with the teacher. These passages have been typed from the handwritten originals.)

Day 1

Tai: Mrs. Reed I would like you to think up something like rainwater or coke and sugar and we would both try it and tell what happen Monday.

Mrs. Reed: Okay! I have an idea for us to try. Dissolve as much salt as you can in ½ cup of water. (Do you think heating the water would help to dissolve more salt or less?) Tie a string on a pencil and put the pencil over the cup, letting the string hang down into the salt solution. (Cut off string if it is too long, it should reach just the bottom of the cup.) Now put it where you can see it and record any changes you see.

Day 2

Tai: Today swooshed by. I am going to do that exsperient. I'm going to keep record every minute up to five. I think heating the water would dissolve it faster.

Mrs. Reed: Good! I'll do my experiment, too.

Day 3

Tai: I did my experiment and all my water evaporated except a little but I left it overnight with some salt and I used warm water and most of the salt stayed in the cup and then I started making my record I waited one minute and I saw the salt coming together and every time I made a recort the salt would start coming together on the string . . .

Mrs. Reed: My experiment is still working! The water in the cup is evaporating, but most of it is still there. I'm getting some salt crystals growing on my string.

Day 3

Tai: Where is your cup at in the house? I put mine in the kitchen.

Mrs. Reed: I have my experiment sitting on the counter in the kitchen, too. Did you find the measure of water we were to have used? My crystals are growing a little everyday. Are yours?

Day 4

Tai: Yes ½ of a cup. Mine is still trying to dissolve. If you can bring yours tomorrow to see what is happening . . .

Mrs. Reed: I won't bring my experiment until Monday. It got bumped twice so it is just now "growing." I'll bring it on Monday.

Day 5

Tai: OK I'll bring mine.

Mrs. Reed: I will try to remember my salt crystals, too . . .

Day 6

Tai: Your experient looks like mine exept mine isn't on the side of the glass.

Mrs. Reed: Do you think it would be interesting to look at those crystals through a microscope? What would you see?

Day 7

Tai: I do think that would be nice to look through a microscope could I? I don't know what I'll see unless I do it.

Mrs. Reed: I'll get a magnifying glass if you'll bring in your experiment, too. Why do you think the crystals continue to grow?

Day 8

Tai: As the water evaporates the salt goes up in the air with it.

Day 9

Tai: I meant to tell you I spilled the exsperient but I couldn't bring it on the bus cause it would spill.

Mrs. Reed: Oh! dear! Now I can't see your experiment!

Two pages of this student's dialogue journal are shown on the following page to show how the science experiment dialogue is one of several topics interwoven in the written conversation between Tai and her teacher.

The second example that follows shows the same teacher using more explicit strategies for focusing this student's thinking, in a situation where it is more difficult for him to use his thinking and reasoning skills on his own.

Day 1

Gordon: I really don't care if I don't make hot dog griddles or whatever you call them. And also I don't think that you were fair when Dino hit me. You didn't even say anything to him. He got of really easy and it just isn't fair. What's wrong with getting cuts. Its just that my friends give me cuts. But I don't really care.

Mrs. Reed: I did not see Dino hit you—I saw you hit Dino. Did you have to hit him? Was there no other possible way of handling that problem? You tell me what is wrong with taking or giving cuts in line? It sure makes you happy when four or five people in front of you give cuts to their friends doesn't it?

Day 2

Gordon: I did not have to hit him. But I felt the need too. Yes there were other ways of handling the problem. But I didn't think of them at that time. Well one thing wrong is people don't like it.

This student begins with a complaint about the teacher's "unfairness" and gives some information about what happened. The teacher adds to his description some relevant new information about the occurrence from *her* point of view. The teacher does not initiate the topic, but she focuses the student's attention on his own behavior and responsibility for making understanding problems. Would you see if you can help? Yes I would have to talk to you about Joan. Now I'm glad I got that over. Today I got to Guenevere but I felt good. I am so happy cause it might be staying after tomorrow. No I never did rain winter in or cup but when it going again I will. Mrs Read I would like you to think up want thing like noinwater or coke and sugar and we will both stay it and tell what I hoppen Monday, Thur. Jan 24. Thanks for your help. You not only help but you are trying to set a good example for other.

Okay! I have an idea for us to try. Dissolve as much salt as you can in a cup of water. (As you think, heating the water would help to dissolve more salt in less?) Tie a string on a pencil and put the pencil over the cup, letting the string hang down into the salt solution. (Cut off string if it is too long; it should reach just the bottom of the cup) Now put it where you can see it and record any changes you see.

You are doing great as the costume planner and as Tonio's matter! Keep it up! Today washed by. I had you doing the play. I am going to do that tomorrow. I'm going to keep record over ... much. Stop to turn. I think -

choices in order to help him "rethink" the problem. She suggests that there were alternative actions that he could have taken. She models a way of thinking about a fight by raising questions that require a reflective response from the student: Was there something else I could have done?

The student's response at this time shows that he has understood the teacher's thinking and entered into her framework of meaning (but we note that she has also entered into his, using his language and talking about his concerns). The reflective questions about a concrete situation can be internalized and become part of an inner "dialogue" the student can use independently later.

A Closer Look: How Does Dialogue Work?

This section takes a closer look at the way in which conversational participation in a dialogue works to help students internalize more flexible and mature ways of thinking about the world and their experiences. Discussed first are some obvious differences between unfocused, classroom interactions and the thoughtful, directed dialogue already described.

Then, the concept of "interactional scaffolding" is described as a partial way of explaining how dialogue can work. We want to stress "partial" because such research concepts are still inadequate to explain all that occurs in language interactions.

Finally, a set of "conditions for dialogue" is described which facilitate the process of thinking together, and which you already may be using, or may find helpful to use, in your classroom.

Involvement without Much "Thinking"

There is a major difference between just having students respond freely and talk about whatever they know and engaging them in a structured topic discussion which demands their thinking. Of course, there is value in developing children's use of language through discussion circles and sharing time. But there is no evidence that indicates that an unstructured discussion with no specific goal really involves students in actively confronting different viewpoints or acquiring new concepts.

An example of the point that just any language interaction does not automatically involve cognitive "scaffolding" is found in the following transcript of a language arts lesson (Shuy, 1980). The transcript is of a second-grade teacher and her class discussing Abraham Lincoln and shows extensive student-teacher language interaction. At the start of the lesson, the teacher has just read a short poem about Lincoln that contains the lines:

> When Abraham Lincoln was a boy,
> He never had a store-bought toy.

Teacher: Was Abraham Lincoln unhappy because he didn't have a store-bought toy?

Students: No.

Teacher: No, because hardly any of the children had store-bought toys. What do you think Abraham Lincoln played with when he was little? Any ideas?

Students: (not intelligible)

Teacher: OK, now try to think now. He was way out there in the woods.

Student: I know!

Teacher: What would he play with?

Nancy: Animals?

Teacher: Animals. He probably had some pets. What else? George?

George: He had the Bible book?

Teacher: He did have the Bible book, but he didn't play with it. What else would you play with if you were way out in the woods, and didn't have any toys?

Student: Dirt.

Teacher: Bill.

Bill: Carve, carving.

Teacher: Yes, he probably carved some things out of wood. What else, Robert?

Robert: He play with mud.

Teacher: He probably made some things with mud. What else?

Student: Out of dirt.

Teacher: Uh, huh. With dirt. He probably had all kinds of ways he could play. Uh, huh, Julie?

Julie: With sticks and stones.

Teacher: He probably did play with sticks and stones.

Students: Break my bones. (laughter)

Teacher: You could have a game with sticks and stones.

Several S: Uh, huh. Break my bones.

Teacher: Sure you could make sticks like tic tack toe. (Crosstalk among students increases.)

Rosie: Sticks and stones will break my bones, but words will never hurt me.

Teacher: That's a poem. How many of you know that one? (hands) Uh, huh. OK.

Teacher: What do you think Abraham Lincoln played with when he was a boy? All right, let's let Emily say what she thinks.

Emily: Animals.

Teacher: She thinks animals. He probably loved having a pet.

Student: Played with squirrels?

Teacher: Played with squirrels. Maybe he had a little pet squirrel. You'd have . . .

Student: They bite fingers.

Teacher: They do bite your fingers. So when would you get a pet squirrel? When would you have to get a pet squirrel, Jenny?

Jenny: . . . (unintelligible) gloves . . .

Teacher: Well, maybe he didn't have any gloves. When would you get a pet squirrel, John?

John: When they're old.

Teacher: When they're old. When they don't have any teeth? Well, that's a good idea. When would you get a pet squirrel? (to another pupil)

Student: When it's a baby.

Teacher: When it's a really tiny baby. OK, when you get an animal when it's a baby, what can you do?

Teacher: Yes, you can train it. Juan, what did you want to say?

Juan: Um . . . he could play with deer.

Students: (Much unintelligible crosstalk to each other.)

Teacher: It might be fun to have a little wild animal for a while. Do you think he kept them all the time?

Students: (More unintelligible crosstalk to each other, ignoring teacher.)

Teacher: We've talked about Abraham Lincoln. Now . . . I want to go over what we've talked about. . . . (Teacher goes on with next point.)

The teacher ensures that many students contribute ideas from their own experience. But the students are controlling the topic of discussion—when they stray off the topic of Abraham Lincoln, the teacher follows *them*. The teacher does not provide an initial goal or problem to be thought about or solved, and she does not make explicit the comparisons or conclusions which could be drawn. The students know what they are to discuss—something about Abraham Lincoln's toys, but not *why*. At the end, it is hard to define what the students have learned from the discussion, although much talk occurred.

To be fair, the teacher's goal here may be one that is an appropriate goal of classroom oral communication: letting every child contribute by "giving everyone a turn." However, we have seen in the earlier excerpt from the seeds lesson that participation by most of the students does not have to be sacrificed in order to achieve cognitive focus and mutual construction of knowledge.

The teacher's purpose may have been to get students to see how different Abraham Lincoln's life was from their own; but if so, neither we nor the children know, as she never states her point. She simply allows children to talk about pets and wild animals from their own experience. The teacher does not model strategies for focusing attention on a problem or questioning or making comparisons; the discussion is circular and ends up in a clutter of information. At the end of this segment, most students are talking with each other, probably about pets, and have tuned out the teacher.

In analyzing a number of videotaped classroom lessons, Roger Shuy found that teachers like this one, who structure all language interactions with students by just "letting everyone get a turn," cannot "build vertically toward larger knowledge . . . but inch forward slowly, never fully revealing the right answer" or goal (Shuy, 1980). What is lacking in the lesson is not language use, but a *goal*-directed use of language to bring into contrast different ideas and to find their relationships.

Concept of Interactional Scaffolding

What teachers can do best (and what no textbook, skill pak, or computer is designed to do) is to engage individual students in active mental processing of their current experience and knowledge in such a way that both new concepts and general strategies for thinking are introduced. Students need these concepts and strategies to understand themselves and the world around them. The examples show how teachers can engage students in thinking together with them while going through a process or problem.

Recent research into classroom interaction shows that this type of focused, guided interaction has a *direct* connection to student learning and achievement. What some researchers call a cooperative, conversational partnership about significant topics (Cahir and Lucas, 1981) and which some call "interactional scaffolding," allows the student to build on and use the teacher's *actual thinking* process (or that of a more advanced peer) to reach a goal or solve a problem which the student could not do unaided.

We usually think of the relationship between language and thought as a one-way street:

Have a thought or idea ⟶ Express the idea in language

But an interactive perspective enlarges the field of vision to include the social and mental activities which lead to a particular linguistic utterance.

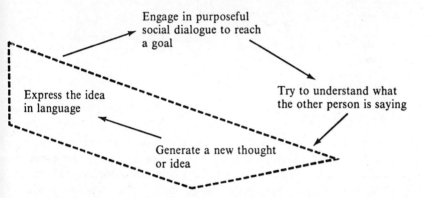

Of course, if we only look at the events within the dotted line, as the first diagram does, we will not see the earlier interaction between thought and language.

In a dialogue about a shared goal or problem, not only is there a struggle for comprehension of the other speaker's or writer's statement, but the process repeats itself, in a special pattern, with each person's statement building on the others. Visualized as a conversational "ladder" with both persons contributing different rungs, this process could look like Figure 1.

For some students, the teacher may need to do relatively little scaffolding; for others, at first, the teacher may need to take some of the student's turns. Scaffolding works when the student has an interest in a problem or is motivated to become engaged in the process. Often, the goal may be clarified only as the process is worked out. As mentioned, this kind of conversational partnership is familiar among friends, who reach for a *mutual* understanding of a problem or experience. Each person has the freedom and responsibility to contribute to the discussion whatever he or she knows without being "put down" or negatively evaluated if a response is off track.

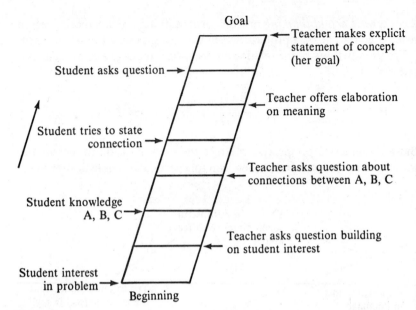

Figure 1.

Eventually, the student, by *internalizing* the teacher's language strategies, should be able to take over much of the process of thinking. The teacher's questions become internalized as self-guiding questions: "What comes next?" and "What's the connection between what I did and what happened?"

The students' statements are not sufficient to accomplish the task initially. The teacher appropriates them into his or her own knowledge structure (or "schema") at the right time (as we saw in the seeds lesson) to reach the goal. With repeated interactions, students incorporate the teacher's strategies into their own thinking and begin to carry out the task independently.

A helpful example of this is found in a transcript of a teacher helping a kindergarten student learn how to narrate a story that she has just heard. When reading the transcript, look at how the student's "turns" lengthen and how the teacher uses questions to support and extend the student's thinking by filling in the necessary information so that Karen can complete the task (McNamee, 1979). At the end (line 72), Karen has even internalized question-asking and directs the teacher to help her when she needs it!

The Five Chinese Brothers Story

Karen (five years old) retells the story of The Five Chinese Brothers to her kindergarten teacher. (Karen has just heard the story five minutes ago with the rest of the class.)

1. *Teacher:* Tell me the story of The Five Chinese Brothers.

2. *Karen:* I don't know this.

3. *T:* What could the first Chinese brother do?

4. *K:* I forgot.

5. *T:* Remember he went fishing?
6.   How did he find all the fish?

7. *K:* He drink the water.

8. *T:* Right.
9.   Now what could the second one do?
10. *K:* I forgot.

11. *T:* Oh remember they tried to cut his head off?

12. *K:* That's the one with the iron neck.

13. *T:* And the next brother . . .

14. *K:* could stretch and stretch.

15. *T:* Karen, you do remember!
16.   You thought you didn't but you do.

17. *K:* (her face lights up) I thought I didn't but I do.

18. *T:* Now how 'bout the fourth.

19. *K:* (silence)

20. *T:* Remember they tried to burn him?

21. *K:* Oh that's the one who couldn't be burned.

22. *T:* Now the last one, the fifth one.

23. *K:* The mother.

24. *T:* Remember the brother they put in the oven so he couldn't breathe?

25. *K:* Then he could hold his breath?

26. *T:* Right.
27.   Forever.
28.   What happened with the first Chinese brother went fishing?
29.   What happened?

30. *K:* He drank the water.

31. *T:* Then what?

32. *K:* The boy came?

33. *T:* See you do remember!

34. *K:* He said "can I go fishing?"

35.   He kept begging.

36.   "OK, I'm going to make a sign for you to come back."

37.   Then he drank the water.

38.   He made a sign for his hands to come back.

39.   And the boy only made faces.

40. *T:* What a nasty boy.

41. *K:* He thought he was going to burp

42.   and all the water came out

43.   and the boy disappeared.

44. *T:* So then what happened?

45. *K:* He had to go to the judge.

46. *T:* Yeah

47. *K:* "Can you only to say my mother goodby?"

48.   "It's only fair."

49.   And the second Chinese brother came back to his place.

50.   That was the one, that was the one that had the iron neck.

51. *T:* So what happened with the one with the iron neck?

52. *K:* They tried to cut his head off.

53. *T:* Were they able to do it? (laughing)

54. *K:* (laughing) No.

55.   Or he could go to the judge.

56.   And the judge said . . . oh no, I *know* this.

57.   The Chinese brother said "Do you only to bid my mother goodby?"

58.   and he said its only fair.

59.   So the four Chinese brother came back to his place.

60.   That was the one who could stretch and stretch and stretch.

61.   (Karen's face is lit up, eyes shining) They tried to throw him in the water

62.   but he was ordered to go to the judge

63.   and the judge said . . . I mean the Chinese brother said "Do you own me to bid my mother goodby?

64. "It is only fair."

65. And the fifth Chinese brother came back to his place.

66. That's the one that . . . that was the one that . . . I'm talking about the fifth.

67. That was the one can be burned.

68. They tried to burn him

69. but he was ordered to go to the judge.

70. The Chinese brother said "Do you owe me to bid my mother goodby?"

71. She said "it's only fair."

72. What comes after the fifth?

73. *T:* Now let's see, they couldn't cut his head off, they couldn't drown him, they couldn't burn him,

74. so finally what did they try to do?

75. *K:* They stuck him in the fire?

76. He couldn't be fired?

77. So he was ordered to go to the judge.

78. And the Chinese brother said, "Do you owe me to bid my mother goodby?"

79. She said "it's only fair"

80. and that's all.

81. Does something else?

82. *T:* So they couldn't drown or burn or cut off his head.

83. Remember the oven?

84. *K:* Oh yeah.

85. They put him in the oven.

86. It was filled with fire.

87. So they tried to get rid of him.

88. That's all.

89. *T:* Did they get rid of him?

90. *K:* Oh no, I know they couldn't! (she laughs, obviously pleased with herself)

The theory of interactional scaffolding is based on the original work of Vygotsky (1978), as developed by others (Cazden, 1979; McNamee, 1979; Wood, Bruner, and Ross, 1975). The theory assumes that only through a social dialogue can young students learn how to think about experience.

The interactional scaffolding can include all of the levels of knowledge organization suggested by Benjamin Bloom in his taxonomy of knowledge: recalling, understanding, relating, analyzing, synthesizing, evaluating (1956). Interactional scaffolding, however, describes how children participate in and understand all of these levels *before* they are able to use them independently. Since Bloom looked only at students' independent, noninteractive thinking abilities, his taxonomy is often taken to mean that primary schoolchildren can operate only at the lowest levels. In fact, many students will make an *evaluative* comment at the end of the dialogue, showing that they did follow and understand what the teacher was saying and can follow the reasoning all the way to the goal. By giving students many opportunities to participate with them in a dialogue, teachers are giving them the opportunity to internalize all of the levels of cognitive representation that Bloom suggested.

Conditions for Dialogue

By examining what is common to the examples in the second section of this chapter, we find a set of conditions teachers can establish to ensure that students are engaged in active mental processing, or "thinking," in language interactions or written dialogues. Although the examples just cited seem very ordinary in their language, they are not accidental or unsystematic. The teachers involved have established conditions which appear to include:

> *a common goal* which both or all participants want to accomplish, and which is understood by each;

> *modeling* by the teacher of strategies for reaching that goal, within the language interaction, as it proceeds;

> freedom for participants to try out *alternative answers* or *strategies* at each step in reaching that goal, without any external penalties for being "wrong"; and

> conscious, verbalized *feedback* on the effectiveness of the mutually constructed progress toward the goal by pointing out the causal relationships between different actions or combinations of actions and the outcome. This verbal feedback occurs only after enough successes and failures have occurred for the information to be meaningful to the learner.

The first example, the seeds lesson, shows how the teacher established those conditions in terms of her language strategies. The following chart shows a simplified version of the teacher's language in the left column and describes and labels in the right-hand column the strategies used.

Examples	Teacher Strategies
"*What does* a plant need in order to grow?"	Establishes *goal* and focuses attention on relevant aspects or attributes of the event or experience.
"It has to have *water.* They have to get *sunlight.*"	Identifies and compares aspects by explicitly naming and categorizing.
"And *after* the seed begins to get some sunlight and rain, something happens?"	Incorporates child's prior experience and world knowledge into discussion.
(Response)	
"Yes, it comes up, and Rachel says there's a little plant inside of that seed so the *plant does something?*"	
"A plant must have—water, sunshine, for seed to come up and a stem will come out of the plant and leaves."	Makes explicit the relationship inherent in the experience which constitutes its meaning (knowledge basis for predicting similar experiences in the future).
"Those are some good answers. But what is this part? Well, before it gets to the flower?"	Gives explicit *feedback* on effectiveness of mutually constructed activity.
"Now I want you to be some little plants for me." (Has children physically enact sequence.)	Connects knowledge to students' own experience, activity.

This example pinpoints how the teacher embedded in her conversation with the students a clear set of strategies for thinking in such a way that they could actively participate with her in constructing the answers, without first knowing everything about plants and seeds. Each child had ample opportunity to try out possible answers without being penalized, while the teacher fitted them into place in the best sequence.

Another instance of teacher-student dialogue can be found in dialogue journals, in which it is shown how the same strategies are used in helping a student understand that he can learn and is not a "dummy." The student is a sixth-grader who speaks Spanish at home and has limited proficiency in English.

Student-Teacher Dialogue	Teacher Strategies
Day 10: *Eduardo:*	
Mes. Reed, I cant do it I ges can't do it. I em a dime. my cetres [sisters] tel me the dime and all my famele tel me the dime my mom tel me I have a good mind Mes R I want to lorn efi dont I no I can lurin sumer [learn some more] on reed and on spell mor	
Mrs. R.:	
Good! If you want to learn you will. I will be happy to help you—but I cannot learn for you. 7×8=56, what is 8×7 6×9=54, what is 9×6	Frames common goal and process: "I will help, but I cannot learn for you." Focuses attention on relevant aspects of event: learning, will to learn, and doing (times tables).
Day 11: *Eduardo:*	
Mes R I now more fracens and mor timstebol and to reed mor and rid [write] mor I like thes day	
Mrs. R.:	
You must read more and write more every day. I will make you some math cards to study at home.	Gives explicit feedback on what actions are needed to achieve goal.
Day 12: *Eduardo:*	
I don't want to lurn. I	

genh [change] my mind
I het school I want to
be a dime.

Mrs. R.:
You can be what you
want to be. If you can
read and write and do
math you'll be better at
whatever you decide to
be.

Makes explicit causal relationship inherent in the experience.

Day 13: *Eduardo:*
Mes R I now Im a
dume and I want to be
a dume I dont want to
lurn nothen Good by

Mrs. R.:
I care! You have a mil-
lion dollar brain! Some-
day when you are driv-
ing a big fancy car you'll
be glad you worked.
You are not dumb!

Connects goal and activity to
student's own experiences, frame
of reference.

Day 14: *Eduardo:*
Then you [thank you]
Mrs. R it you cares and
my mom dus cares to
and one of my sestrs
cares too.

This example shows that even very brief statements by a student reflect
his or her thoughts. Usually, teachers respond to student writing by
focusing on errors in language forms. In dialogue writing, this teacher is
responding to the student's thinking and focusing him on understanding
the problem. By allowing the student to express his thoughts without fear
of being corrected for errors, and by "listening," the teacher is able to
participate with the student in a mutual effort.

The written dialogue with Eduardo about his desire to do better in school
continued all year. By spring, the teacher's efforts had paid off: Eduardo
did change his way of perceiving himself and came to believe that if he tried
hard, he could do sixth-grade work. Here is a sample from Eduardo's
journal:

Spring 1979

Day 80: *Eduardo:*

> Mes. R. I had a good dy I can do berer an everythin and I can.
> Mes. R. I hope I can gate my gurnol and I well rite more and
> raed more . . . and I had a good reces and a good lunch I play
> far and I had a good day and I I got ever bory out in sococ
> and a sococ ges ones they got me out and we wan all the
> games and we play And I had a good day in math I got 100
> and Mer M.he was happ and I had a fantatic day Mes. R. I we
> be good and I love all the world Good by

> *Mrs. R.:*
> Wow! I could not believe you wrote so much in one! That is
> good. That is super good. If you play fair the other children
> will like you better. You raised your hand and answered
> questions very well today. When you listen and think you are
> very smart.

This typical entry from his journal in the spring shows that Eduardo has
incorporated into his own thinking much of how the teacher thinks: "I can
do berer [better] an everythin," "I will rite more and raed more." His entry
reflects a much more positive self-concept, greater fluency, and a better
command of written English conventions

What about Questions?

Most teachers have been taught that the way to stimulate cognition in
students is to ask them lots of "higher-order questions" or wh-questions,
which are supposed to get the students thinking about *why* things happen,
in *what* order, and *how*. These are questions that focus on relationships,
causality, and meaning. While this practice has helped teachers move away
from questions that demand little thought, the focus on the frequency and
type of *teacher* questions is misleading. It suggests that teacher questions
alone, without the surrounding context of a thoughtful discussion which
interests students, can bring about genuine thinking. Perhaps this comes
from a memory of the idealized Socratic dialogue, but if so, such a focus
distorts that kind of discussion, which actually began with his *disciples*
asking Socrates questions, not the other way around.

J.T. Dillon has recently argued rather strongly against the typical
interrogative question-response-evaluation pattern found in many classrooms, in which the students wait for the teacher to ask questions, and do
not participate actively. Dillon suggests that teachers first of all use
questions only when genuinely perplexed, and secondly, use alternatives to

questions in their discussions (Dillon, 1981). Among the alternatives he suggests are making open declarations of your own state of mind, declaring one's perplexity about the student's meaning and giving the student a chance to rephrase, inviting the student to elaborate more, and allowing/inviting other students to raise questions about what someone has just said.

Both research and good common sense suggest the following about questions in the context of a genuine interaction:

> Move away from interrogation of students, with teacher as authority or critic, toward a shared role in disciplined inquiry into why things happen, etc.
>
> Ask questions when they are genuine—when you really do not know what students are thinking or why, just as you would with a friend.
>
> In thinking together, your real aim is to *encourage the students' questions,* of the teacher or of each other, which come out of genuine perplexity. By talking out loud about what puzzles you, you can help students formulate questions about *why* things happen.

In a genuine dialogue, which involves a mutual effort to understand an idea, an object, or an experience, everyone can ask questions about what they do not understand. The frequency and type of questions your *students* ask is the most obvious sign of whether your classroom discussions (or dialogue journals) involve real thinking on the part of the students.

Do Dialogue and Social Interaction Really Help Students Think Differently?

The problem with this kind of thinking together is that it does not automatically produce a product that can be assessed or graded. As teachers experience greater pressures to be accountable for children's learning on an almost daily basis, it may even become harder to justify time spent on activities—such as "just talking" with students or carrying on a written dialogue—which are never graded. Genuine thinking may be very exciting for both students and teacher but much harder to measure than whether students can fill in the right blanks to show that they have memorized some facts. Teachers are right to ask if there is theoretical and empirical research support for the value of such interactive dialogue.

Cognitive Development Is Interactively Facilitated

Most teachers are familiar with Piaget's theory and research into the way children's minds develop through cognitive "stages." Although Piaget emphasized that his theory was an *interactive* one, in which the child's mind developed through direct interaction with the world of objects and people, the mechanisms of interactive development were not well understood until very recently. Now research has begun to study the *process* of cognitive development and the mechanisms by which new operations are formed. What has been found is that language interaction appears to play a major role in facilitating transitions from one stage to the next. A typical experiment goes like this:

> A child who is not at the stage of understanding the "conservation" of liquids when the visible shape or appearance of the container is changed, is asked to work with two other children who *do* understand conservation. The nonconserving child is the "operator" who must divide up juice equally so the two other children "have the same" amount even when their containers are of different widths or heights. The two "conserving" (more cognitively advanced) children are to judge if the division is fair, and can argue or explain how to do it, and why to the child who is pouring—in effect, to teach through dialogue. (Perret-Clermont, 1980)

In many experiments using this task, the findings are that:

> after one or two experiences, a significant number of nonconserving children had acquired the concept of the conservation of liquids;

> this change was *not* a matter of verbally "imitating" what the other children said—in posttests, the students came up with *different* (but equally valid) arguments to explain why the amounts were the same, than the arguments that they had actually heard in the teaching situation; and

> these changes are durable over time and reflect genuine reorganization of thought.

The "mechanism" for effecting this change is the verbal conflict which occurs in viewpoints as the children discuss which glass has more. During the teaching situation, children who are nearly ready to move into this new stage of concrete operational thinking (usually five to seven years of age in our culture) are confronted with contradictions between their way of describing and explaining events and the way the conserving children explain it, as they talk together. These contradictions set up the imbalance or disequilibrium in their thinking, and demand that they adopt a more flexible view: "There's the same in both glasses because this one's wider but this one's taller."

Other researchers have shown that such changes cannot be produced by having children memorize and practice saying the "correct answers." When children are simply taught by an adult to say lines perfectly in an experimental situation, they cannot solve a new problem (Sinclair, 1969). But children involved in the situation in which *genuine* arguments occur about which glass has more are led to integrate two different ways of thinking into one concrete operational principle.

What these studies indicate for classroom practice is that having students involved in tasks in which they must use language to solve a problem allows them to begin working at a level of cognitive operations one step up from where they can work unassisted. Gradually, the processes first experienced and understood in interactive situations are internalized and made an integral part of each student's own thinking. This internalization occurs not at the factual level of learning—memorizing the right answers to teacher questions—but at the conscious level of learning how a more experienced member of the culture "thinks" through a process in order to *ask* questions. The process of internalization involves transforming overt language utterances into covert or "inner speech." In a way, human learning is a matter of learning how to ask a series of questions of oneself deliberately to focus attention, to search out the connection between events— which is called *meaning*—to "take on" the adult's or teacher's turns as well as one's own in directing the search for meaning.

Social Interaction Affects Reading Performance

In a study of reading in the Kamehameha Early Education Project (KEEP) in Hawaii, the language interaction styles of two teachers were contrasted in teaching the same group of children a reading lesson (Au and Mason, 1981). One teacher used a culturally familiar language experience, the Hawaiian "talk-story," as a way to help students understand the reading lesson. In the talk-story, everyone can join in to build a story narration without waiting to be called on individually. The teacher does not control each individual child's opportunity to have a turn. The second teacher followed a traditional style of calling on each child individually to give the right answer; children had to wait and raise hands before speaking.

The talk-story group produced a much higher level of academic engagement in reading. Also, the students who participated in the culturally familiar interactive participation gave more on-topic responses related to the story that they were reading and discussing, and made more logical inferences (Au and Mason, 1981). The real difference between the two styles was that in the talk-story class, teacher and students were all equal participants in the discussion. Students were not thinking about whether what they said would be "right" or "wrong" from the teacher's perspective. Instead, each child had many opportunities to initiate sensible ideas, and a second child could build on the first child's statement as soon as the second child understood what might be a good next response. Children did not have to wait for the teacher to tell them if they were right; they could just go on *thinking* about what they knew and join in freely. This conversational style of dialogue focuses the children on what they know, and on making connections. One result of the greater amount of really concentrated thinking in the talk-story classroom was that those students had *more* time for discussion of reading and for sustained silent reading than did the students taught in the traditional elicitation manner, which tended to take up most of the available time.

Interaction Impacts Reading Achievement

The results of a large-scale study by Jane Stallings of classroom interactions in a large number of high school remedial reading classes lend impressive support to the argument that direct student-teacher language interaction is a primary—and powerful—force for learning (Stallings, 1980).

The classrooms were observed and the various activities recorded by trained observers. For analysis, observed activities were divided into "on-task" and "off-task." On-task activities were further divided into interactive and noninteractive categories. The *interactive* on-task activities included discussion/review, reading aloud, drill and practice, and praise and support in reading tasks, and supportive, corrective feedback. The *noninteractive* on-task activities included classroom management, silent reading, sustained silent reading, and written assignments. Off-task activities included organizing, social time, and disciplinary activities. The researchers initially expected that most of the on-task activities would be positively associated (statistically correlated) with reading gains. But surprisingly, none of the *noninteractive* on-task activities, such as silent reading or filling out workbook assignments, were positively associated with student reading gains. In fact, significant *negative* associations were found. This means that the more time students spent in noninteractive activities, the *lower* their reading scores.

All the activities positively associated with reading gains involved language interactions—discussion, teacher feedback, oral drill and practice. What made the difference for these remedial readers at the secondary level was engagement in focused interaction using language. The study also found that students at the lowest reading levels (first to fourth grade) gained most from the interactional instruction activities. Off-task activities directed at just managing the classroom had the same kind of negative association with reading gains as did noninteractive instruction.

Interaction Encourages Independent Thinking

Most teachers will want evidence that having students do more cooperative social interaction tasks will lead to truly *independent* thinking. It is one thing to be able to solve a problem cooperatively with someone else helping; it is another to do it alone.

Evidence for growing independence stemming from the cooperative situation can be found in the study of student discussions of problems in the dialogue journals described earlier. Because the discussions cover several months of the school year, there is an opportunity to observe the gradual process by which the student incorporates some of the teacher's thinking about an event or problem, and then uses those concepts and ways of constructing the world independently or voluntarily.

These examples are from the journal of a sixth-grader who wants to do better in math but does not know how to accomplish the goal (Staton, 1982b).

Day 22

Gordon: Math was great today. I think I should move up in about a month.

Teacher: You really listened well in math today! If you work hard and learn to listen, there is no reason you can't move up.

Day 33

Gordon: I feel I'm getting better in math. I feel that I can move up in the next test.

Teacher: You've been listening better in class. Now if you are thinking, too, you'll really do well.

Day 49

Gordon: Math is really coming along for me. I really do like it.

Teacher: Super! I like math, too! You are fun, before you even start the assignment you say, "I don't get it." Then I say, "Read it to me, Gordon." You do read it, then what happens! It is fun for me to see you really thinking it out.

The excerpts show the student making the same assertions that he is doing better without any awareness of what kind of effort he will have to make. The teacher keeps reminding him that he must keep *trying, listening,* and *thinking* if he is going to do better and move up. She describes his actions for him, filling in the apparent gaps in his knowledge of the relationship between his actions and the consequences.

Later in the year, Gordon has incorporated the teacher's ideas that *trying hard* and *listening* are essential for doing well. He begins to use these ideas independently in evaluating his own actions, described in the following excerpts. The teacher introduces yet another new idea: understanding is the key to math being "easy."

Day 87

Gordon: It is fun doing something new in math. And it is also fun, especially when I try my hardest.

Math was pretty easy today. Desmils really isn't hard. But I kind of (had) a bit of trouble doing my work. But I'll keep on *trying to do good* [emphasis added] on it. Okay.

Teacher: Good! Decimals are easy—if you understand them.

When Gordon falls back into his earlier pattern of hating every new concept because he does not understand it, the teacher is ready with a reminder:

Day 99

Gordon: I did terrible on the math homework from last night. Math was totally terrible. I hate math. I really do hate it!!!!!!!!

Teacher: Come on! Give yourself a chance. You "hate" every new math idea and in a couple of days you're saying "I like this—it's easy." You'll catch on—let me help.

Day 100

Gordon: That is not true. I did not say that about fractions. Did I?

Math was pretty good today. Even though we had more division which I really do hate. But it was a little bit better today. I am kind of getting used to it. But I still hate division. Hate it.

Eventually, Gordon begins to internalize not only the teacher's ideas, but also her processes of reflection, of comparison, which are first available to him on an interactional, interpsychological level through the dialogue. At year's end, he has begun to evaluate his own performance in terms of this new concept of *understanding* it, and he now looks forward to new concepts.

Day 118

Gordon: Three of the problems on that test were kind of hard. But I think that *other than these three I did pretty good* [emphasis added]. Are we going to go on to *something different* [emphasis added] on Friday. I hope so, this is really getting kind of fun.

Gordon: I like the math work that we did today. I finished both of the math papers. I finished the last one with just five minutes to go before math time was over.

Summary

Research results concerning the importance of interactive language use emphasize the necessity of language interaction focused on learning events or tasks for developing students' thinking processes. Beyond age seven, the major kind of thinking that develops is reflective thinking about relationships in increasing independence of contextual cues. Teachers need not laboriously teach students how to think this way—they do so naturally and endlessly. But students do need opportunities to use this kind of thinking on a variety of problems and tasks in many different contexts, or their potential ability to think effectively will not develop into competent performance.

Piaget greatly emphasized the need for language interaction as the child grows older. Only language, he said, can integrate many different ideas or "operations" into new structures of thought (Piaget, 1967). Piaget saw logical reasoning as "arguments we have with ourselves, and which reproduce internally the features of a real argument" in which two persons are expressing opposing viewpoints. In a genuine dialogue, the outcome of an argument is a synthesis of these two viewpoints into a higher-order way of construing the world. Involving students in such dialogic thinking allows them to observe, practice, and incorporate another perspective into their own thinking.

What makes oral or written dialogues about topics of mutual interest such excellent learning experiences is that the learner is continually required to make sense out of a different viewpoint to continue the conversation. Gillian McNamee, a classroom researcher, has described how the adult "continually makes demands of the child that are just beyond the child's grasp, and the child then struggles to find coherence in what the adult is saying. . . . The child is continually having to work to make sense out of the adult's questions" (1979).

What Can I Do?

What can you as a teacher do about engaging students in more thinking together? Many teachers may find it difficult to increase the amount of genuine, engaged dialogue in class because they are so used to looking only at observable student behaviors. The first step, then, is to acknowledge that difficulty and struggle with those natural feelings of guilt and uncertainty. By really increasing the amount of focused, purposeful thinking that you and students do together, the lower-order skills and facts that you already teach will be that much more easily acquired.

The kinds of language interactions described in this chapter are not isolated games to be played once a week, or a unit on "critical thinking." Instead, you need to focus on the everyday processes of a classroom inter- action, and ask yourself: How much genuine thinking do *I* do, aloud or in writing, with my students? Do my questions seek information *I* do not know, and express my perplexity?

This section suggests a few ways to increase valuable, structured thinking in the classroom and lists additional resources that you may be able to use. First, it is important to assess your classroom practices and see how much interaction may already be happening. Second, some ideas and resources for restructuring class discussions and student interaction are presented. Third, types and examples for developing written dialogue interactions are described.

Assessing Your Classroom

Evaluate your daily class activities. You need to see how much interaction occurs and where the possibilities are for restructuring. Note how much

	Academic Areas or Classes	
	Reading	Social Studies
Activities (total time)	50 min.	50 min.
1. Whole-class presentation (one-way teacher monologue)	20 min.	5 min.
2. Whole-class discussion/ review	10 min	5 min.
3. Small-group or panel discussions of activities with teacher participation	0	0
4. Small-group or paired discussions without direct teacher participation	0	20 min.
5. Individual student-teacher conferences	0	10 min. 6 students involved (overlaps with activity 6)
6. Individual student seat work or other independent activity	20 min.	20 min. (overlaps with activity 5)
7. (add your own)		
8. (add your own)		
9. (add your own)		

time is actually spent thinking together and in what contexts. You may feel comfortable with just observing yourself for one or two days. Or, you may ask a friend—peer or resource teacher or someone from an inservice training program in your district or university—to observe your class several times (or to stay for an entire typical day if you are in a self-contained classroom). The observer records the amount of time spent in each type of activity, using a simple checklist, such as the sample pictured. (You can modify this to make it fit your situation.) The checklist tells you how much *opportunity* for dialogue is available. The chart has been filled out to indicate how different academic areas might show very different patterns.

With this kind of record, you can decide where you need to increase focused conversations in which you and students participate mutually in finding out and asking why. Effective classroom dialogue discussions have to occur at the right moment when there is a genuine problem or event to talk about in which everyone has opinions, ideas, and information.

Step two would be to review some of your classroom discussions to see if you are already using the scaffolding principle and establishing conditions for dialogue. Tape record one or two class discussions and then listen to the recording at home; it would even be worthwhile to transcribe ten to fifteen minutes so that you can study whether students are becoming actively engaged in the discussion. Remember, there is no one right sequence in these dialogues. Here is a brief list of questions to ask about your discussions.

Is the problem or goal explicitly stated?

Do I focus students' attention on relevant aspects of the process that we are engaged in by describing and identifying them—am I thinking aloud as I talk?

Do I use "who, what, when, where, and how" questions, and reflective questions to guide students' thinking?

Do I elaborate and expand what students say, and suggest alternative viewpoints or strategies?

Do I encourage students to take on more of my turns in constructing the discussion, letting them elaborate on an answer, and, *especially,* giving students opportunity and responsibility for asking questions?

Do I provide an explicit statement of what we have discussed, making clear the principle, meaning, or logical relationship as part of the evaluation of the dialogue?

Example: "This morning we have found out that writing is a way of learning how we think; I especially liked what Gordon said about understanding his own feelings better *after* he'd written them down."

Not: "You all contributed very nicely to our discussion."

As a result of the self-assessment suggested above, you may already have decided on some changes in your dialogues with students during whole-group or small-group discussions. These last two sections describe two additional options for increasing the amount of interaction, small-task groups, and dialogue writing.

Small-Task Groups for Cooperative Learning

Small-task groups are optimal for creating more opportunities for students to interact effectively. Teachers are already familiar with the value of peer groups for developing social skills; the following examples stress ways of grouping students and structuring tasks so that cognitive development through dialogue is enhanced.

Each group should have students at differing levels of cognitive development who are asked to work cooperatively to solve a common problem, such as getting enough information to figure out how to make something work. Research has shown that in heterogeneous peer groups, the more cognitively advanced students *continue* to progress in their thinking as a result of working with *less* advanced peers (Perret-Clermont, 1980; Slavin, 1980). The reason seems to be that both less and more cognitively advanced students benefit from the presence of cognitive conflict, and both progress as a result of the need to elaborate their ideas, offer reasons for why things happen, or explain how they would solve a problem. Thus, teachers need not be concerned that heterogeneous small groups will hold back more advanced students, *as long as* there is a task requiring social cooperation and coordination and integration of different perspectives to achieve the goal.

By asking students to work cooperatively, and by setting up a task which can only be accomplished if everyone contributes, interactive mental processing is required to integrate different ideas. Also, interactional scaffolding by the teacher may be much easier to accomplish with smaller groups.

Paired Learning Tasks

Primary-age students are learning about weights (or any other scientific concept). A simple game can be devised in which children must work together in pairs with a balance scale to solve the problem of finding the right combination of weights from among blocks of different weights of the same size. Each child has the same set of six blocks of different weights (Cooper, Ayers-Lopez, and Marquis, 1982).

The children are to work together, with each child responsible for one side of the balance. The task is self-evaluating: students will know when they are right. This game allows students to discuss what will work and to find the right combination. Any similar task in which two partners must contribute equally to the outcome and must discuss possible solutions will do as well.

If material or equipment is limited for this kind of group task, a learning center can be set up, and children can work there in pairs while other activities are going on. A very important extension of this task is to ask a member of a pair who knows how to play it to teach another child who does not know.

Jigsaw

Jigsaw is a cooperative learning process for students from kindergarten through graduate school (Aronson, 1978). Students are assigned to small heterogeneous teams, and the task to be learned and materials are divided into as many sections as there are members on each team. For example, a biography might be broken into "early years," "schooling," "first accomplishments," and so on. A study of plants might be divided into "food sources," "chemical manufacturing," etc. A study of a country might be segmented into geography, culture, industry, transportation, and government.

First, members of the different teams who have the same section form "expert" groups and study together. Each then returns to his or her team and teaches the section to the others. Jigsaw requires that students depend on and learn from each other.

Additional Resources: Student Grouping

Aronson, Elliott. *The Jigsaw Classroom.* Beverly Hills, Calif.: Sage Publications, 1978.

Peer Review/Editing Groups

Small-task groups are especially helpful in writing. The group's task is to discuss aspects of the writing assignment before writing and then to critique in a helpful way first (and second and third) drafts. These peer review groups are a way to have students take on the responsibility for determining the purpose of the writing task, and then apply this purpose as the goal of a particular assignment. For example, if a class is learning to write persuasive letters to spur someone to take action, the groups can discuss before writing what evidence is needed, how specific to be, or how to organize an argument. After a draft has been written by each member, the group's task is to read and make helpful suggestions as an audience before a second draft is written.

Additional Resources: Peer Review and Editing

Hawkins, Thom. *Group Inquiry Techniques for Teaching Writing.* Urbana, Ill.: ERIC Clearinghouse on Reading and Communication Skills and the National Council of Teachers of English, 1976.

Holbrook, Hilary Taylor. "Johnny Could Write When He Was a Kid." *Language Arts* 58 (October 1981): 864–66.

Moffett, James. *A Student-Centered Language Arts Curriculum.* Boston: Houghton-Mifflin, 1973.

Dialogue Journals and Dialogue Writing

For many years, writing has been idealized as a way of developing thinking. And when we read a clear, coherent piece of writing, we say it is evidence of a "good mind." Recently, teachers have begun to find better ways to make writing for students a real "tool of thought," an active process for creating and transforming and practicing reflective, conscious thought. Keeping a dialogue journal is one way to engage students in actively thinking about their learning and personal experience. Other kinds of dialogue writing can occur in letter correspondence or focused journal writing in content areas such as math, history, or composition.

Dialogue journals are private, written conversations between students and the teacher on a daily, semiweekly, or sometimes weekly basis (Staton, 1980; Staton, Shuy, and Kreeft, 1982). (Journal writing works best if it is done often with brief entries.) As discussed earlier, a number of examples demonstrate that students are free to write about whatever concerns or topics that *they* feel are most important. The writing is *functional*; that is, students and teachers write directly to each other, using language to get things done in an active way. Students ask questions, complain about lessons, describe what happened on the playground or at home, reflect on why things happen, express personal feelings, and even argue with the teacher about the fairness of assignments—in other words, they think in written language.

The teacher writes a direct, personal response to the *content* of the student's writing, rather than commenting on its form or style, and also brings up new topics of interest. In responding, the teacher may describe what happened in a disputed event from another perspective, explain in more detail the reasoning behind an assignment or decision, and ask reflective questions that require the student to engage in some rethinking. The teacher's responses are natural elaborations and extensions of the students' thinking about issues and experiences.

The journals also give students an opportunity for reflective, deliberate rereading of what they wrote earlier. Because of the informal conversational style with a question-answer format, a student must often reread his or her own entry to understand the teacher's response. Students who have kept a dialogue journal not only like the opportunity to share their thinking with the teacher, but quickly understand that this is writing *to* think. One student explained the difference between dialogue journals and other writing:

> Well, reports is, you have to look up facts and everything. But in journals you can just look it up in your mind, and write what you think (Nicky, Spring Interview, 1981, in Mrs. Reed's classroom).

Another student said that she liked writing in the dialogue journal much better than completing worksheets on a content area.

> The worksheets make you answer questions, but the dialogue journal makes *me* ask the questions, and then the teacher helps me think about possible answers.

Teachers are using dialogue journals at all age levels—often their use has grown out of asking students to keep a personal journal in which the teacher at first made brief comments. When the student responds in turn to the teacher's comment, a dialogue is begun. However, dialogue writing in whatever form is quite different from ordinary teacher-student discussions, in which the teacher is *evaluating* how well the student wrote but is not interested in or contributing to the topic itself.

Leslee Reed, the Los Angeles teacher whose use of dialogue journals has been most intensively studied, says that she began using dialogue journals as a way to *learn* more about what her students were thinking. After using them daily for seventeen years, she still says:

> Oh, I'm learning, I'm learning, I'm learning! Especially with this class I have now, with so many cultures, there's such richness. I don't think I've ever grown so much in my life as I have this year in understanding the problems of different cultures, trying to fit into this pattern of American life. Plus, as a teacher who has taught for a great many years, I'm sometimes so sure when I'm teaching a lesson what the effect will be, that it does me good to see in the journals something that I totally missed. I have used a cliché or an idiom that literally blocked out everything I taught up to that point. It's like a challenge.
>
> I find that journal writing is sort of the kernel of my teaching. When I sit down to do journals, I am doing a kind of résumé of my day, and of each child. As I'm writing each child I'm mentally thinking about that child. As I'm reading each journal I'm seeing if what I sensed as a teacher came through to that student. And often it comes through then in my lesson plans, that this did not go over well. I'll need to get this over from a different point of view. So it becomes a planning tool, a core from which I'm planning not only tomorrow's work but next week's work, too. For me, it makes my whole school year flow, because

I have a constant finger on the pulse of the children. I know quite accurately what every child is doing and not doing.

Like everyone else, I get exhausted from teaching, but when I sit down to do my journals I get exhilarated. Sometimes their advice to me is hilarious, you know, telling me what I should do. This feedback is so good for me and I really do look forward to it. I can be just dog tired and sort of go "well, I've got to get to my journals," but the first thing you know, I'm so involved in my journals that I'm no longer weary. (Reed, 1982)

Strategies for Getting Started

Dialogue journals allow students to write anything about whatever topics that they wish without worrying about what others think of what they write, or *how* they write it. Only the content of their thinking matters, not the forms, spelling, or paragraphing, for example. When you start these journals, say simply that they are a way to *communicate,* to talk with you. Following are key aspects in implementing effective dialogue journal communication.

First, there are the *logistics* of keeping a dialogue journal. Here is the way most teachers have found that it works best.

Small, bound journals (not spiral notebooks) with covers that can be individually decorated are most appropriate. Students are impressed when they fill up a whole book and get a new one.

In elementary school classes, journal writing should be allowed to occur at free times or transition times all during the day, rather than at one assigned time. Elementary school students need to be able to write as soon as questions, ideas, or problems pop into their heads; they usually forget what they really felt and wanted to say if they have to wait until a set time.

It is important to establish a regular place and time for journals to be turned in, and handed back: they should not be "collected" like other papers. A corner of a room or a "journal bag" can be used.

Teachers should write back immediately; short, brief exchanges seem to work better, and are easier. Most teachers take the journals home each night and spend about an hour responding, which also doubles as relaxation and "thinking about tomorrow" time.

The journals should be given back to students first thing in the morning, and they need enough time to read your response and write in return.

For younger students, it may be helpful to set a minimum length for any entry—such as three sentences—so that no one can complain about having to write "too much" when there just isn't anything to say. This keeps the dialogue going over dry spells.

At secondary levels, teachers will probably need to modify the approach, and some in-class time will be needed for journal writing. High school teachers have found that once or twice a week turnaround is practical and still allows for sustained, thoughtful conversations to develop. It is also "OK" to suggest a maximum length for older students' entries, and to stress that they are writing directly *to* you, not just filling pages with thoughts.

Just as important as the logistics are your responses. They will help students to "dig deeper" into themselves and to express more of their ideas, opinions, feelings, and values. Some tips for responding:

> Respond to their topics first, acknowledging the importance of what they are writing about and commenting on their topics before you introduce a new or related topic of your own.
>
> Ask genuine questions, ones *you* do not have the answers to either, but would like *their* ideas and personal opinions on. Be careful not to ask two or three questions consecutively—that is teacher talk!
>
> Make your response interesting by talking about how *you* feel, what your opinions and concerns are. As you develop greater rapport with individual students, you can share your personal experiences and fears just as you would with a close, trusted friend.
>
> Write about as much as the student writes, not more. This is very important to equalize the power between you, as an experienced writer, and a beginning writer, as we saw in the example from Eduardo's journal.
>
> In your response, draw the student out. Ask questions which can help the other writer elaborate and add to a topic he or she has introduced. (This means avoiding yes/no questions such as, "Did you like today?" But: "Why do you think that problem happened?")
>
> Use a direct, informal style of writing—write down what you would say if you were responding orally, including phrases and exclamations.
>
> Try to answer the student's questions as completely and honestly as you can. But if you do not know the answer, or wish not to answer, say so. You can set boundaries for the discussion; so can each student.
>
> Try not to lecture or give advice. Instead, offer ideas and choices and ask them in turn what *they* think. Some students will try to make you

a "Dear Abby," and demand that you solve their problems. Remember that your job is to help *them* think it through, not to have all the answers.

Be patient and try not to do it all in one turn—you'll get more chances and so will they.

Focused Dialogue Writing in the Content Areas

How do you get students to really think about math, history, the writing process, or learning a foreign language? How can students develop meta-cognitive, conscious strategies for directing their own learning? As students move beyond primary grades, teachers need to be concerned with helping them become independent, self-directed learners. Independent learning requires that students think for themselves in new situations, learn to ask questions, and have strategies for consciously transferring and applying their knowledge. Dialogue writing provides a way for students to reflect consciously with their teacher or instructor about the processes and difficulties of learning and the general principles and concepts which are at the heart of the particular subject matter. (See also the chapter by Thaiss and Thaiss in this volume.)

Dialogue writing on a regular basis can focus on the learning process and assignments in almost any area. In the first part of this chapter, an extended dialogue about science illustrates one way of using dialogue writing to encourage students to reflect on their learning. In the chapter's third section, the dialogue on math involves discussions about the content of mathematics.

Essay-Dialogues

A student's first draft of an essay or story can become the basis for an extended dialogue in writing between the student and teacher concerning possible elaborations and revisions. Many teachers *do* write back with good comments on student essays—sometimes called "response" writing or evaluation. But a dialogue approach developed by Wilmington, California, teachers allows students to respond in turn and extends their reflective thinking about the content of their writing and approach to presenting it.

In the following example, an eighth-grade student wrote a first draft (typed), discussing a story the class had read. The teacher then asked questions to elicit more elaboration, and the student's responses led to further comments by the teacher.

The Pigman

Well, John's parents are people who like to have things their own way or at least his father is that way. In the story John called his dad Bore.

When John told Bore that he wanted to be an actor his father told him he was stupid. Instead of listening to John he told him he should grow up to be a business man. His father is very pushy. But on the other hand his mother is just the opposite. She is very clean and doesn't like the house getting dirty. She also gets hyper when John and his father are having the slighest discussion.

Lorraine only has a mother. Her mother is very supious about boys. She's a nurse and is always complaining about her job. She's always telling Lorrane about her appearance and how hard it is to bring up a child by herself.

No, I don't think I could handle having parents like that. They seem to expect too much out of you. It really doesn't seem like they care. They have too many family problems. It doesn't seem like they even want to settle any family problems. They don't listen to each other. They neglect there children, except for Lorraine's mother who is over protective.

[Teacher:] Very accurate account of their problems! (A)
Let me pose a very difficult question and see if you can answer it: **WHY?**

1 Why do you think J's dad thinks acting is stupid?

2 Why do you think his mother is "hyper" and cleans all the time?

3 Why do you think h's mother is always criticizing her appearance?

4 Why do you think L's mother is suspicious of men?

[Student:] 1. Maybe when his father was young he wanted to be an actor. Maybe he just didn't have the potentials to be an actor. He saw he could not be an actor so he decide that acting was stupid.

Good point. John's parents does say his parents were afraid. Maybe they imagination in some way. enough him.

2. She's probly just afraid of Johns father. He throws a fit if it doesn't go right for him at work. Very possibly true! She's afraid of something for sure!

er comments in script; student comments in block printing.

I agree. *

Maybe we can be even more specific and say it won't happen, I don't want anything to that happened her? *

3. She probably doesn't want the boys to be tempted by her daughter. In the story she asked her daughter if she thought her skirt wasn't a little too low. So I think that she doesnt what anything to happen to her daughter.

4. She doesnt trust men because of what happened to her. Her husband left her. She put her trust in him thats why.

Essay-dialogues retain the notion of *functional* interactive writing-as-thinking and, as these examples show, use students' first drafts as points of departure for reflection and discussion by both student and teacher. Many teachers find that students devalue their own writing and do not really take time to think about what they write on the teacher's comments. Engaging the student in a "thinking" dialogue *in* writing is one way for a teacher to demonstrate the value of the student's thoughts as the basis for the teacher's own comments. Secondary school teachers in the Wilmington, California, school district who came up with this adaptation report that the average time required for students to submit revised essays dropped from a month to less than two weeks when dialogues were used as a means of feedback instead of corrections on spelling and grammar.

Additional Resources: Written Dialogues

Dialogue Journals: A Commonsense Approach to Communication, a handbook on dialogue journal communication (by Leslee Reed and Jana Staton), is in preparation and will be available in 1984. Write to Jana Staton at the Center for Applied Linguistics, 3520 Prospect St., N.W., Washington, D.C. 20007, for publication information.

Thaiss, Christopher. *Learning Better, Learning More: In the Home and Across the Curriculum.* Washington, D.C.: Basic Skills Improvement Program, U.S. Department of Education, 1983. (See chapter in this volume.)

A Note on Beginning

This chapter is only a point of departure for your own creativity and ingenuity in strengthening the kinds of language interaction already occurring in your classroom. Our interactional perspective has looked at a student's use of language not as a product to be judged or measured, but as part of an ongoing cognitive process. We want you to understand the cognitive demands on the student of being involved in dialogue and the resulting growth in thinking processes and strategies. So rather than being concerned with forms of language, we have stressed the *cognitive* functions of language interaction and invited teachers to reexamine their own interactions with students, and their students' interactions with each other. Those of us who have studied what teachers and students actually do in interaction are convinced that this is the heart of the learning process, and that there is a lot more going on there than you might realize. We are not suggesting that you do something entirely different or new, but we hope that you have become more aware of the value of what you already do, and of the essential role that you play in students' development when you demonstrate what it means to "really think" about something in such a way that students can participate actively with you in the process.

The teacher who gets genuinely perplexed by an event and begins to think about it together with a student or a group of students becomes part of the student's "internal dialogue," as Bruner suggests. By sharing a dialogue in written or oral language, the teacher's thinking can become part of the student's own thought.

References

Aronson, Elliott. *The Jigsaw Classroom.* Beverly Hills, Calif.: Sage Publications, 1978.

Au, Kathryn Hu-Pei, and Mason, Jana. "Social Organizational Factors in Learning to Read: The Balance of Rights Hypothesis." *Reading Research Quarterly* 17, 1 (1981): 115–52.

Bloom, Benjamin S., et al. *Taxonomy of Educational Objectives: The Classification of Educational Goals.* New York: McKay, 1956.

Bruner, Jerome. *Toward a Theory of Instruction.* Cambridge, Mass.: Harvard University Press, 1966.

Cahir, Stephen, and Lucas, Ceil. *Exploring Functional Language.* Washington, D.C.: Center for Applied Linguistics, 1981.

Cazden, Courtney. "Peekaboo as an Instructional Model: Discourse Development at Home and at School." In *Papers and Reports on Child Language Development.* No. 17. Palo Alto, Calif.: Stanford University, Department of Linguistics, 1979.

Cooper, Catherine; Marquis, Angela; and Ayers-Lopez, Susan. "Peer Learning in the Classroom: Tracing Developmental Patterns and Consequences of Children's Spontaneous Interaction." In *Communicating in the Classroom,* edited by Louise Cherry Wilkinson. New York: Academic Press, 1982.

Dillon, J. T. "To Question and Not to Question During Discussion: Questioning and Discussion." *Journal of Teacher Education* 32 (September/October 1981): 51–55.

Dillon, J. T. "To Question and Not to Question During Discussion: Non-Questioning Techniques." *Journal of Teacher Education* 32 (November/December 1981): 15–19.

Green, Judith. *Research on Teaching as a Linguistic Process: A State of the Art.* In *Review of Research in Education,* 11 (January 1983). American Education Research Association.

Griffin, Peg; Newman, Dennis; and Cole, Michael. "Activities, Actions and Formal Operations: A Vygotskian Analysis of a Piagetian Task." Paper presented at the International Society for the Study of Behavior Development. Toronto, 1981.

Lucas, Ceil. "Stop Talking, Y'all, at the Same Time: Evidence for the Teaching and Learning of Turn-Talking Strategies." Paper presented at Linguistics Society of America, Winter Meeting. New York, 1981.

Lucas, Ceil, and Borders-Simmons, Denise. *Language Diversity and Classroom Discourse.* (NIE-G-80-0072.) Washington, D.C.: Center for Applied Linguistics, 1982.

McNamee, Gillian. "The Social Interaction Origins of Narrative Skills." In *Quarterly Newsletter of the Laboratory of Comparative Human Cognition* 1 (October 1979).

Perret-Clermont, Anne-Nelly. *Social Interaction and Cognitive Development in Children.* New York: Academic Press, 1980.

Piaget, Jean. *Six Psychological Studies.* New York: Random House, 1967.

Reed, Leslee. "The Teacher's Perspective." In *Dialogue Journal Writing as a Communicative Event, Vol. II: Research Papers.* J. Staton, R. Shuy, and J. Kreeft. (NIE-G-80-0122.) Washington, D.C.: Center for Applied Linguistics, 1982.

Shuy, Roger. "Teacherese: The How of Talking in Classrooms." Part IV, *Participant Perspectives of Classroom Discourse,* Greta Morine-Dershimer, Morton Tenenberg, Arnulfo Ramirez, Roger Shuy, and Gary Galluzzo. NIE final report (NIE-G-78-0161.) Research Foundation, California State University at Hayward, 1980.

Sinclair, de-Zwort H. "Developmental Psycholinguistics." In *Studies in Cognitive Development,* edited by D. Elkind and J. H. Flavell. New York: Oxford University Press, 1969, 315–69.

Slavin, R. E. "Cooperative Learning." *Review of Educational Research* 50 (1980): 315–42.

Stallings, Jane. "Allocated Academic Learning Time Revisited, or Beyond Time on Task." *Educational Researcher* 9 (December 1980): 11–16.

Staton, Jana. "Writing and Counseling: Using a Dialogue Journal." *Language Arts* 57 (May 1980): 514–18.

Staton, Jana. "Discussion of Problems in Dialogue Journal Writing." In *Dialogue Journal Writing as a Communicative Event, Vol. II: Research Papers,* J. Staton, R. Shuy, and J. Kreeft. (NIE-G-80-0122.) Washington, D.C.: Center for Applied Linguistics, 1982a.

Staton, Jana. "The Development of Topic Understanding: Analysis of the Dialogue in Math." In *Dialogue Journal Writing as a Communicative Event, Vol. II: Research Papers,* J. Staton, R. Shuy, and J. Kreeft. (NIE-G-80-0122.) Washington, D.C.: Center for Applied Linguistics, 1982b.

Staton, Jana; Shuy, Roger; and Kreeft, Joy. *Analysis of Dialogue Journal Writing as a Communicative Event.* Final Report and Research Papers. (NIE-G-80-0122.) Washington, D.C.: Center for Applied Linguistics, 1982.

Vygotsky, L. S. *Mind in Society: The Development of Higher Psychological Processes,* edited by M. Cole, V. John-Steiner, S. Scribner, and R. Louberman. Cambridge, Mass.: Harvard University Press, 1978.

Wood, David; Bruner, Jerome; and Ross, Gail. "The Role of Tutoring in Problem-Solving." *Journal of Child Psychology and Psychiatry* 17 (1975): 89–100.

Using the New Technologies in Language Communication Education

Nancy S. Olson, American Society for Training
and Development, Inc.

It is Saturday morning, and video game arcades are the biggest draws in the shopping mall. At home, children tune in to "Tom and Jerry" or "Discovery."

The average American child voluntarily spends twenty-eight hours weekly involved with electronic media, estimates Mary Alice White of Teachers College, Columbia University, and another twenty-five hours, mostly assigned, with print materials. We have entered what she calls the "Electronic Learning Age," and educators must realize that outside the classroom new technologies are changing how children give and receive information.

White, who directs the Electronic Learning Laboratory at Columbia University, says that children by age three or four "have learned that music and sound effects, and sometimes changes in types of voices, are cues to make them look at a TV screen. They are familiar with words as a spoken source of information, but words are secondary to the visual image on the screen."

In most classrooms, however, because the spoken word is the primary means of instruction, children need to be taught when and how to pay attention, according to White. Since the 1950s, teachers have said children do not listen the way they used to, and "I'm sure it is true that they do not," she says.

Television has taught that "learning is entertaining, that it is immediate, and that it is fun," she explains, while schoolwork is often hard. In addition, teachers tend to be "print people" by virtue of their own print education; they draw on a pedagogy developed largely through study of how children learn from and with words. Image learning raises new questions for educators, says White. She is convinced that teachers must stop fighting new technologies and start learning how they work. They must recognize that they are competing with music, sound effects, and technical effects—"everything technology has come up with to keep your children's eyes glued to that TV screen." Teachers should not expect students to pay attention all the time, she continues. They should develop cues that tell students what is important to listen to. And teachers should study electronic learning to see what they can use as a bridge to print learning.

The work of Dan Anderson at the University of Massachusetts and that of White at Teachers College suggest that children, when they watch television, pay attention primarily with their eyes to grasp information, and use the sound coming from a television set to orient themselves. Young children playing with toys in one of Anderson's experiments turn to the television when certain auditory cues come on, such as an upsurge in music, children's voices, or certain technical effects. "But these act as cues to look, and their information is gotten primarily from looking," says White.

When children enter the first grade, they have spent a minimum of four years "learning with their eyes, and they're primarily, we think, visual learners," says White. In school they are expected to be auditory learners. "We're facing an entirely new ball game here," she says. "How do you get images out of the heads of children by asking them with words? 'Tell me, pupils, what image do you have in your head of so and so who was on the news last week?' What I'm wrestling with is how to be able to come up with some kind of imaginative technique of using images to retrieve images. I haven't solved it yet, but that's the frontier we're at. It's a whole new world in research."

The Power of Television as a Curriculum Tool

For more than a decade, television has been used as an instructional aid in the classroom, yet the skills to use, analyze, and learn from television are still underdeveloped in the educational community. While instructional television is available in 74 percent of all classrooms, according to the Corporation for Public Broadcasting, the National Center for Education Statistics reports that only 17 percent of teachers are trained to use it.

Many instructional television programs that focus on language are available or being developed. One example is the Agency for Instructional Television's ThinkAbout series of sixty fifteen-minute lessons that help strengthen reasoning skills of fifth- and sixth-graders and review and reinforce their mathematics, communication, and study skills. The Think-About series uses an integrated approach to curriculum that blends skills presented in clusters. Twelve of the sixty programs highlight basic communication skills; each program deals with both receptive and expressive language skills.

In ThinkAbout's "Collecting Information" cluster, entitled "Where Do I Go?" two boys who sight a UFO while camping try to identify what they saw by interviewing people, doing library research, and reasoning. Throughout the program, the characters are shown using communication skills, always for a real purpose. Students can see how these skills can be applied in their own lives.

"The Write Channel," a series developed by Mississippi Educational Television, provides third- and fourth-graders with opportunities to practice sentence-combining. In this series of fifteen fifteen-minute programs, an animated character, R. B. Bugg, interacts with live characters. Bugg covers news stories for WORD-TV. When he returns to the TV station with stories, an editor assists him in combining simple sentences by using coordinating and subordinating conjunctions, and in making his sentences more interesting with adjectives, noun clusters, and phrases. The series shows Bugg rewriting and invites children to help Bugg think up endings for some of his unfinished stories.

"Zebra Wings," also from Mississippi ETV, stimulates the imaginations of fifth- and sixth-graders and promotes their creative writing skills. The series host interacts with a panel of three children in discussing poetry, short stories, fables, myths, and newspaper articles. Many of the programs take viewers "on location" to stimulate creativity, and some programs solicit responses from viewers.

Don Kaplan, author of *Video in the Classroom: A Guide to Creative Television,* encourages educators to produce student-created television in schools. For example, he thinks that with a minimum of media hardware, students can play games consisting of taping improvisational activities that encourage student self-awareness, spontaneity, and creativity while helping them to become familiar with the equipment and its techniques. He sees video as a valuable tool for improving visual and verbal skills that enhance interpersonal communication in the classroom.

"The true power of video as a curriculum tool is that it goes beyond a single subject area, and allows the teachers to integrate various components of their existing curricula into one all-embracing educational experience," says Joanne Fredrickson, project coordinator of an ESEA (Elementary and Secondary Education Act) Title IV-C project, "Developing Core Curriculum Through Video."

In Fredrickson's video project, students and teachers in twelve elementary schools in Albuquerque, New Mexico, use the skills of critical thinking, organizing, sequencing, perceiving, visual and auditory discriminating, communicating, researching, analyzing, creating, and cooperating as they write and produce video programs.

Interactive Video

Video has long been popular among speech teachers as a means for student self-critique of language use and delivery. But now some video users are branching out of the closed classroom into interactive video. Over the past seven years, the Unified School District of Irvine, California, has become through cable television a tuned-in community.

Irvine educators have established a Unified Information System in which two-way interactive cable television links twenty-four schools, the public library, city, the University of California at Irvine, and every home with a television set. Students in four or five schools join in a discussion of "Music from Beethoven to Kiss"—with more students from other schools invited to participate. Other programs, most of which are devoted to acquiring the basic skills, make it possible for students across the city to share lessons, research, learning games, school news, discussions with experts, and videotapes received from students in foreign countries.

Irvine Superintendent of Schools A. Stanley Corey believes that productive learning occurs when communication technology serves four purposes: (1) provides economical one-to-one interaction among teachers and learners; (2) offers access to information resources beyond the school site; (3) enables personal control of and responsibility for learning; and (4) allows "fluid time," unconstrained by traditional concepts of class scheduling.

QUBE, a two-way cable system in Columbus, Ohio, allows an instructor and students to communicate in a limited manner during the broadcast of a college course. Each subscriber has a push-button control that allows selection of thirty channels and one of five response choices. When students respond to questions asked by the instructor, answers are transmitted back to the computer at the cable company's station. In this way, the instructor knows who is participating in that particular session. The instructor can receive answers both collectively and individually when members of the audience activate response buttons.

The "New Technologies"

Although today's students are quite familiar with television, there are other new technologies that are making their way into the classroom, such as the videodisc, cable TV, microcomputers, and other electronic learning aids. The much publicized "electronic learning revolution," however, has been slow to occur, due partly, some think, to teachers' fears of the new machinery and of their being replaced.

Videodiscs

Some hail the videodisc as being the most important new teaching tool on the horizon. The videodisc is special in educational settings because it allows students to pace their own instruction by manipulating a few simple controls. For instance, in addition to watching and listening to a segment straight through, learners can view a video sequence frame by frame, in slow motion or speeded up, or "freeze" a particular picture for careful analysis. Hooked up to a microcomputer, the videodisc can become a computer-controlled interactive learning center. Students will be able to answer questions posed by the microcomputer while viewing presentations that reinforce and test learning.

The California School for the Deaf in Riverside is testing a system to teach language development using a disc player interfaced with a microcomputer. The school's three-year project has produced two twenty-seven minute videodiscs featuring "Dusty," an old miner who travels magically to various places in a modern community: an airport, a hospital, a fast-food restaurant, a grocery store, a lake, a go-cart raceway, a water-slide, and others. Students are automatically branched through activities that require them to acknowledge captions appearing on the screen, sequence events, recognize correctness of grammar and syntax, respond to questions, categorize, spell, capitalize, punctuate, and construct sentences and questions. Students respond primarily with a light pen, which they touch to the computer's television screen to indicate their answers, or by using the keyboard during spelling tasks.

The videodiscs contain only visual material (for instance, one image is of Dusty sprawled on the rocky ground), while the computer generates all printed material appearing on the screen (over the above image, the computer generates the instruction, "Make a sentence or question," the words "falling," "not," "like," "does," "he," and the punctuation mark "."). The student would touch the light pen on a box beside each word or punctuation mark to indicate his or her sequence in the sentence.

Since the computer puts the captions and all printed tasks on the television screen, rather than having any text permanently embedded on the videodiscs, many different language concepts and instructional objectives can be achieved while using the same video material.

The project also provides for total individualization. The system allows the learner to proceed through the program at his or her own pace, with remedial instruction inherent in the branching software program. The teacher is provided a printout documenting student progress including recommendations for classroom remediation.

"The students respond personally and candidly to the characters they see on the television screen," note project designers Rod Brawley and Barbara

Peterson (1983), "and are enticed into the more difficult language tasks through exciting and motivating video segments."

The U.S. Department of Education estimates that only about 150 to 200 elementary and secondary schools in the United States currently have videodisc players. Lack of software that maximizes the disc's potential for participative and interactive use may account for the lack of educational use. However, software developers predict that in about two years, videodisc titles will be available embracing the entire range of curricula.

Surveying the Scene

Marc S. Tucker is currently assessing the potential of the new technologies in elementary and secondary education through a project funded by the Carnegie Corporation. He and his fellow researchers are highly optimistic about the new technologies—microcomputers in particular.

Tucker suggests that a future scenario for classrooms will be a student sitting in front of a console that contains a personal computer, a videodisc player controlled by the computer, a television screen, and a device to connect the console to a variety of telecommunications systems.

What Tucker sees as the problem, however, is inadequate software. He says that thus far the new technologies have been used to "push facts into students—what Mao Tse Tung called 'stuffing the duck'" (Heard, 1982, p. 12). Tucker warns against relying on computer vendors and educational publishers to develop good software in response to market demands.

Computer innovations are already being adopted rather rapidly in affluent school districts, with implications for increasing inequalities between rich and poor districts. "Although it's not clear yet that using the new technologies will confer an enormous advantage in learning, it is clear that they definitely will do so with respect to learning how to use a computer," says Tucker.

The Office of Technology Assessment, a Congressional research agency, is concluding a two-year project, part of which examined the impact of the new technologies on elementary and secondary education. In preparing part of the study, Linda Roberts, of the Department of Education's Office of Libraries and Learning Technologies, visited schools across the country to determine where there is significant application of computer technology.

It is difficult now to generalize, she says; the field is changing day by day. According to Roberts, much of the instruction is drill and practice, but a few districts are going beyond that to use the computer for more advanced learning tasks.

There is a push to get away from using computers solely for mathematics, says Roberts, and to make their use interdisciplinary. "One sense I have about the future of all the technologies," she says, "is that they are means, tools, not ends. We must look now at the content—what we are trying to do with the tools."

Computers in Writing

In the next five years, the biggest impact in the computer area will be in writing, predicts Robert Taylor, of Teachers College, Columbia University. "Computers," he says, "will make clear that writing is a process. Students will not mistakenly think then that some people can write and some people can't. They will see that it is a refinable process." Microcomputers, programmed as word processors, make writing easy and fun, says Taylor, and lead young writers to write more, which leads to better writing.

For example, with word processors, students have the freedom to instantly shift letters, words, and paragraphs on the computer screen or to "erase" them and bring them back later. "The computer can also automatically correct such things as spelling and punctuation. This will lead to debates about learning to spell, similar to the debates about calculator use in mathematics," says Taylor. But such debates over spelling would be trivial, he thinks. What is important is that the computer teaches students to rewrite with ease. "*Nobody* likes to rewrite," he says.

In addition to ease in rewriting, Taylor thinks another important application of the computer to writing is the possibility for instant reorganization. This gives students a healthier view, he says, makes them less anxious, and gets them out of the "Gee, I can't write" syndrome. Says Taylor, "If we can do anything to improve the way students feel about writing and the ease of writing itself, by all means we should do it. If this means taking away the mechanical drudgery, then do it."

Computers also make it possible for students to transmit drafts and documents to other students or to the teacher to call up on their own terminals to read and comment on. ARTNET, a full-blown electronic mail system, now operates out of Florida's Southeastern Regional Data Center on a UNIVAC 1100/81A. The network, which was spearheaded by Florida's Poet Laureate Edmund Skellings, allows interactive multi-port computer interaction among Florida's nine state universities, and plans are underway to expand the system to elementary and secondary schools. On each campus, faculty and students compose two- and three-dimensional graphics and text on computers and transmit their work around the state. Says Skellings: "If the typewriter gives the artist a personal printing press, the electric color memory computer gives the artist a personal publishing house."

Skellings sees this technology not only as the writer's tool but as art itself. "The computer program has become the new American poem," he says. "This new, colorful, animated poetry fulfills the desire of McLuhan to break the black and white of Gutenberg and fulfills Karl Shapiro's plea for poets to break out and off the static printed page" (Blair, 1983).

Another new trend in computer-assisted instruction is being tested in Riverside, California, where Classroom Curriculum Corporation's "Dial-a-Drill" helps students in grades one through eight review and practice basic learning skills at home. At a prearranged time, for example, eight-year-old Allan answers the telephone at home and is greeted by a machine voice. The voice, called a Digital Speech System and housed in the instructional computer in the county superintendent's office, guides him through a series of vocabulary exercises offering practice with synonyms, antonyms, definitions, and word categories. For instance, he is asked to identify the most appropriate word to finish a sentence in his workbook. "Excellent work," says the voice after a right answer; "Try again, Allan," says the voice patiently if he makes a mistake. During the six- to ten-minute lesson, children control the pace of the drill while the computer adjusts the level of difficulty according to performance. The computer follows pathways or strands that guide students to the most appropriate level of questions among the thousands banked in its instructional system.

In the first lesson, students learn how to use their push-button telephones as keyboards and to punch "go" and "repeat." "Go" is the # sign on the phone and is equivalent to the return key on a computer keyboard. Students spell by pressing the letter buttons on the telephone.

The program, designed by Patrick Suppes, professor of philosophy, education, and statistics at Stanford University, is part of the newest trend in computer-assisted instruction (Beyers, 1983). Suppes says that "Dial-a-Drill" improves students' basic skills by providing supplemental course-work in mental arithmetic, reading, and spelling.

"Dial-a-Drill" costs a school approximately $40 per student per year for at-home lessons. Each student's performance is tracked and the computer provides progress reports in each topic.

Although computers traditionally have been used for drill and practice on basic concepts and skills in subjects like math and science, some fear that they will never progress effectively beyond this. Richard Anderson of the University of Cincinnati, who has written computer programs for English grammar and composition, feels that after his twelve years of experience with computers that the computer is best suited for "concrete, skill-mastery composition, skills such as grammar and spelling, skills with clear-cut right and wrong answers."

He says, "The computer can tell a writer that a comma is in the wrong place, ask what kind of paragraph the student has just read, ask which is the topic sentence." But he adds that computers will never be able to identify "style" in writing or "creativity."

But the advantages, according to Anderson, are that each student, alone and unembarrassed, can work with a computer terminal. Self-image is enhanced because students "control the fanciest tool to come down the pike." They move at their own pace, and "nobody gets mad at them."

With computer use, says Anderson, teachers are freed for human creativity during classroom instruction; the computer handles the remedial, skill-mastery, and right-and-wrong-answer-type instruction. The teacher can concentrate on "style."

Researchers cite several reasons why students have a positive attitude about being instructed by computer:

> Because students set their own pace, they absorb and comprehend material without inconveniencing anyone else.
>
> They can make mistakes without embarrassment; only the computer knows.
>
> They get immediate feedback that their answers are either correct or incorrect.
>
> The computer bases its evaluations solely on performance, not on such things as the student's relationship to the teacher. (Clement, 1981, p. 28)

Two popular myths perpetuated by opponents of the use of computers in the learning process seem to have been disproved in the literature (Clement, 1981, p. 29). The first is that computer-based instruction is dehumanizing. In reality, Clement reports that the opposite seems to be true if student self-reports can be believed. "Most students find the computer exciting to work with," calling it "friendly," patient, and undismayed by their mistakes, according to Clement.

The second myth is that high student acceptance of computer-based instruction is due to the novelty of the experience. Longtime computer users do become more critical of computer breakdowns, but their feelings remain positive, says Clement. Students tend to spend more than the prescribed time at the terminals.

Beverly Hunter, of Human Resources Research Organization in Alexandria, Virginia, suggests that it is essential for students to spend plenty of time on the terminal to use it with ease. "It's rare in elementary schools today that kids have that much machine time. You can't learn to master writing on a terminal in a few weeks," she says. "A good system for kids would have a built-in 'Typing Tutor' which would teach them how to type," she adds.

Hunter's own twelve- and fourteen-year-old sons now compose writing assignments on a home word processor. With word processing, she says, they find it easier to begin to rearrange and reorganize, to edit and correct grammar and spelling, to put in headings. "With hand writing," she says, "this is a difficult process. They're bored after two or three drafts. They have writer's cramp. With word processing, the mechanics of reorganization are trivial, and when they're through, they have a pretty product."

For those students whose work is sloppy, this may be the first time that they have "a pretty product." "Word processing opens up the possibilities of striving for perfection," she emphasizes.

Nancy Taylor of Catholic University agrees that in traditional writing instruction, many students fail to proofread and edit their products. "Text editing on the computer overcomes the mechanical aspects which often deter children's revision and development of written work, such as problems in reading their handwriting, difficulties in inserting corrections or elaborations. In addition, the computer can be programmed to remind the child to proof certain things before signing off" (Wall and Taylor, 1982).

Researchers at Bell Laboratories in New Jersey have developed "Writer's Workbench," the first extensive collection of computer programs for analyzing written text and encouraging modification and addition. "Workbench" was designed for professional writers at Bell, but Colorado State University researchers are adapting it to student use. A series of "Workbench" programs runs automatically on every paper students type into the computer as part of Colorado's pilot program.

"Workbench" analyzes student writing for *organization* by highlighting organizational weaknesses in formal paragraphs and essays; *development* by drawing attention to short or underdeveloped paragraphs by comparing them to paragraphs of good papers submitted; *find be* which calls attention to all forms of "to be." Thus students are alerted to common weaknesses in their writing—excessive reliance on weak, colorless "to be" verbs. These are among several other programs designed to improve writing.

Another unique feature of computer-based writing instruction is that teachers can compare the student's original and revised versions, evaluate progress, and record and monitor student achievement of learning objectives in individual progress files. Through the computer storage system, the teacher, principal, child, and parents have evidence of the student's progress in writing.

Taylor adds that through the computer's imaginative visual display capabilities, children may enjoy their skill lessons and be interested in further computer work.

Kathleen Gilbert, who teaches math, English, and computer programming in Colorado, suggests that combinations of computer graphics, color, sound, and changing displays will assist student writing—in composing new forms of poetry, for example. In a computer program being developed by Gilbert, students will describe parts of speech and grammatical rules to the computer, and the computer will then display a variety of sentences based on those rules.

Gilbert thinks that the computer is a powerful tool for fostering new forms of learning. For example, students can interact with the computer to compose a story. Imagine the computer requesting a time, place, and setting for a story, she suggests, and the student responding at the terminal. The story unfolds then as a collaboration between student and computer (Gilbert, 1981, p. 13).

The U.S. Department of Education has funded Bolt, Baranek, and Newman, a research group located in Cambridge, Massachusetts, to develop a microcomputer-based curriculum to help teach writing to upper elementary school students. "At the highest level," says Andee Rubin, supervisor of Software Development, "we want to provide the tools and environment that will help students write."

The program being developed has several components. Using text editors, students will compose written works and exchange information with each other. For instance, says Rubin, a student can type, "What happened on 'Hill Street Blues' last night?" and other students in the class can respond. The student who asked the original question can bring up on the screen the responses that have been made or print them out in hard copy form.

In addition to exchanging information with each other, students will make their writing public, the way adults do. They will put together a class newspaper on the computer that can be read either on screen or on a printed copy. "Students will be able to make the text look physically attractive," says Rubin, "with publication aids that provide formatting, such as centered titles and different typefaces."

Costing from $200 to $2000, printers are fairly expensive, she says, but the program's developers think that they are essential. "In terms of writing," she says, "we think it's crucial to have paper. You can't buy a minimal system and use this program."

In addition, a "message system" on the computer will enable students to send messages to each other within the class or possibly across the country. "We're finding kids write more on the text editor," Rubin says. Why? "My guess would be that they don't have to worry about spelling and such matters. They can go back easily to make changes. They're freer to get down what they want to say."

Microcomputer Effects on the Writing Process

Colette Diute, a psycholinguist at Teachers College, Columbia University, thinks that the speed of output of microcomputer text editors affects the writing process. Her research with students at the United Nations School in New York is focusing on how the computer frees the writer of the cognitive burdens of writing.

She is working with three groups of students: one that uses a word processor, one that writes with paper and pencil, and a third that writes with a word processor that prompts them to check such things as spelling, usage, and sentence structure errors. The reason for prompting in the last group is not to focus on errors, but to see what it takes to encourage students to revise.

Says Diute, the students "love writing on the computer." They report that writing is a lot easier, and she feels that they also revise more. When they do not need to recopy, she says, they are freed to compose. Students are no longer forced to compose and evaluate and edit at the same time.

The Writer's Assistant, a computer program developed by researchers at the University of California-San Diego, is now used by fourth-graders in Oceanside, California. The program is composed of a screen editor, software that allows students to rearrange a text, and spelling verification.

With the capability to rearrange text, students can separate each sentence from a paragraph to see more easily, for example, if it is a run-on or a fragment. Students verify spelling by moving the cursor over a word on the screen that they are uncertain about; the computer phonetically matches that word against words in the computer file. If a child has written "sale," the computer might come up with "sail" and give a brief definition. Seeing that that is not the correct word, the student types in "no," and the computer searches further.

With this approach, the writer must first make a guess at the correct spelling, then the individual receives spelling verification. This program differs from traditional computer spelling verification in that traditionally the computer checks every word against a built-in dictionary after the writing is complete.

Spelling verification came about because a teacher in Oceanside had her students write out the word or words that they did not know; she would check each student's word list. Now the computer handles this task.

The Writer's Assistant spelling verification is easy to personalize with words students need, says Jim Levin, assistant research psychologist at the University of California who is working with the Oceanside students. He says that spelling verification is also the most popular command, based on the number of times students use it.

The Writer's Assistant is a powerful tool for researching the writing process, says Levin. Since it keeps a detailed "trace" of the keystrokes made by the writer in generating and changing copy, researchers are using this trace data to study the processes involved in writing.

For example, two boys, Gerry and James, used the Writer's Assistant to create a story called "Dragon Tamer." Researchers were able to analyze the boys' low-level processes like spelling or typing correction. At one point, Gerry and James changed "so*n*ʈ" to "sor*¢¢*r" to "sorcery."

The Writer's Assistant also keeps track of higher-level, more global actions, such as large-scale deletions of previously entered text, as well as insertions of next text. For example, the original title of the story was "Dragon Slayer." At the end of the writing process, Gerry and James changed the title to "Dragon Tamer" because they had modified the theme of the story from winning the king's daughter's hand in marriage by slaying the dragon to slaying or taming the dragon.

Levin thinks that the Writer's Assistant is important because it allows the teacher to observe different problems novice writers experience and then provide the needed individual support. "For novices, much of the effort of writing is distributed externally, both over other people in the setting and over inanimate resources like print and computers. As the novice writer becomes an expert, this external support becomes less necessary, as more of the cognitive processing can be done by the writer. Our goal in designing microcomputer-based environments for writing has been to create settings in which the support provided by the environment can be reduced dynamically as the writer progresses to expertise."

Levin says that it is "crucially important" that children use the computer in pairs. Demands on teachers are then substantially reduced because most problems that arise for one student can be handled by the other. Students also cooperate to improve their work. "In contrast to the stereotype that computer use leads to isolation of students from their peers, this paired student use generates substantially increased interaction between peers, compared with other classroom activities" (Levin, Boruta, and Vasconcellos, in press).

These interactions most often mutually benefit both students. When one child encounters a block in writing, the other child who has a different viewpoint can offer alternative approaches. And, for research purposes, having pairs of children use the computer generates "ecologically valid 'protocols' of the children's writing processes, as each child explains to the other what actions to take and reasons for those actions when there is a conflict."

Students who were tested before and after four months of Writer's Assistant use showed positive results when compared to students who wrote with paper and pencil. The students who had access to the program increased the average number of words per writing sample from 45.1 to 74.1 words. The control class showed virtually no increase in average length of writing sample (prescore—44.6; postscore—46.4).

The writing quality rating was based on a four-point scale, with the judge blind to the classroom from which the samples were collected. The judgments were "holistic," with adherence to topic and organization emphasized while mechanics of spelling, punctuation, and so on were de-emphasized. The qualitative score for the experimental class increased from 2.00 to 3.09 after four months of using the Writer's Assistant. The control classes had a prescore of 2.27 and a postscore of 2.24.

When asked, "How is writing with the computer different from writing with paper and pencil?" most students responded positively with comments like, "It's funner and easier than writing with paper and pencil. Also it does not hurt your hand."

Levin said that there were two negative comments. One student complained about accidentally hitting the wrong key and making his writing disappear; another felt limited by not being able to do drawings as part of his writing.

In the spring of 1982, the Oceanside students began communicating with students in a small town 150 miles northwest of Anchorage, Alaska, via computer hookup. Students in the two states are expected to share class newspaper articles and then to send individual messages. It is anticipated that teachers will also communicate with each other, which could be particularly helpful to teachers in rural Alaska who may need the advice of a colleague.

This exchange of messages brings even greater social resources to the educational setting, broadening the range of peers available for children to draw upon for learning and problem solving. Microcomputer electronic message systems have tremendous implications, says Levin, especially for education in remote or isolated areas.

Microcomputers in Oral Language

W. Patrick Dickson, of the Wisconsin Center for Education Research, has developed microcomputer software to teach young children speaking and listening skills. His work involves the kind of communication that is specific and measurable, such as directions on a map.

Dickson developed two communication games in which players must help each other rather than outdo each other. In one game, each of two players sits in front of a video screen which has an array of cartoon faces, abstract drawings, or other pictures. The player who is "speaker" tries to give enough information about one of the pictures so that the "listener" can distinguish which picture the "speaker" is describing. Players get up to three chances for each array, and tones tell if the listener's choice is right or wrong.

In Dickson's second game, children practice oral language to describe locations and relationships: players give each other directions to a location on a map of a model city shown on the computer screen.

Dickson says that the games elicit rich, noncompetitive interaction from students, and such cooperative activities promote communication as well as social interaction.

Research on interracial friendship and cooperation in schools fostered by team learning leads Dickson to speculate that these computer games can be used to deliberately bring together individuals who otherwise might not interact—black with white, English speakers with non-English speakers, boy with girl.

Although games can certainly be played without using computers, micro-computers make it possible to adjust the difficulty of the games to the abilities of the players. "That means," says Dickson, "we can individualize without any intervention of the teacher. The computer monitors the activity, and if the kids are making a lot of mistakes, it will simplify the display. If they're making no mistakes, it can make the tasks more complex" (*Wisconsin Center for Education Research News,* Fall 1981/Winter 1982, p. 2).

Another advantage is that computers are stimulating. The machines can get and hold attention with color, sounds, motion, and light, and children can interact with them. And, they offer teachers recordkeeping capabilities for each student. The teacher can then get a better sense of a child's speaking and listening abilities or suggest pairing students that have complementary needs and abilities.

Dickson hopes that he will eventually be able to help teachers to accurately assess children's oral communication abilities with this kind of computer game.

Another project from the Wisconsin Center is focusing on designing interactive microcomputer programming to teach action verbs to children with physical and developmental disorders. Believing that action verbs are critical to children's spoken language development, communication disorder specialists want to develop ways to assess the children's comprehension of verbs and their ability to use them.

Actions represented by up to twenty-five verbs, such as "walk," "sit," and "run," will be demonstrated by moving cartoon figures to be shown in split-screen pairs and be accompanied by verbal instructions, test sentences, or questions presented by microcomputer. Children with minimal motor control can use special sensitive micro-switches, light pens, or "joy sticks" to reach beyond their physical restrictions and learn language through interaction with the computer.

Because not much study has been done in this area—particularly in verb comprehension—researchers anticipate doing fundamental research in early semantic development during the three-year project.

Drawbacks of Computer Instruction

Although classroom use of microcomputers is increasing, and many teachers are enthusiastic, only a comparatively few microcomputers are used in language courses, primarily in elementary and middle schools. Market Data Retrieval, Inc., surveyed the country's 15,500 school districts and found that 17 percent—or 15,000—of the nation's schools have at least one microcomputer. TALMIS, Inc., a microcomputer industry market research firm, estimates that there are 90,000 microcomputers in schools today—the vast majority of which are used for math and science and computer-use classes. TALMIS predicts that by 1985, there will be as many as 400,000 microcomputers available to U.S. students.

The complaint heard most often from all parts of the country regarding use of computers for instruction concerns the poor-quality software currently available. As more and more educators begin to use the computer in the classroom, they will become more discriminating purchasers, and even programmers.

For the three best-selling machines (the Radio Shack TRS-80, the Commodore PET, and the Apple II), some good software is available, according to Karen Billings, director of the Microcomputer Resource Center at Teachers College, Columbia University. But several problems exist: much of the software does not fit teachers' needs; software developed for one machine cannot be used on another manufacturer's model; and it is expensive. Schools commonly blow the budget on hardware at the expense of software.

Poor-quality software and the incompatibility of different manufacturers' software led the Minnesota Educational Computing Consortium (MECC) not only to set up a software dissemination network, but also to endorse a single manufacturer's microcomputer equipment for use in the state's schools. Now, Minnesota schools, and those in other states, can purchase software from MECC and receive it via telephone hookup in minutes. MECC also runs workshops for teachers and spends an estimated $40 million annually to help schools make the best use of computers.

According to *Electronic Learning* (November/December 1981), good-quality software should:

be free of "bugs" or "glitches" (technical problems or errors); should load properly and run smoothly; and should be error free. As one educator points out: "It's amazing how many programs have simple spelling errors in them."

take advantage of the machine's unique capabilities without substituting flash for substance. It should be more than a workbook on the screen and should enhance learning of certain tasks better than a teacher or a text. Word-processing programs and Typing Tutor (from Microsoft) demonstrate the power of the computer while satisfying important instructional objectives as well, according to Jane Mestrovic, a math teacher at the Chapin School in New York City.

provide positive reinforcement while helping students to understand wrong answers. Bob Jackson, regional coordinator of instructional computing for Fairfield County in Connecticut, says software should help kids understand concepts and rules. "So much of the spelling software that's out, for example, never gets to the rules of spelling. The word is either right or wrong. If you tell kids they're wrong without telling them why, not much learning will take place."

include some diagnostic and branching features. Most educators agree that good-quality software should attempt to determine the student's level and adapt to individual needs. One program that educators frequently mention that exemplifies these objectives is Typing Tutor. The program keeps track of the time between the student's keystrokes and places those "slow to find" keys into the drill section.

be creative and stimulate creativity among users. Students should not be locked into computer-imposed right and wrong answers. Some educators think that the game format is a creative use of the computer and believe that learning will take place faster while playing a computer game that requires learning to play successfully.

allow for easy teacher modification. For example, in a program that provides drill and practice with vocabulary words, teachers should be able to add more difficult words for above-average students and easier words for slower learners.

provide clearly written operating manuals, support materials, and activities.

A study of classroom use of microcomputers by New York City's Bank Street College of Education indicated that their potential for improving learning is limited for the present by several factors:

Student access to computers is sporadic and erratic.

Computers are rarely integrated into classroom work.

Good software is in short supply.

Claims about instructional value of microcomputers are largely unsubstantiated.

In addition, some educators fear that increasing computer use will have negative consequences, such as overemphasizing problems and ideas that lend themselves to quantification. Other educators are concerned that computers reinforce students' giving the quick, superficial answer.

Says Joseph Weizenbaum, professor of computer science at Massachusetts Institute of Technology (MIT), quoted in the *New York Times:* "Abraham Maslow once said that to him who has only a hammer, the whole world looks like a nail. To him who has only a computer, the whole world looks like a computable domain. You introduce a new symbolic system, and one begins to interpret the world in such terms. The danger is that we will end up thinking like a computer and that the only things we will recognize as legitimate problems are those where quantification and calculation play a big role."

Some educators see computers and other technology as further splitting American schools into the "haves" and the "have nots." "At the heart of the equity issue," says Linda Roberts of the U.S. Department of Education, "is who is going to benefit from the technology and who is not? We must ensure that all students become knowledgeable about a variety of electronic learning devices and their multiple uses."

One obstacle to creative use of computers, suggests Joyce Hakansson, a computer consultant and former coordinator of computer education at the Lawrence Hall of Science in Berkeley, California, is the fear of some educators that discovery learning may erode the traditional authority of the teacher. Some teachers do not want to compete with computers for the attention of students; others are used to being the information providers and now find that they know less about computers than their students.

Computers are not the first "technological breakthrough" that educators have witnessed over the years. Some are reluctant to jump on this electronic bandwagon, pointing to the unused language labs, teaching machines, the dusty 8mm projectors, and video monitors.

But many are enthusiastic. Marvin Minsky, a founder of the Artificial Intelligence Laboratory at MIT, and his colleague Seymour Papert, creator of LOGO and other computer languages, see in computers the opportunity for changing our methods of education. Says Minsky:

> The computer provides a more flexible experience than anything else a child is likely to encounter. With it, a child can become an architect or an artist . . . dealing with a computer, at least as Papert and I see it, allows a child to have a whole new set of attitudes towards making mistakes, which we call finding "bugs." We have not been able to find

any other word for it. It does not seem to get taught in schools where the concern is to teach the "truth." . . . Seymour wanted to develop a working place for a child in which it would be a positive achievement when a child can find the things that can go wrong. If you know enough of them, you get close to something like the truth. This is what happens with children who use computers in the schoolroom environments that Seymour has set up, and, in this, the computers are essential since their behavior is so flexible. We hope that when a child does something that does not quite work out, he will say, "Oh, isn't it interesting that I came out with this peculiar result. What procedure in my head could have resulted in something like this?" The idea is that thinking is a process and if your thinking does something that you don't want it to do you should be able to say something microscopic and interesting about it and not something enveloping and evaluative about yourself as a person. (Bernstein, 1982, pp. 123–24)

References

Bernstein, Jeremy. *Science Observed: Essays Out of My Mind.* New York: Basic Books, 1982.

Beyers, Charlotte. "Telephone Gives Drill New Twist." *Electronic Education* 3 (October 1983): 52–53.

Blair, Marjorie. "Florida's Poet Laureate 'The Best Will Recognize the Worth Immediately.'" *Electronic Education* 2 (November 1982): 11–12.

Brawley, Rod, and Peterson, Barbara. "Interactive Videodisc: An Innovative Instructional System." *American Annals of the Deaf* (September 1983): 685–700.

Clement, Frank J. "Affective Considerations in Computer-Based Education." *Educational Technology* 21 (April 1981): 28–32.

Crowell, Doris C. "Educational Technology Research: Should We Teach Children How to Learn from Television?" *Educational Technology* 21 (December 1981): 18–22.

Electronic Learning 1 (September/October 1981): 1–72.

Electronic Learning 1 (November/December 1981): 1–84.

EPIEgram Equipment. "The Ultimate Wired Community." 9e (October 1980): 1–2.

Fletcher, David B. "Oral Language and the Language Arts Teacher." *Language Arts* 58 (February 1981): 219–24.

Gilbert, Kathleen. "Electronic Teaching, New Responsibilities." *Media Methods* 18 (December 1981): 13.

Heard, Alex. "Researcher Seeks to Assess How the Revolution in Information Technology Will Affect Schools." *Education Week* 1 (February 2, 1982): 12–16.

Hennings, Dorothy Grant. "Input: Enter the Word-Processing Computer." *Language Arts* 58 (January 1981): 18–22.

"Into the Electronic Learning Era: Implications for Education and Psychological Research: An Interview with Mary Alice White." *Educational Technology* 21 (September 1981): 9–13.

Kaplan, Don. *Video in the Classroom: A Guide to Creative Television.* Knowledge Industry Publications, 1980.

Kimmel, Stephen. "Hte Proofreader Porgrams." [sic] *Creative Computing* 8 (March 1982): 14–19.

Levin, Dan. "Microcomputers: Out of the Toy Chest and Into the Classroom." *Success By Design* (the best from *Executive Educator*): 5–7.

Levin, James A.; Boruta, Marcia J.; and Vasconcellos, Mary T. "Microcomputer-based Environments for Writing: A Writer's Assistant." In *Classroom Computers in Cognitive Science,* edited by Alex Cherry Wilkinson. New York: Academic Press, 1983.

Miles, Paul L. "Student Video Self-Critiques." *Communication Education* 30 (July 1981): 280–83.

Smith, Charles R., and Kiefer, Kathleen E. "Using the Writer's Workbench Programs at Colorado State University." *Sixth International Conference on Computers and the Humanities,* edited by Sarah K. Burton and Douglas D. Short. Rockville, Md.: Computer Science Press, 1983.

Strickler, Darryl S., and Farr, Beverly. "TV as a Tool to Improve Basic Communication Skills?" *Language Arts* 56 (September 1979): 634–40.

TC Today (Newsletter of Teachers College, Columbia University) 10 (Fall 1981): 4–5.

Wall, Shavaun M., and Taylor, Nancy E. "Using Interactive Computer Programs in Teaching Higher Conceptual Skills: An Approach to Instruction in Writing." *Educational Technology* 22 (February 1982): 13–17.

Wisconsin Center for Education Research News. "Microcomputers: New Wave in School Practice and Education Research." (Fall 1981/Winter 1982): 1–3.

Integrating the Language Arts

R. R. Allen, University of Wisconsin

Robert W. Kellner, University of Wisconsin

A growing number of educators are calling for the integration of the language arts. Undergraduate language arts methods textbooks reveal the folly of teaching the language skills in isolation from each other. Teachers are told that "the Language Arts are so strongly interrelated that no single skill can be taught in isolation" (Tiedt and Tiedt, 1978, p. 4), and that "the strands of language study are so interwoven that speaking, listening, reading, and writing activities are almost indistinguishable" (Burns and Broman, 1979, p. 3).

Many researchers in language development and language learning also stress the strong interrelationship of the language arts. For example, Loban's research with 338 children revealed that "those who were in the highest quartile of reading and writing ability at grade six were the same subjects who were notably powerful in oral language in the primary grades." On the strength of this evidence he concluded that "there is no hope of building a successful program in reading or writing on an inadequate base of oral language" (Loban, 1978, p. 104).

The call for integration is sounded as well by leading professional organizations. The National Council of Teachers of English devoted the entire April 1977 issue of *Language Arts,* the official journal of the Elementary Section, to the theme "Integrating the Language Arts." A casual perusal of almost any issue of that journal will reveal articles testifying in behalf of language arts integration and in the spring of 1984, NCTE published a full collection titled *Integrating the Language Arts in the Elementary School.* Similarly, William Work, Executive Secretary of the Speech Communication Association, has observed that it is counterproductive "to think of reading, writing, listening, speaking, and viewing as separate behaviors." Rather, he urges that we see human communication as "a dynamic complex of interdependent systems involving different 'mixes' of thinking and speaking and listening and reading and writing and viewing and feeling" (Work, 1978, p. 336).

Have these calls for integration changed actual teaching practices? It appears not. Ironically, while many elementary language arts textbooks advocate integration, they contain separate chapters on reading, writing, speaking, and listening. And in the schools, the integration of the language arts peaks in kindergarten and declines as grade level increases. By the time the child reaches secondary school, language arts instruction is neatly fragmented into separate courses. On the college level, the fragments are divided even further.

This chapter was motivated by the disparity between what is advocated and what is practiced in language arts teaching. The remainder of this section describes an integrated kindergarten classroom and identifies two major approaches to extending such an integration throughout the elementary and secondary levels. Subsequent sections will describe model designs of integration used in elementary and secondary settings and will consider the advantages of integration.

Integration: An Illustrative View

On a crisp February afternoon in Sun Prairie, Wisconsin, eighteen kindergarten students met with their teacher, Mary McDonnell, in the kindergarten complex of the Royal Oaks Elementary School. It was an ordinary day for the students. They hung their coats in the cloakroom and entered the classroom, which was bedecked with the red-and-white trappings of an impending Valentine's Day.

The afternoon began with an intimate gathering of the children in a semi-circle around the teacher in the front of the room. The children were asked to identify the day and the date from a colorful calendar posted on the front wall. The teacher then took attendance as she said "good afternoon" to each child by name. Each child responded by saying "good afternoon." A volunteer was handed a card by the teacher and enthusiastically led the daily name cheer: "Give me an R; give me an A; give me a C; give me an H; give me an A; give me an E; give me an L—Rachael, Rachael, Rachael!" Rachael looked pleased.

The teacher then drew word cards from folders for the children to read—first common names, then colors. The children called out the words in unison. It was then time to invent words around the sound [æ]. Under the teacher's direction, the words *cat, mat, hat, fat, rat, pan, man, fan, Nan,* and *Ann* were sounded (and we learned from *Ann* that two n's still say [n]). A volunteer wrote sentences on the chalkboard using the sounded words: "Cat sat on a mat," "Fat rat sat on a hat," and "The man sat on a fan." After the teacher dictated the last sentence, and the student wrote it correctly, the teacher said, "I tried to fool you by using 'the' in the last sentence; you can't sound out the word 'the'." The student replied, "You can't fool me; I'm too smart."

Taking their places around circular tables, the children prepared for a listening exercise. As the teacher played sounds from an audiotape, the children drew pictures of the objects which make the sounds on a workbook page entitled "Donald Has a Dream." Donald had dreams of a dog, a doorbell, a drum, and a duck. The children were then asked to share one of their dreams with classmates and to talk about the way the dreams make them feel. They all agreed when a little boy said that it was "scary" when he dreamed that a monster with a blue face came into his bedroom.

Next, the children were directed to an open space near the piano for additional listening games: This is what I can do, now I pass it on to you; Simon says; and "music (and instructions) to move by" presented by a record player. The teacher then played the piano as groups of students sang "Four of Us Were Singing"—first in English and then in German.

The children next dramatized "Three Billy Goats Gruff," picking their own replacements when it was time for a change in "cast." Then, the teacher presented a slide/talk show on the theme, "If you were born in Alaska." Following the show the teacher asked questions about what the children had seen and heard. A milk and cookie break ensued.

As this narrative illustrates, Mary McDonnell was successful in integrating the language arts into the entire kindergarten curriculum. Her students communicated about days and dates and music and Alaska (and milk and cookies, for that matter). In an hour of instruction, an intelligent and creative teacher had provided a skillful integration of the language arts —reading, writing, speaking, and listening. Additionally, she had provided opportunities for children to practice social amenities, to practice group rituals, to fantasize, to express feelings, to follow directions, to take turns, to dramatize, and to engage in informative listening.

Major Approaches to Integration

Many teachers still teach the language arts in a fragmented way. During the school day, time periods are designated for reading, spelling, punctuation, handwriting, composition, and the like. Such instruction may be criticized for promoting an unnatural view of language. Language is not simply a collection of unrelated elements; rather, it is a process through which ideas and feelings are shared with others.

This traditional approach represents an extreme pole on the integration continuum (Figure 1). This extreme represents fragmentation rather than integration of the language arts. Sub-skills or elements are studied for their own sake in separate time slots. When sub-skills are so isolated, students do not experience the process of using language to accomplish their communicative goals.

At the opposite pole of the continuum, language is perceived as a tool for learning—a way of thinking about the concepts inherent within all subjects. Students write, speak, listen, and read as avenues for comprehending, interpreting, analyzing, evaluating, and creatively responding to the content of various subjects.

Those who argue for such a global integration of the language arts point out that language learning differs substantially from the learning of other subjects in the school curriculum. They question, in fact, whether the language arts should even be considered a separate discipline. Instead, they perceive language as "the main ingredient in our symbolic life," which "not only operates within every aspect of our lives but . . . [serves] to integrate the diversity of experience into a harmonious whole" (Moffett and Wagner, 1976, p. 42). Thus, they conclude that the proper way to teach the language arts is to encourage their use as students explore ideas across the curriculum and in everyday life.

At first glance, the notion of global integration may seem troublesome to teachers. It appears to demand a high level of teacher creativity, extensive planning, access to multiple resources, and administrative commitment. Teachers may also fear that total integration of the language arts will lead to neglect of the "content" of language instruction.

Given these reservations, teachers may wish to assume a more moderate level of integration in order to gain confidence and familiarity with this new approach. Such a moderate stance is represented by the midpoint of the continuum. In this approach, reading, writing, speaking, and listening are blended and used to reinforce each other. In designing communication

Language Arts as a means, a tool across the disciplines	Language Arts as communicative forms, as a means unto themselves	Language Arts as separate disciplines
Life experiences	Interrelated language acts	Separate time slots
Language unlocks all learning	Unifying principles	Isolated skills
Communicative goals	meaning	Elements studied for their own sake
Communicative growth	audience	Lack of communicative purpose
	context	
	content & form	
	Communicative goals	
	Communicative growth	

Figure 1. An Integration Continuum.

activities, the teacher attempts to use all of the language arts. To arrive at this stage on the continuum, a teacher would need to be concerned not with time blocks, but with student communicative needs and interests along with unifying principles inherent in all communicative situations—purpose, audience, context, the marriage of content and form, and those skills needed to transmit a particular message vital to the sender and the receiver. A teacher needs to see that communicators always face these issues at all levels of sophistication.

The following section describes sample models of integration representative of the moderate stance. The perceived advantages of such an integration will be examined in the final section.

Models of Integration

Since there are a number of models of integration, the three models discussed here are meant simply to illustrate the range of such models available to teachers and educators. The first model focuses on K–8 grades, the next program is intended for K–10, and the final example is directed at the secondary level.

The first two models are part of the National Diffusion Network which contains 200 programs consisting of validated, U.S. Office of Education approved projects. These nationally disseminated projects have demonstrated significant student achievement, cost-effectiveness, and suitability for adoption in nearly any school district. The secondary model is a new, teacher-developed curriculum currently being piloted in a number of Wisconsin secondary schools.

Individualized Language Arts Model

An integration of the language arts can take many forms. One program is the Individualized Language Arts Project from Weehawken, New Jersey. It has been most successfully used at the K–8 levels and has been adopted in a host of states. The project seeks to improve teacher competence in the methodology of writing instruction and to develop student proficiency in composing skills.

Inherent in the program is the integration of reading, writing, speaking, and listening. The Weehawken model merges these language acts within a "Communication Spiral"—a series of suggested procedures that may be adapted by participating teachers. Depending on student readiness and achievement, teachers may decide to enter the suggested sequence at different points, may skip steps, or may repeat a procedure.

There are eleven steps in the Communication Spiral of the Individualized Language Arts Program (Ezor, 1974, pp. 8–11).

Step 1: Begin with a shared experience involving content areas (e.g., science, social studies, art, health). This shared experience may involve an interesting reading, a television program, a play, a painting, a musical selection, an event, or a personality in the school or in the news.

Step 2: Have students talk about the shared experience through small-group or whole-class discussion. Student talk is a necessary step before any writing occurs.

Step 3: Plan a specific writing activity aimed at carrying forth the interest generated by the discussion. The writing activity should be carefully explained so that students understand the purpose for writing and the intended audience.

Step 4: Supply students with a starter technique. One starter involves formulating one or more complete sentences from a series of words and/or groups of words (phrases or clauses). This technique is called "sentence synthesis" because a student creates sentences with a variety of words from his or her sight and/or oral vocabulary.

Step 5: Let students write a first draft.

Step 6: Have students silently proofread the first drafts. Next, have them read their drafts aloud to the teacher, a friend, a small group of students, or to the entire class. A number of different strategies may be used to stimulate interaction (e.g., mini-conferencing, peer-group advising, or listening to and discussing audio recordings of the writing). Throughout this stage, emphasis should be given to the clarity of the student's message, its originality, its audience appeal, and its intended effect. At this time, only secondary attention is given to matters of form and to surface features.

Step 7: Post a "Checklist of Directions" that identifies matters of content and form that should be of interest to student writers as they revise their drafts. A checklist might include such questions as

> Can I make my composition more interesting by using some of the words I have learned in reading or class discussion?
>
> Am I using all the words that I can in my story?
>
> Am I sure of the meaning of each word or do I need to use my dictionary?

Step 8: Assist students in applying the "improver" techniques to their first drafts. Improver techniques involve different ways of revising sentences or paragraphs. Students can improve either by adding or deleting certain words, combining sentences, or moving different words or phrases. These techniques can also be applied to larger units of thought.

Step 9: Direct students to read their messages aloud again. This time the improved drafts receive the attention of a classmate, a small group, or the whole class. The teacher may vary audience size as the topic and task demand. By having students read the improved writings aloud, the teacher advances the notions that listening is important and that writing is communication to real audiences.

Step 10: Conduct a formal or informal evaluation of final student drafts. During the final evaluation, both teachers and students should pay particular attention to how well the paper has fulfilled its purpose and satisfied the demands of audience.

Step 11: Initiate or create a new shared experience and begin the communication spiral again. It should be noted that a spiral may be scheduled over a three or four day period.

To illustrate these steps in the communication spiral, consider how they are implemented in a fourth-grade classroom. After reading and discussing *Charlotte's Web,* the teacher and students decide that "friendship" is a vital topic. The teacher leads a discussion of friendship and prompts questions and comments about such concepts as loyalty, trust, giving, and sacrifice. Words important to the students become "key" words which are written on the chalkboard.

The teacher suggests "friendship" as a possible writing topic; the students agree. After some additional talk, they decide that they will write paragraphs describing friendship. The students further agree that they may refer to people in the class or outside the class in their writings. One student suggests as a starter sentence the notion that "Friends must give and receive." Others agree.

Since the students have previously used this "sentence synthesis" starter technique, they go right to work, glancing periodically at the "key" words on the chalkboard. While the students write, the teacher circulates to answer questions and provide encouragement.

After the rough drafts are finished, students are given a few minutes to read their paragraphs silently. Then they pair off and read paragraphs to each other. The students are told to talk about how well the paragraphs develop the original topic sentence, and they exchange comments and suggestions.

The teacher then discusses editing tips for revising paragraphs and writes each tip on the chalkboard. Students ask questions and make comments about the tips. As they rewrite and edit their paragraphs, the teacher again circulates—questioning, encouraging, and praising.

When the students have completed rewriting, they meet in small groups to read the paragraphs to each other. After the small groups complete discussions, the teacher leads a whole-class discussion of such questions as: Why must friends both receive and give? Does the use of real people in the paragraphs improve or weaken the description? What things did you really like about some of the paragraphs read in your groups?

The preceding illustration demonstrates how a classroom stimulus, such as *Charlotte's Web,* can inspire a blending of the language arts as students complete the communication spiral. In addition to writing, students read, discuss, compose in groups, listen attentively, follow directions for writing and oral reading, and interact in dyadic, small-group, and whole-class structures.

In validating the Individualized Language Arts system, educators gather data from experimental and control groups in a number of settings. One study of the Weehawken project revealed that students in the experimental group wrote longer, richer, and more varied sentences and recorded significant gains in vocabulary and T-unit scores. Students in the experimental groups also surpassed students in the control groups in such matters as organization, punctuation, spelling, and overall clarity (Ezor, pp. 2–3).

The authors have found that ten to fifteen hours of workshops are needed to train teachers to implement the twenty-two writing techniques that are included in the Communication Spiral. These techniques—"starters" and "improvers"—promote skillful teacher intervention in the composing process. Information about training and materials for this model are available from each state education agency.

Model for Language Improvement

In Kenosha, Wisconsin, a K–10 Title I program, "Academic Improvement through Language Experience," offers students in this industrial community an opportunity for marked language improvement (Kenosha Unified Schools, 1978, p. 1). The Kenosha Model is based on the philosophy that students can talk about what they have experienced, write about what they have spoken, and read about what they have written. Communication skills are developed around the concept of writing about and discussing the student's experiences. Experiences contributing to the program's success include field trips to local businesses and industries, visits to summer camps and forest areas within the school district, and in-class experiences such as food preparation, art, or media projects.

In a typical lesson, students in the fourth or fifth grade enjoy the experience of "getting to know senior citizens" (Kenosha Unified Schools, 1978, p. 88). They visit a local nursing home and converse with selected residents. Back in school, the students discuss their experience, generate a vocabulary list, and begin planning a letter or note to a pen-pal at the nursing home. The teacher reviews the parts of the letter (heading, greeting, body, closing, signature) and encourages students to include photographs of themselves.

Subsequent activities include a number of options. Students can invite several nursing home residents to visit the school to share with the children their special talents or experiences. One resident may decide to show the children how to make a stained-glass object or a yarn flower. Students can learn to make the object by following directions written on an experience chart. Other follow-up activities may include remembering residents on special occasions, interviewing and tape recording grandparents who tell about their experiences, and reading library selections to develop student awareness and understanding of aging people.

Overall, the objectives of this experience, cultivated over several days, encompass: conversational and interviewing skills; skills useful in writing thank-you notes, letters, and vicarious stories; listening skills through attending to different speakers; and library skills. Through such a language experience, students discuss, read, write, listen, and think as they enjoy communicating with elderly people.

Out of the thirty nationwide adoptions of the Kenosha Model, the Waterloo School District in Waterloo, Wisconsin, was awarded a Certificate of Recognition for exemplary replication of the Kenosha Model (Jenkins and Plaisted, 1981, pp. 9–11). Two Waterloo staff members, resource teacher Barbara Plaisted and reading specialist Martha Jenkins, created a variety of lessons especially for grades 4–6. One such experience involved a visit to a local pickle and sauerkraut factory.

This lesson had several goals, including observing and sequencing the pickling process, developing pride in the local community, learning new vocabulary related to the visit, improving oral reading fluency, and developing direction-following skills. Twenty new words ranging from "preservatives" to "crunchy," "tumeric" to "alum," were generated by students after the visit. During the visit, students had a pickle-tasting session and listed words describing taste, feel, smell, and appearance. Students toured the pickle factory, took photographs of the pickle-making process, and later wrote captions for each photograph.

Follow-up tactile activities included making pickle-ham-cream rollups according to proper directions. Also, students made pickled vegetables as Valentine's Day gifts. On thank-you notes sent to the pickle factory, the students created pickle-like prints by using cut pickles and printing ink. Students also wrote a creative story about "Pesky Pickle Pet," performed a choral reading of "Ickle Me, Pickle Me, Tickle Me, Too" by Shel Silverstein, and used the tongue twister "Peter Piper Picked a Peck of Pickled Peppers."

To validate the Kenosha Model, the Peabody Picture Vocabulary Test, the Peabody Individual Achievement Test, and the Gates-MacGinitie Reading Test were administered in schools with pupils from low-income families. It was found that students demonstrated an average growth in excess of 1.5 months per month in the program.

Students at the adopter site in Waterloo demonstrated an average gain of 1.7 months per month in the program on a standardized reading test. In addition, outside evaluators, who examined pre- and post-instructional writing samples and cumulative folders, noted improvements in vocabulary, sentence syntax, and paragraph development.

The Kenosha Model and its exemplary Waterloo Model offer a language experience approach with a special resource room, outreach activities, and a rich variety of integrated language arts lessons. If teachers in small towns with limited resources can design meaningful learning activities, think of the learning potential available in more diverse communities.

The Wisconsin Alternative Curriculum Design

> In the real world, people use communication to serve a variety of functions or purposes. We use communication to give and receive information, to persuade others, to share feelings, to engage in imaginative thought, and to interact socially. Further, communication in society is directed toward specific audiences ranging from oneself, to another, to a small or large group, to a mass audience. As we communicate in life, we use a blend of language arts or processes. We read, write, speak, or listen as the occasion demands.
>
> If the above is true in the real world, then students being prepared to communicate effectively in that world ought to initiate a variety of messages differing in purpose, intended audience, and language form.
>
> Wisconsin Department of Public Instruction, 1981

This statement identifies the three major components of the design: functions of communication, audience contexts, and integration of the language arts. These components are reflected in two separate documents: a curriculum for grade nine and one for grade ten.

The Wisconsin Alternative Curriculum Design is based on a matrix (Figure 2) developed in 1977 by R. R. Allen. Through familiarity with the five major functions of communication and the five major audience contexts for communication, teachers can develop curricula that reflect the variety of functions and audiences served by communication in society.

The Functions of Communication

In 1976, members of the Speech Communication Association's National Project on Speech Communication Competencies sought to identify the major functions (uses, purposes) of communication in everyday life. Borrowing from the earlier work of Wells (1973) and Halliday (1973), they concluded that communication is used for the purposes of informing, expressing feeling, imagining, ritualizing, and controlling (Allen and Brown, 1976). Each of these functions will be considered in turn.

Informing—People communicate for the purpose of informing in a wide variety of contexts: authors write informative essays; teachers

Dimension One: Functions of Communication

	Informing	Expressing Feeling	Imagining	Ritualizing	Controlling
Mass Communication					
Public Communication					
Small Group Communication					
Dyadic Communication					
Intrapersonal Communication					

(left margin, rotated) Dimension Two: Communication Contexts

Each cell involves both message initiation and message reception skills.

Figure 2. A Matrix for Generating Curricula in Communication.

lecture and distribute handouts to inform; and students write informative reports, give demonstration speeches, and participate in discussions about information. As receivers, people read the morning paper, search out information in the library, watch the evening news on television, and read their favorite "self-help" book before retiring for the night.

Expressing feeling—Affective communication is a necessary and powerful ingredient of life. People initiate and receive various messages expressing positive and negative feelings about themselves and others. They express positive feelings of love, appreciation, and admiration, and negative feelings of disappointment, anger, and frustration. A variety of forms are used for affective messages: poems, greeting cards, love notes, hate mail, pats on the back, a glance, a glare, a raised eyebrow, a prayer. As empathic readers and listeners, people try to see the world from the perspective of the person communicating so that they may celebrate or commiserate as appropriate.

Imagining—The imaginations of students may be engaged through a wide range of creative communication activities. Students may be given opportunities to dramatize, fantasize, tell stories, invent limericks, brainstorm, theorize, role-play, and pantomime. Through appreciative listening, viewing, and reading, students may enjoy the results of creative efforts of others whether that creativity is revealed through literature, film, television, stage, or face-to-face encounter.

Ritualizing—Many communication exchanges are largely ritualistic in nature. On any given day, people engage in such ordinary speech acts as greeting, leave-taking, introducing, teasing, commenting on the weather, and demonstrating social amenities. They perform rituals appropriate to home, school, church, bus, elevator, and office settings. Rituals are used in conversations, interviews, small-group discussions, parliamentary debates, ceremonial speeches, letters, diaries, printed invitations, thank-you notes, and announcements. As listeners and readers, people note and often respond to violations of social expectations and ceremonial requirements. From, "Hey, it's my turn," to "Point of order," they demand that ritualistic requirements be honored.

Controlling—People seek to influence the thoughts and actions of others by using such diverse strategies as threats, commands, arguments, psychological appeals, and entreaties. Controlling messages take such diverse forms as television commercials, printed advertisements, legal briefs, editorials, election posters, and schoolyard squabbles. When on the receiving end of a controlling message, one is well-advised to be a critical listener, viewer, or reader.

Communication Contexts

As people communicate for various purposes, they also communicate in diverse contexts. Communication scholars often categorize contexts by the size and/or distance of the audience.

Intrapersonal communication—Intrapersonal communication simply means talking to oneself. It takes such forms as rationalizing, goal-setting, speculating, praising, blaming, and debriefing. Intrapersonal messages may be thought, verbalized, written in diaries, or scrawled on "to do" lists.

Dyadic communication—Two-person communication is both pervasive and important. On a given day, one crosses paths with a relatively large number of people with whom one engages in dyadic exchange. Certain of these exchanges are with people who are of the greatest significance in one's life—parents, offspring, friends, life companions. The ability to establish and maintain such dyadic relationships is important to a happy and fulfilling life.

Small group communication—Two conditions are necessary for an assembly of people to be considered a small group: they must be in face-to-face contact, and they must be psychologically aware of each other. A group of strangers on a city bus are not a small group; they become one when the bus stalls in a flooded underpass and they begin discussing their predicament. Among the most significant small groups in life are families, peer groups, teams, clubs, and classroom groups.

Public communication—Public communication tends to involve larger groups of people in situations in which initiator and receiver roles are relatively fixed. Public messages are given in such diverse settings as auditoriums, banquet rooms, courtrooms, street rallies, and rock concerts.

Mass communication—The communicator and the audience in this form of communication are physically separated, necessitating the use of technology in bringing the message to the audience. Messages are often initiated by groups and are often intended for large, heterogeneous audiences. Common mass communication forms are radio and television programs, films, audiotape recordings, newspapers, and magazines.

Generating Learning Activities from the Matrix

After becoming familiar with the five functions of communication and five communication contexts, teachers may use the matrix to generate learning activities representing differing communication functions, contexts, and modes. In the Wisconsin Alternative Curriculum Design, twenty teachers generated a reading, writing, speaking, and listening activity for each of the twenty-five cells in the matrix for grades nine and ten.

For example, in developing ninth-grade learning activities for the center cell of the matrix—Imagining/Small Group Communication—the Wisconsin teachers chose to focus on the theme "Happy Families." Students begin by reading the play *You Can't Take It with You* by Kaufman and Hart. They take roles and read aloud about a loosely constructed, do-their-own-thing family. Following the reading, class discussion focuses on questions dealing with family role expectations, humor in families, rules and structures in families, the peculiarities of each character, and specific contrasts with the traditional family.

For the writing activity, entitled "Raising the Roof," students in small groups are asked to write a poem offering a comparative view of three families from a bird's eye view. As a prewriting activity, the teacher leads a discussion of catalogue poems using David Wagoner's "While Looking through the Yellow Pages." Following the discussion, groups of students are given telephone directories from outside their locale. Each group is directed to choose thirty to forty yellow page listings that evoke interesting sensory images (e.g., The Tots and Teens Shop, Pizza Palace, 28 Flavors of Ice Cream). Next, using the white pages, the groups find three interesting names of people around which families may be imagined, and attributes and interests may be assigned. After matching the families with the images, each group creates a twenty-line poem that offers a comparative view of the families while focusing on sounds and images. When the poems are completed, the groups are asked to give them titles and share them with the other groups.

For a listening activity, students view two television programs featuring "idealized pictures" of a family. Students are asked to create lists of the positive and negative qualities of the families in the two shows that they chose. They share the lists with the class and a comparison of these idealized families is developed through classroom discussion using a chalkboard listing of family qualities.

As a final activity, the students work in triads as they come to a consensus regarding their idealized family. Each triad must agree on an ideal mother, father, sister(s), and brother(s), and on an ideal home setting. Each group prepares and presents an oral report in a creative format in which each member contributes to the report.

Through this series of activities, students would give sustained attention to the nature of communication in family relationships. They would know more about family roles, family expectations, family rules and structures, and the attributes of harmonious family life than they did when instruction began. Additionally, they would have had a chance to engage in appreciative reading and listening and a chance to ponder the charactertistics of plays and television dramas that contribute to receiver enjoyment. Finally, they would have experienced two opportunities to initiate creative messages and to experience the joy of imagining.

Advantages of an Integrated Curriculum

The systems discussed in the preceding section are based on the premise that integration is preferable to isolation in teaching the language arts. Among the advantages that may be assigned to integrated language arts curricula are the following.

Encourages a Better Balance among the Language Arts

It is widely recognized that the study of literature dominates secondary school and college English curricula. In Wisconsin, for example, 65 percent of students in grades nine through twelve are taking literature courses, only

33 percent are taking composition or writing, and less than 20 percent are enrolled in a speech course (Department of Public Instruction, 1978–79). This skewed orientation has had serious consequences. In May of 1979, the University of Wisconsin System Basic Skills Task Force reported that "25 percent of our freshmen enter without the basic skill competencies needed for success in traditional entry level courses" (pp. 5–6).

When the reading of literature is integrated with writing, speaking, and listening activities, a better balance is achieved. In the Wisconsin Alternative Design, equal attention is given to each of the language arts. John Fortier, a Wisconsin language arts coordinator from Rhinelander, noted "the most significant characteristic of the new curriculum is its balance of activities among the four areas of listening, reading, speaking, and writing. This curriculum recognizes that these four areas must function together rather than exist separately."

Promotes Development of a Sense of Audience

James Britton and his colleagues have indicated that "the growth of a sense of audience, the growth of the ability to make adjustments and choices in writing which take account of the audience" is an important factor in the development of writing ability (Britton et al., 1975, p. 58). A sense of audience is also helpful as students read various types of printed messages.

When writing is taught in isolation in separate composition courses and reading is isolated in literature courses, the sense of audience may be difficult to develop. But when reading and writing are integrated with speaking and listening, the student is encouraged to view communication as a purposeful activity in which speakers or writers address flesh and blood listeners or readers. Blankenship and Stelzner (1979), in providing a rationale for teaching speaking in the writing classroom, observe that "the very face-to-face nature of much oral communication reminds the . . . [student] of the transactional nature of discourse" (p. 1).

Provides Rich and Varied Language Experiences

When the language arts are integrated, the curriculum is substantially enriched. By its very nature, oral communication is varied and multifaceted. People communicate orally for a variety of reasons, to a number of audiences, in a variety of contexts. The language arts curriculum is substantially broadened in scope when one includes messages that are spoken or performed, listened to or viewed.

Oral messages seek to inform, influence, dramatize, express feeling, and conform to social expectations. As we know, speakers talk to themselves, each other, small groups, public audiences, and mass audiences, and oral discourse occurs in such diverse settings as auditoriums, buses, classrooms, dining rooms, elevators, lunch counters, nature trails, stores, and zoos. Oral communication varies in form from pantomime to public speech, from conversation to courtroom ritual.

Blending the language arts also enriches each of its parts. In as much as writing is improved by opportunities to communicate orally (Emig, 1977), speaking is improved by first organizing ideas in writing. Similarly, reading and listening often inspire and improve writing and speaking.

Encourages Experiential Learning

A number of scholars have noted the fun that children have as they learn language in non-school settings (Goodman, 1980, p. 602; Nilsen and Nilsen, 1980, p. 603). Through active play, children acquire language with joy. When the language arts are integrated, teachers are more likely to use small group rather than whole-class structures. Play serves a central role in newer approaches to children's language study. "The activity has literally become a game with children performing game-like operations: guessing, searching, figuring out, solving puzzles, pantomiming, leading, inventing, and of course thinking" (Hennings, 1978, p. 37).

Each system of integration discussed in the previous section is based on active student involvement in language learning. Children learn about language by using it in purposeful communication.

Increases Communication Potentialities

In the real world, students communicate for differing purposes, with a variety of people and with varying degrees of success. How unlike that real world is the world of the classroom, where the student communicates both orally and in writing to an audience of one—the teacher. The artificiality of the school writing experience was reported by Britton and his colleagues in this way: "In school . . . it is almost always the teacher who initiates the writing and who does so by defining a writing task with more or less explicitness. Not only does he define the task but also nominates himself as audience. He is not, however, simply a one-man audience but also the sole arbiter, appraiser, grader, and judge of the performance" (Britton et al., 1975, p. 64).

In the integrated language arts classroom, communication is not perceived as something one does with the teacher in a guarded fashion. Rather, students communicate with each other individually and in small groups. They initiate messages as self or as role-player, and study and initiate messages representative of diverse media and forms.

In the richness of the integrated language arts curriculum, students acquire what Blankenship and Stelzner (1979) call "fuller awareness of all the possibilities of language" (p. 3). Students who are apprehensive and ineffectual when writing for the teacher may be confident and effective when writing for peers. Britton and his colleagues (1975) have noted the dramatic change which "comes over adolescent pupils' writing when it is genuinely directed to a peer audience" (p. 63).

Similarly, when students communicate through varying modes for varying purposes, they discover that everyone has communicative strengths and weaknesses. Some students have excellent facial expression, some gesture naturally, some use eye contact effectively, some speak with animation and fluency, some have excellent handwriting, some are skillful in using communication media, some are empathetic listeners, some are skillful in performing cultural rituals, some are gifted in pantomime, some have a dramatic flair, some are critical listeners, some are skillful questioners, some present information with clarity, and all have the potential for experiencing success in some aspect of communication.

Focuses Attention on Communication as Process

It is fashionable today to talk about writing as a process rather than a product. Increasingly, educators have come to realize the importance of talk during that stage of the writing process when ideas "incubate." For example, Britton and his colleagues (1975) note that "of all the things teachers are now doing to make their pupils' approach to writing more stimulating, and the writing itself seem a more integral part of the manifold activities of the classroom, it is the encouragement of different kinds of talk which is the commonest and most productive factor" (p. 29).

It is important that students come to see all communication as a process. There is something about oral communication instruction that encourages such a perspective. Instruction in public address has always offered a view of the speaker with an intent, making choices as a message is shaped and adapted in the light of audience beliefs, expectations, and values. Instruction in interpersonal communication has always viewed communication as a transaction between two or more people in which the roles of sender and receiver change as the process unfolds. Instruction in mass communication has always viewed such messages as a complex process involving multiple senders, intervening technology, and heterogeneous and distributed audiences.

Having evaluated the Wisconsin design, Pauline Pray, Steven's Point Senior High School English Chairperson, noted that the process orientation of the curriculum is a "major way of avoiding the product trap, where what we create as communicators is divorced from the dimensions of the interaction which produced it. In this curriculum students are actively engaged in the process of communication: they act, react, discuss, evaluate, plan and act again in a rich variety of pertinent experiences."

Observations

When examining model programs that purport to be integrative, one soon discovers that talking and listening are used as tools for achieving reading and writing improvement. While many of these programs can demonstrate validity by changing scores on reading and writing measures, student growth in speaking and listening skills has not been demonstrated. It is important that model programs of integration demonstrate success in improving oral communication skills as well as written communication skills.

If authentic integration is to take place in the secondary school English curriculum, changes must occur. The secondary school teachers who implemented the Wisconsin Alternative Curriculum Design soon noticed that literature receives less attention than in traditional secondary English curricula. When an attempt is made to balance instruction in the language arts, the current preoccupation with literature at the expense of the language arts must be corrected. The assumption that teaching of literature leads to growth in student reading and writing skills must surely be questioned. One wonders what value was taken from the literature-dominated secondary school English curriculum by the matriculating students in the University of Wisconsin system who could neither read nor write at a level commensurate with basic college survival.

Finally, teachers who choose the path of integration will find their professional lives substantially enriched. In the Wisconsin Alternative Curriculum Design, traditional teachers of English marveled at the wealth of messages that becomes available for consideration when speaking and listening are assigned equal importance with reading and writing. Similarly, teachers of speech communication were delighted by the realization that literature offers insights that illumine the nature of human communication in the oral tradition and that writing has value as a pre-speaking activity much as speaking has value as a pre-writing activity. Teachers of different disciplines have much to learn from each other when they cross disciplinary boundaries seeking integration.

Questions for Consideration

At what point on the "Integration Continuum" would you place your teaching of the language arts? Ideally, at what point would you like to be?

If you were to place the three model programs of integration on the "Continuum," where would they fall? In your estimation, which of these models holds the greatest potential for your school?

Do all of the advantages of integration pertain to your school situation? Which advantages are most attractive to you?

If you wished to increase the integration of the language arts in your school, how would you begin? What problems would you encounter? How might these problems be resolved? On what people or resources in your area might you draw?

References

Allen, R. R., and Brown, Kenneth L. *Developing Communication Competence in Children.* Skokie, Ill.: National Textbook Company, 1976.

Blankenship, Jane, and Stelzner, Sara Latham. *Speech Communication Activities in the Writing Classroom.* Urbana, Ill.: ERIC Clearinghouse on Reading and Communication Skills, 1979.

Britton, James; Burgess, Tony; Martin, Nancy; McLeod, Alex; and Rosen, Harold. *The Development of Writing Abilities 11-18.* London: Macmillan Education, 1975.

Burns, Paul Clay, and Broman, Betty L. *The Language Arts in Childhood Education.* 4th ed. Chicago: Rand McNally College Publishing Company, 1979.

Emig, Janet. *The Composing Process of Twelfth Graders* (Research Report No. 13). Urbana, Ill.: National Council of Teachers of English, 1971.

Ezor, Edwin. *Individualized Language Arts: Diagnosis, Prescription, Evaluation.* Weehawken, N.J.: Weehawken Board of Education, 1974.

Goodman, Yetta M. "From a University Faculty Member." *Language Arts* 57 (1980): 601-3.

Halliday, M. A. K. *Explorations in the Functions of Language.* London: Edward Arnold, 1973.

Hennings, Dorothy Grant. *Communication in Action: Dynamic Teaching of the Language Arts.* Chicago: Rand McNally College Publishing Company, 1978.

Jenkins, Martha, and Plaisted, Barbara. "ESEA Title IV-C Adopter/Adapter Evaluation Report." Waterloo, Wis.: Waterloo Public Schools, 1981.

Kenosha Unified Schools. *Kenosha Model Sampler.* Kenosha, Wis.: 1978.

Loban, Walter. "Relationships between Language and Literacy." In *Perspectives on Literacy,* edited by Richard Beach and P. David Pearson. Minneapolis, Minn.: University of Minnesota, College of Education, 1978.

Moffett, James, and Wagner, Betty Jane. *Student-Centered Language Arts and Reading, K-13: A Handbook for Teachers.* 2nd ed. Boston: Houghton Mifflin Company, 1976.

Nilsen, Alleen, and Nilsen, Don. "From Authors." *Language Arts* 57 (1980): 603-4.

Tiedt, Sidney W., and Tiedt, Iris M. *Language Arts Activities for the Classroom.* Boston: Allyn and Bacon, Inc., 1978.

University of Wisconsin System. Basic Skills Task Force. *Final Report* (May 1979).

Wells, Gordon. *Coding Manuals for the Description of Child Speech.* Bristol, England: University of Bristol, School of Education, 1973.

Wisconsin Department of Public Instruction. *Enrollment Reports,* 1976 and 1979.

Wisconsin Department of Public Instruction. *The Wisconsin Alternative Curriculum Design in Basic English/Communicative Skills, Grade 9.* 1981.

Wisconsin Department of Public Instruction. *The Wisconsin Alternative Curriculum Design in Basic English/Communicative Skills, Grade 10.* 1981.

Work, William. "Toward Comprehensive Communication Literacy." *Communication Education* 27 (November 1978): 336–42.

Assessing Children's Speaking, Listening, and Writing Skills

Linda Reed, CEMREL, Inc.

It's 4 p.m., and Marlene Harris, a teacher at Kimbark Elementary School, is making her way very slowly through traffic to her southside Chicago apartment after a long week—and only a few surprises—in her fifth-grade classroom. The week was not normal, because next week is testing week, but that isn't all that made it hectic. Cedric's mother finally returned her call about a conference to discuss Cedric's sudden reluctance to talk in the classroom. A new transfer student appeared in the doorway this morning—the teacher received an almost empty record file on him yesterday. Doreen, on the way to school Wednesday morning, saw a dog get hit by a car, and the teacher found it difficult trying to help her sort out her feelings and fears. Judy had helped, though, when she started to talk about how her canary died. No, not too many surprises. With luck, next week will bring no surprises at all.

What happened in Marlene Harris' classroom during the week was not unusual. She is the kind of teacher that stays on top of events in her class-room. She does not want to wait very long before helping Cedric with his problem, because his silence is having an effect on his schoolwork and on the work of his two closest friends. Cedric even refuses to play with them at recess. Harris' plan is to try to get Cedric to start a journal. He can share it with her or with other children as much or as little as he likes.

And the new child. If only some of his other teachers had added com-ments about the child's strengths and weaknesses to the reports in the file. Some samples of his writing would have helped, too. As it is, it will take Harris much longer to discover his needs and to find out how he can con-tribute to the growth of other children in the class. The fact that the child will undergo testing may help to shed some light on the situation, but the teacher will have to look well beyond those test scores to see how he will fit in her class.

It seems as if every semester a child watches a dog or cat die, hit by a car as it dashes out into a busy street. Growing up in Chicago is an education in itself. As sad as it is, it might be good timing for Doreen. The teacher has been nudging Doreen along in her writing, trying to encourage her to write about things that mean a lot to her, but Doreen has long since learned that the important thing is to try to please the teacher. Maybe this accident will help her make the leap into writing that grows out of her own need to express herself instead of her need to please the teacher. Her willingness to talk to Judy about it is a good starting point.

All of the children seem slightly on edge because of next week's tests. After eight months with them, though, Harris feels good about the students' readiness. With the exception of the new student, whose ability is unknown, the students in the class should test out at about the level the teacher has mentally assigned them.

Like most teachers, Harris spends much of her day diagnosing the needs of individual children and making slight adjustments in instruction based on her perception of those needs. To find out those needs, she seeks as much input as possible—the children's talk among themselves and with the teacher, their experiences at home and going to and from school, their writing, results of large- and small-group discussions, information from parents, and results of tests, from quizzes to major criterion-referenced tests to norm-referenced standardized tests

This chapter reviews a number of concepts and issues that are important considerations in the approach toward assessment that Harris uses— concepts and issues that are important regardless of the specific classroom evaluation techniques used. The chapter also describes how a teacher might use several techniques to assess the communication competence of children —techniques that apply equally well at both the elementary and secondary levels.

A Look at the Issues

Teachers have raised a number of issues related to assessing oral communication and written communication, both at the classroom level and at district, state, and national levels. Some of these issues are described on the following pages. Like most educators, we can describe the issues but find it difficult to offer solutions that address the many concerns of classroom teachers. Teachers, themselves, must be the source of the solutions. Like Marlene Harris, the individual classroom teacher will adjust instruction based on his or her own priorities, the needs of students involved, and the teacher's perceptions of what works.

Among the issues discussed in this chapter are those involving the availability of assessment instruments, conflicts in definitions, concerns about curriculum, demands placed on teacher time, and mismatches between classroom instruction and standardized tests.

Speaking and Listening

Assessment of speaking and listening skills is more difficult to discuss than assessment of writing skills because we know so much less about speaking and listening as a curriculum area. Most children begin school already knowing how to use language skillfully, so the goal of classroom instruction has been to give them opportunities to practice their skills and expand them through performing. For example, students' listening skills are sharpened when teachers have them give feedback about or answer questions on information they receive from teachers, peers, and stories read aloud in class.

Teachers have increasingly been told that their responsibility for oral communication instruction goes beyond having children perform and respond to teacher questions. In 1978, Congress enacted the Basic Skills Improvement Act—Title II—which broadened the definition of the basic skills to include "communication, both oral and written." A growing number of states now require that oral communication be made a part of the elementary school curriculum. Speech courses have long been a part of the secondary school curriculum. Barbara Lieb-Brilhart has pointed out, however, that these courses are usually taken by students who are self-assured and confident of their ability to perform orally (1982), rather than by the many students who need to improve skills so they will be able to function effectively when they leave high school.

Although many school districts now require explicit instruction in speaking and listening, they have not been able to answer many important questions—Just what is oral communication? What is the best curriculum? And how can speaking and listening skills be assessed?

Educators and researchers have not been able to agree on the definition of communication competence. However, Larson and his colleagues, in a study of the literature (1978), found that certain notions were common to all or most definitions. Larson's group developed a definition incorporating those major concepts: "We have chosen to define communication competence as the ability to demonstrate knowledge of the communicative behavior socially appropriate in a given situation. . . ." (p. 24). This definition is common to most definitions in these aspects:

Ability to demonstrate	This implies a performing function, a set of skills that the individual

	demonstrates and that can be examined.
Knowledge	Communication competence is influenced by a person's linguistic capability.
Communicative behavior	The definition is restricted to behavior that is related to communication.
Socially appropriate	The communication is subject to socially prescribed rules. Communication behavior that is appropriate at home may not be appropriate in the principal's office, just as communication behavior that is appropriate in America may not be appropriate in the Far East. Competence, then, is to some extent determined by degree of adherence to cultural norms.
In a given situation	The communicator must take into account all of the elements of the context in which the communication occurs.

Although speech communication educators agree that teaching speaking and listening skills should be an integral part of the school curriculum, they do *not* agree on how children should be taught communication competence. Brown and his colleagues (1979), through a review of the communication education literature and classroom observations, identified five major approaches to instruction in oral communication:

1. The Component Skills Approach—the teacher focuses attention on mastery of clusters of specific skills.

2. The Communication Activities Approach—students experience a variety of oral communication activities that prepare them to engage in situations found in everyday life.

3. The Participant Network Approach—students receive systematic instruction in interpersonal, small-group, public, and mass communication.

4. The Referential Communication Games Approach—students engage in activities that build the speaker's ability to describe an object—a

referent—so that a listener will be able to identify the object.

5. The Functional Communication Approach—instruction focuses on developing a wide range of communication skills and behaviors in five areas—feeling, informing, controlling, imagining, and ritualizing.

Regardless of the approach that teachers use in developing children's communication competence, formal assessment procedures are difficult to establish. Informal procedures, like those Marlene Harris uses, have been used in classrooms as long as there have been teachers. She encourages children to talk to her and to one another, and she listens closely and watches how they listen to and respond to one another. She has them work in small groups and assesses both the manner in which they solve problems and the actual solutions. She asks children questions and encourages them to ask questions of her and their peers. She encourages children to perform and to evaluate themselves, while asking other children to offer suggestions.

Most formal communication competence tests present problems to school districts. Although speaking and listening are inseparable acts (for example, even if I am speaking aloud alone in the middle of a field, I am listening to myself), most tests of communication skills separate speaking from listening. Tests of listening are usually multiple-choice, paper-and-pencil tests of literal comprehension (Brown, Backlund, Gurry, and Jandt, 1979; Larson, Backlund, Redmond, and Barbour, 1978; Lundsteen, 1979; and Rubin, Daly, McCroskey, and Mead, in preparation). Although many tests of speaking ability involve speaker performance, test and rater reliability and time and equipment needs present serious obstacles for teachers and administrators (Brown, 1982; Rubin et al., in preparation).

Choosing a test for assessing communication competence can be a confusing experience. First, if a school district has established its own goals and developed an instructional program to match those goals, it is unlikely that the district will be able to find a published test that measures the skills students have been taught (Rubin et al., in preparation). In addition, a wide range of skills is assessed by published tests. Some measure students' attitudes about communications, some measure communication apprehension, and many test the ability to recognize Standard English in a written passage (Brown, 1982; Rubin et al., in preparation).

State education agencies and school districts nationally are making attempts to solve the problems inherent in tests of speaking and listening ability. These improvements, however, are very slow in coming, and may be even slower in reaching the classroom teacher. Teachers who have a mandate to include speaking and listening instruction in the curriculum are justifiably concerned about teaching skills that even the "experts" find difficult to assess.

Writing

One of the original three Rs, writing has always been an explicit part of the school curriculum. In most classrooms, teachers have students learn about the conventions of writing in an established sequence, from learning to write their names and the names of familiar objects to writing short sentences, to putting sentences together in paragraph form to, finally, constructing themes and essays. It is believed that if children master the mechanics and have opportunities to apply that knowledge through writing assignments, they will become reasonably good writers.

The fact is that most students do learn to write—they "write" grocery lists, letters, checks, postcards—but few use writing as a means of learning, of stretching the mind, just as only a few of us leave school as avid readers. Some children who started school eager to learn discovered that writing meant punishment—"I will not throw spitballs. I will not throw spitballs. I will not throw spitballs. . . ." Many discovered that teachers cared more about periods and commas, and spelling and awkward sentences than about how children felt or the messages they tried to convey.

Over the past decade, a group of educators and researchers have urged that schools take a new look at writing instruction. They suggest that teachers view writing as a series of processes, and that they encourage children to do so. Learning how to write, they suggest, must be experienced in a classroom environment that encourages risk-taking and that builds on young children's extensive knowledge of language. The teacher's role is as a warm, accepting respondent who creates a trusting relationship with each child. In the early stages of writing—prewriting and drafting—children concentrate on working through their ideas and feelings about a topic. Only in the later stages—revising and editing—do they become concerned with organization, structure, and mechanics. Most important, children write as often as possible.

What does this mean for the teacher? It may mean looking for additional opportunities to have children write in the classroom, being careful that time is not taken away from other subjects. It may mean finding ways to ensure that children will still be able to score well on the year-end standardized test that will focus on their mechanical skills. It will surely mean finding creative ways to give children feedback on all of the additional writing they will do.

Dealing with the Issues—A Careful Balancing Act

Teachers have long been aware of the issues surrounding assessment of writing instruction and, to a lesser degree, of the many issues involved in assessing children's speaking and listening abilities. Every teacher has had to come to grips with his or her own beliefs about instruction in these areas and with how those beliefs match the priorities of the principal, district administrators, parents, and others who influence their classroom decisions.

Teachers like Marlene Harris must ask—and answer—a number of questions before they finally decide how they will assess the progress of students.

What methods of assessment match the goals that I have set for my instructional program? What are the most effective means of measuring the objectives that I have established? Each year, elementary level teachers are faced with planning an entire, year-long educational program for the children entering their classes. The previous year's program may form the foundation for this plan, but the new group of children will have different strengths and needs and new combinations of backgrounds, experiences, and attitudes toward school.

Decisions made by teachers at the secondary level are more narrow in focus but are just as detailed. For example, a science teacher must decide not only what concepts to teach in what order, but also how much time to give to each, how to structure the classroom, what techniques to use to encourage student participation, whether there might be ways to do integrated projects with teachers in other subject areas, and what additional outside resources might be available to the class.

Questions of classroom management, time management, how to help children with special needs, efficient handling of the paper load generated by students and by the school administration, and how to maintain appropriate levels of communication with parents and other caretakers are important at all levels.

Teachers must make many specific decisions regarding instruction in writing, speaking, and listening. For example, do they want children to write once a day, once a week, or as the opportunity arises? Will a specific time be set aside for writing, or will children be encouraged to write whenever they feel the desire or need to do so? Will children be encouraged to view writing as a process, with the development of ideas the goal in the early stages and attention to details important in the later stages? Or will children be asked to spend a specific period writing and then hand in a polished piece for grading? The period can range from fifteen minutes for a piece for which the topic is assigned to a month for special projects.

The choices made by the teacher will determine the assessment techniques and the classroom organization strategies that will be used. This is especially true in speaking and listening instruction. Will the children be encouraged to do assignments individually, or will they be encouraged to talk with classmates and perhaps to solve problems in small groups? Will oral communication instruction be accomplished as an integral part of all of the subject areas, or will a specific time be set aside each day or week for instruction? Will children be asked to perform periodically in front of classmates (show and tell, oral book reports, speeches, dramatic improvisations)? Or will they be asked to work together to solve problems related to situations that they are likely to encounter in and out of school? Might a combination of approaches be best? Will the focus be on individual performance or small-group work?

The decisions that the teacher makes regarding these questions and many others will determine the methods of assessment he or she will select. Marlene Harris, for example, has clearly defined the approaches that she will use in the classroom, and she has developed specific means of assessing achievement of her goals:

Harris' major classroom goal is to help the children recognize the relationships among things—to give them experiences that will allow them to draw on their knowledge of a variety of subject areas. She learned long ago, from another teacher, that integrating the subjects allows her to give far more attention to all of them than trying to teach them separately. Harris' assessment techniques are also flexible. Her overall strategy is to listen to the children, to talk with them, to ask them questions, to encourage as much communication as possible. This gives her day-to-day information about whether they are grasping what she is trying to teach them. This strategy helped her especially in the case of the Korean twins she taught several years ago.

When the twins walked into her classroom, she turned them over to several other students. They were to be special assistants to the teacher to help the twins with such things as where to go for lunch, what the bells mean, where to return workbooks at the end of the day. But they were also to help the twins with their language, and they were to report each day to other students in the class about something they had learned about the twins' language. It was a fascinating experiment, and the twins, who were ten years old, taught the class a great deal. Most importantly, Harris discovered that they were very bright and that, given the opportunity to use their own language to read and write, they progressed at normal rates. It was a hectic year but a rewarding one.

Harris knows that the success of the students, many of whom are from minority families, will depend to a great extent on their ability to use language appropriate to the situation. Using the family dialect is appropriate at home and with friends, but students will not have opportunities to become executives in major corporations if they do not understand that they will need to use standard spoken English during interviews. So Harris gives the children many chances to use language in a variety of settings, and she gives individual children help with specific skills when they need it. When they have been practicing a specific skill, she has them speak and write, using situations that will let them practice. Then she asks them to evaluate their own success and to seek feedback from peers. For these situations, Harris has developed a variety of rating forms.

So that children will be able to keep track of their own growth, Harris has created a file of portfolios. Each portfolio has samples of the child's writing (Harris has finally decided that one sample a week is enough; during the first two years, the files became bulky and unmanageable for children to work with, so the system was self-defeating), tapes and transcripts of the child's speaking, and samples of projects they have done that have integrated several subject areas. Some students decide to keep personal journals in the file, so that Harris can respond to their entries.

The children in Harris' class *will* have to take standardized tests, an inevitable fact that she has long since accepted. Now, however, she has developed a strategy that pleases her and that will let the children achieve a measure of success when they take such tests. She teaches children to deal with such tests by giving them similar tests at frequent intervals. Her tests cover material the children have focused on. She asks them what they feel they should be tested on and how they feel the test should be structured. They help determine how long they should have to complete the test and what the criteria for success should be. It has proven to be another useful technique for informal diagnosis—just talking about what should be on the test gives Harris a great deal of information about what the children have learned. Surprisingly, they move from being skeptical and unsure of themselves to being fairly sophisticated test creators—and takers—by the year's end.

What do I know that I have to do; that is, what are the constraints placed on me by groups or persons outside the classroom? Given those demands, what alternatives do I have? Teachers do not develop goals for students, instructional programs to meet those goals, and assessment strategies in a vacuum. Student needs and factors that fall outside the control of the teacher must be considered. For example, the principal, superintendent, or even the State Education Agency may have identified goals that narrow the range of choices the teacher has in designing the instructional program and the plan for assessing the program. Textbook publishers also influence teachers' planning. And the community's preferences concerning language and literature always influence curriculum planning.

Although there are many ways in which the teacher can feel constrained, resourceful teachers turn constraints into opportunities. For example,

> Your principal requires that you have your students write a theme once a month and that the grade for that theme be entered in the grade book, supposedly a sufficient amount of "essay" writing for the junior high level.
>
> Fortunately, your principal has not regulated the way in which you should go about developing the process for those once-a-month essays. So, you can start at the beginning of the month, encouraging students to begin to think about a topic, to jot down ideas, to read and to talk

about their ideas, to share thoughts with one another. A month is a generous amount of time considering the amount of time that we usually give students to write. Students can write and talk with the teacher or peers about the first draft by the beginning of the second week, can try a second draft by the beginning of the third week, after they have had time to mull things over. (Some may have decided on a different twist or a new topic altogether.) They will have the third week and part of the fourth week for more revision and for editing. You as the teacher have the option of developing a rating scale and having students rate each other's papers and suggesting a rating for your consideration, or of rating the papers yourself.

What do I want to know about students' progress and how often will I need some measure of their growth? As teachers, we are responsible for ensuring that students learn what we teach them. We have always had a sufficient variety of methods for determining whether students have mastered the details and the concepts. Children are tested regularly—quizzes, chapter tests, mid-semester exams, and finals—their homework is graded, and they are subjected to standardized tests, usually once a year.

Most teachers, however, are uncomfortable with simply testing students, recording grades, and waiting until the next test to see if students have corrected any problems that they might have. At least this is true in reading and mathematics. After-school classes, small-group attention, and help from special educators are available to children who are high-risk learners.

But children who have difficulty learning how to write, who are reluctant speakers, who have poor listening skills, and who are unable to organize their thoughts—let alone speak them or put them on paper—have seldom received such individual, specialized attention. Children learning English as a second language or who are under pressure to master the standard dialect of English must compete for attention with twenty-seven or more children each year throughout their school careers. Teachers are aware of these children and their needs, but they have been given no training and little or no assistance in how to deal with such children.

As they develop plans for assessing the students' progress, teachers usually rely on two different categories of assessment procedures. The first is *formative* evaluation. This takes place in the classroom on a daily basis and is designed so that necessary adjustments can be made in the instructional program. These adjustments are made so that the needs of individual children will be addressed and the goals of the instructional program will be met. Formative evaluation includes such informal procedures as classroom observation and conferencing, and such formal procedures as quizzes, tests, and assessment of written work and oral performances.

The second category is *summative* evaluation. Such assessment is done at the end of an instruction period to determine what has been learned and to what degree the instructional program has been successful. Year-end standardized tests are a good example, as are the grades on students' report cards.

During the primary grades, ongoing diagnosis and adjustment of instruction for individual children is an integral part of the system that most teachers use in assessing children's progress. Daily or weekly diagnosis and appropriate adjustment of the instructional approach for individuals decrease as children move through the intermediate grades, and virtually disappear by the time students reach high school.

Also, as children grow older, the techniques used to judge their progress are increasingly related to paper-and-pencil activities. Paper-and-pencil tests can be useful for assessing many skills. However, it is important that teachers look beyond the convenience of such measures to the fact that many educational goals cannot be assessed through using tests that ask children to fill in the blank, decide whether a statement is true or false, make a choice among four items, or underline the incorrect word in a sentence.

In writing instruction, for example, such tests will not give the teacher information in several important areas:

> Do students understand that effective communication must be purposeful and must be directed at an audience?
>
> Can students who are able to answer the items accurately on a paper-and-pencil test apply the same principles and rules in their own writing when appropriate?
>
> Are students able to develop an idea, organize thoughts, and put those thoughts on paper?
>
> Do students believe that writing can be an effective means of learning about, communicating with, and controlling the world around them?

Similar questions can be asked about using such tests to measure growth in speaking and listening abilities.

What can I do effectively, given the limitations on my time and other instructional responsibilities? What adjustments must I make if I adopt a particular method or group of methods? For a teacher who asks children to write a "theme" or "essay" once a week, it may be difficult to imagine creating a classroom environment that encourages them to write as often as they feel the need or desire to do so. And encouraging a classroom of young children to ask questions and to solve problems in small groups daily might be out of the question for a teacher who believes that children will learn best from a teacher who maintains control. Questions involving assessment—grading 150 pieces of writing a week instead of thirty, and moving from group to group to listen to as many children as possible daily—seem almost unanswerable.

The key is planning. Several guidelines might apply for teachers who desire to take a look at their current instructional programs with an eye toward improving or changing approaches.

> Your approach may be fine. After looking at the instructional program and analyzing your priorities and those of the principal and parents, you might decide that what you are doing is right for the students.
>
> If you decide that you would like to make some changes, develop a plan for moving gradually to your chosen approach. For example, if your children write an essay once a week and you agree that they should write every day, start implementing your plan by having them write twice a week and move gradually toward the goal, exploring as you progress a variety of techniques for giving feedback to the children. Another possibility is to explore ways to expand writing activities in subject areas such as mathematics and science.
>
> Get the support of the principal and other teachers. You may be able to plan some inservice days that will help you with planning and implementing strategy. If you can interest teachers, you might develop a support team that could be critical to the success of the plan.
>
> Examine your use of time. How much time is actually spent giving direct instruction to students or having them interact with each other in constructive learning situations? Do you spend much time giving instructions, passing out papers, disciplining individual children, erasing the blackboard? You might ask another teacher or a parent to observe you and keep a record of your various activities over several days. It is possible that you will be able to identify large chunks of time that are used inefficiently and that could be devoted instead to constructive interaction with students. Have students help you develop improved classroom management techniques. (Anderson, 1982)
>
> Think about the possibility of training students to assist in evaluating their own communication and their peers'. Time spent to train them now will be time saved for you later. Many of the references at the end of this chapter offer suggestions for how you can do this.

How do I want to communicate with my students and their parents about the progress students are making and about the instructional program? All teachers are familiar with and use the standard, long-accepted methods for reporting student progress—grades on papers and tests, report

cards, parent/teacher conferences, and announcements of results on standardized tests to individual parents and to the local media. Several additional techniques can prove effective for teachers.

Communicate with parents early in the year. Let them know what your
expectations for students are and how you plan to assess their progress. Let
parents know how they can help you. For example, if a child has experienced a death in the family, the parents should let you know right away, so
that you will understand any changes in the child's behavior. Marlene
Harris' talk with Cedric's mother proved very enlightening. His parents
had announced their divorce plans to their children. The other children in
the family were talking about it, trying to change their parents' minds. But
Cedric had clammed up at home, as well as in school.

Student/teacher conferences can be an effective means of assessing
students' progress at any point in a project. Such conferences can be planned
for five minutes weekly, or you can conduct short conferences with children
daily, spending one or two minutes on an assignment, a special concern of
the child's, or a question or suggestion of yours. If possible, every child in
the class should have one or two minutes of private time with you daily.

Portfolios of written work, oral performances (tapes or transcripts), and
work in other subject areas are useful for assessing children's ongoing
progress and for developing children's interest in their own progress. Portfolios allow children to assess their work based on how far they have come
since September or December, rather than how they compare to other
classmates.

Making the Implicit Explicit

Before discussing specific assessment techniques for oral and written
communication, I would like to discuss briefly several factors that play an
important role in the kind of relationship that develops between a teacher
and students. Factors are present in the relationship that will determine
how a teacher views his or her role and whether students view the teacher as
an evaluator or a key actor in their communicative environment.

1. It is very important that teachers view themselves as having real
   choices. If there is a mandate to use paper-and-pencil tests to
   assess students' writing ability, the teacher need not feel that all
   other possibilities are eliminated. The teacher can structure
   instruction and the classroom environment in a way that several
   additional approaches to assessment can be used. Those procedures can be selected to complement the information that the
   teacher gets from the results of paper-and-pencil tests.

2. The kind of assessment strategy that the teacher uses will always depend on the purpose that is to be achieved in the speaking or writing activities. For example, if a child has been asked to develop a strategy to persuade other children to sponsor her participation in a bike-a-thon, the best evaluators of her performance will be the other children. The ultimate evaluation, of course, would be if she actually did participate and if a number of children actually did sponsor her. The children could offer her feedback about why they were or were not convinced.

The teacher may want to assess a student's progress during the developmental stages of a piece of writing or of an oral activity, rather than review the piece for the first time when the student delivers the final product. To accomplish this, the teacher might use frequent, short conferences.

3. A major role that the teacher plays in the classroom is that of a respondent to students. This is true in a large-group discussion as well as in an individual student/teacher conference. How the teacher responds to students' speaking and writing and the degree to which a teacher really listens to and offers feedback to students will have a direct influence on how those students learn.

4. Although children need to have feedback whenever they speak or write, it is not necessary that they be evaluated every time they engage in a classroom activity involving speaking or writing. When students are evaluated, they can be evaluated by peers as well as by teachers, and they should have frequent opportunities to evaluate themselves in an explicit manner. Very young children need not be evaluated at all. As they grow older, children can be given the opportunity to select the pieces of writing or the oral activity for which they will receive a grade.

5. Children must be given many opportunities to interact with peers and the teacher individually and in large-group and small-group activities. The classroom environment must encourage a great deal of talking that is purposeful and meaningful. Such a class will also stimulate lots of writing, with children doing writing projects individually and together and editing each other's work. At the secondary level, brainstorming and discussion should be the norm in any class where students are expected to write. Such opportunities for peer interaction give teachers valuable information about students' growth.

A classroom environment that encourages interaction will be especially helpful for students who are learning English as a second language and for students who speak a dialect other than standard English. Such interactions will help them strengthen their knowledge of the standard dialect and will develop their ability to use it appropriately.

6. The teacher must understand that communication—whether through speaking or writing—is a high-risk activity for young children or teenagers asked to expose ideas or feelings before an audience. Children who are comfortable speaking in front of others or putting their thoughts down on paper are still nervous about command performances. Children who have experienced writing as a form of punishment, have difficulty writing out their thoughts, are reticent speakers, are handicapped in some physical way, speak English as a second language, or speak a dialect different from that of most classmates and the teacher, may be devastated by an order to perform. Teachers must become aware of these individual concerns and make allowances for them. Some help is in the literature. For example, Phillip Lopate has discussed how he helps young students begin to write in a noisy classroom environment (1978), and James McCroskey (1977a, 1977b) has written about ways in which the teacher can help the reticent child.

The bottom line is that the teacher must build a classroom environment in which children know that it is all right to take risks and to express themselves freely. They must have a trusting relationship with the teacher. Trust will not develop if children view the teacher solely as an evaluator of their work. Rather than learning to take risks —and in the process, growing—they will learn to play it safe by giving the teacher what they believe he or she wants.

The Role of Assessment in Developing Communication Competence

As mentioned, evaluating children's communication competence—both oral and written—serves an important instructional function. Whether formal or informal, assessment gives the teacher feedback on the effectiveness of the instructional program and information about where adjustments need to be made. This continual fine-tuning of the educational program is essential if the needs of all the children are to be met.

Children need frequent classroom opportunities to try out skills and to expand their knowledge of what does, and what does not, constitute effective communication. Giving children opportunities to expand knowledge and to build communication competence requires an environment that invites them to fail, and to fail until they succeed. If children are to experiment in this way, they must feel free to take risks and to express themselves freely. They will not expose themselves to possible failure if they do not feel secure in their relationships with peers and the teacher. And children who view the teacher as an evaluator will be unlikely to take many risks.

However, children will accept feedback readily from a trusted adult, one who responds in a constructive way to their efforts to communicate effectively. Feedback must be given in concrete terms and should be related to children's use of language in ways that help them expand their knowledge of communication strategies available in a variety of contexts.

Most importantly, as children develop a trusting relationship with the teacher, they will be less anxious about situations in which the teacher does assume the role of evaluator.

Another important source of feedback is the children's peers. Peer evaluation should be used widely in the classroom. Self-evaluation is also important. A child should not only be able to identify and implement strategies for a given situation, but should also be able to evaluate his or her effectiveness in handling the situation.

The following is a description of another visit to Marlene Harris' classroom. We have learned that she believes in integrating the content areas so that children will understand relationships among various facets of their lives—home, school, community. Here is an example of how she does that and has her students share responsibility for evaluating their responses.

In November, Harris' fifth-grade class had studied the heart and the human body's circulatory system as part of a unit on biology. Their field trip to the Museum of Science and Industry at the end of the unit had given them an opportunity to expand their understanding of the heart and other parts of the body.

One day in early March, she welcomed the class back from lunch and then called out four names—Martin, Sondra, Donna, and Robert. She asked that they get together while the rest of the class was involved in free reading to develop a presentation on the circulatory system—How does the heart work? How does blood move through the body? Why is the heart important? How can we keep our hearts healthy?

"After you make your presentation, we will allow the rest of the class to see if they remember any details that will add to what you have said, and then we will look at the chart we sent off for. Then we will ask you as a group to talk together and tell us how you think you did."

Although Martin, Sondra, Donna, and Robert groaned when their names were called, the class as a whole was not surprised. The teacher does this to them all the time. When she asked why they thought she had picked this particular day to make an assignment about the heart, one student made a good guess. The day before, the newspaper had reported that a young mother of two children had been told that the government had finally agreed to pay for her to be given a new heart.

A couple of points should be noted about the group that the teacher picked. Sondra is a reticent student who still, after six months with Harris, cannot speak in front of class. But she is a great artist and will enjoy helping to do the graphics for the presentation. The teacher has not insisted that all four children speak during the presentation. Sondra surprised Harris by explaining to the class that the red lines were arteries and the blue lines were veins; no small achievement for Sondra. Martin, on the other hand, loves to talk, and so does Donna. But Martin speaks quickly and is difficult to understand. Because they both like to talk, Martin and Donna decide to take turns, which has the effect of slowing Martin down a bit.

Creating a Context for Assessment

Mostly, children need to learn in an atmosphere that is free of formal evaluation and that offers continuing feedback on results of their communication. The contexts in which students are called on to perform can range from very formal situations (for example, giving a speech or writing an essay on a specific topic in a specified length of time) to very informal situations (for example, communicating with a peer about a movie or keeping a daily journal). Students need to be evaluated at both ends of the continuum, and at many points along it, if they are to be aware of the wide variety of situations in which they will need to use effective communication.

Creating a variety of contexts also calls for developing specific criteria for each context. The oral or written language used to persuade a stranger to make a donation to a community improvement project is very different from language used to help a new student in class understand rules and routines. I was impressed recently when my daughter, a ninth-grader, came home and described a "dirty trick" that her English teacher had played on the class that morning:

> She came into the class and said she didn't have our tests graded because her house had caught fire last night. She talked about how frightened she was when she discovered the fire and told us how some of her furniture was damaged by smoke. Then she told us that our tests were in the room where the fire started and had been destroyed.
> "Are you going to make us take the test again?" Two students blurted out almost the same question.
> "I could do that or I could give everyone who took the test an A and just grade the tests for those of you who have to make it up."
> "No fair!" came cries from the two or three who had been absent the day before.
> "This has been very interesting"—my daughter's teacher, again. She went on to tell her class that she was making up the story about the fire—there had been no fire and the tests were safe. But she was amazed that not one student had responded with some feeling of sympathy for what she had experienced the night before.

The students seemed to feel ashamed, of course, but she apparently allowed that for only a moment. They discussed why the students had responded as they did, the appropriateness of what she had done to them, and what other responses from the students might have been appropriate.

Their assignment for the next day was to develop a farfetched story and to tell it to the class, trying to convince them that it is true. Stories would be judged by the class for "believability" on a scale from 1–10.

Assessment Instruments for Speaking and Listening

The rating scale is the primary assessment instrument used by classroom teachers to evaluate students' speaking ability. The scale lists criteria that will be used to judge a student's performance in a particular context. The criteria can be teacher developed or student/teacher developed. The teacher may assign numerical ratings for the criteria (1–5) or may simply place a check mark to show that the criterion has been met. Students listening to the performance can be asked to use the rating scale, too. This is an opportunity for them to exercise listening skills and an opportunity for the performing student or students to receive specific feedback from peers. Rating scales can assess the content and effectiveness of the communication, as well as the student's delivery and language.

Marlene Harris has developed a rating scale that her students use when they are asked to rate their own group presentations (Figure 1). Martin, Sondra, Donna, and Robert used it to evaluate their presentation on circulation.

Planning for the presentation	Circle One	
Did we talk about the purpose for the presentation and what we knew about our audience?	Yes	No
Did we decide what tasks had to be done to get ready for the presentation and who would do them?	Yes	No
Did we talk about how the presentation would be structured and who would do each part?	Yes	No
Did everyone have a chance to contribute information?	Yes	No
Did we remember as much information as we thought we should have remembered?	Yes	No
Did we use our time effectively?	Yes	No
Doing the presentation		
Was the presentation well-organized?	Yes	No
Did the division of responsibilities we decided on work well?	Yes	No
Did we work well as a group, moving smoothly from one part of the presentation to another?	Yes	No
Was our delivery good? (Did we speak clearly and slowly? Did we speak loud enough? Did we keep eye contact?)	Yes	No

Figure 1. Group Self-Rating Scale.

Donald Rubin (Holdzkom et al., 1982) has suggested that teachers should have several additional strategies for assessing children's speaking ability:

> For example, groups involved in problemsolving discussions can be evaluated with respect to their efficiency: the time elapsed and the accuracy of their solution. Dyads engaged in referential or descriptive communication can also be evaluated in terms of communication accuracy. . . . A storyteller might be evaluated according to relatively concrete criteria which indicate consistency between an original story and a subsequent retelling. (p. 143)

Listening skills are generally assessed by having children listen to a short passage and then respond to several questions about its content. One difficulty with this is that it is hard to find a passage that contains information that is totally new to the child. For many passages, it is possible that the child would know the answers to the questions without being exposed to the material. So, the teacher cannot be certain that the child has listened and understood the passage (Lundsteen, 1979).

Teachers who offer children many opportunities to interact in the class and to perform individually and in small groups will increase students' opportunities to improve listening skills. Having peers rate classmates' performances, as my ninth-grader's teacher did, or having them be responsible for offering additional information, as Marlene Harris did, are examples of situations in which children must listen carefully, relate what they hear to their own experience, and offer a relevant response.

Some tests of listening skills ask children to respond behaviorally. Such a test might give children instructions and ask them to act them out, or it might ask children to draw an object based on a description of the object done by another student.

Assessment Strategies for Writing

The most familiar form of testing the writing ability of groups of children has been the paper-and-pencil test, usually the fill-in-the-blank or multiple-choice variety. These tests, which can be formulated by teachers or commercially developed, measure students' skills in specific areas, such as their knowledge of rules of grammar and usage, mechanics, sentence structure, and syntax. The results of tests that are developed by the teacher and that reflect instruction that children have received may provide useful information to the teacher, so that future instruction can be adjusted. But such tests are only *indirect* measures of students' ability to write.

Direct measures of writing ability involve assessing actual samples of student writing. Teachers who teach writing have students write prose—whether it is a paragraph or ten pages—on some regular basis. The prose is graded by the teacher, usually for content and for attention to conventions of language. Because of pressures on teachers' time, many students are asked to write an extended piece of prose only once in a long while, and the teacher does not see the piece until it is handed in as a finished product.

Throughout this chapter, we have been advocating informal assessment procedures that create opportunities for the teacher to interact with students daily. These interactions allow the teacher to assess the student's progress continually and to contribute to it by making necessary adjustments in the instructional program. Teachers who create warm accepting environments in which children are encouraged to write as often as they feel the need or desire to do so will be in the best position to assess the growth of students in writing. In such an environment, children will be free to make errors in writing; for young children, these errors reflect learning in progress.

The following letter, written by Laura, who was seven years old at the time, demonstrates that she knows a great deal about language, despite her self-acknowledged spelling difficulties:

Laura
Dear arin I mite not of speld.
your name rite but I.
fergot how too spel it.
because I am in st. lowis now.
and I have made a lot of.
frens I am vary sarry that.
I haveint rote too you.
but I haveint had the time.
I hope you are haveing fun.
Saye hiy too soesin and.
tart it is vary nise hera
and vary fun oh Im.
sarry I fergot atem well
good biy Love Laura
xoxoxoxoxo

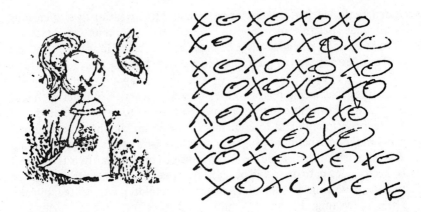

Every year, Laura's teachers have spoken with her parents about her difficulties in spelling. However, her problems remain, as the following work reveals. But these examples demonstrate Laura's growth. She has come a long way, which, incidentally, would have been apparent if the schools that she has attended had maintained portfolios of significant examples of her writing.

In the example below, Laura decided to advertise her new availability as a baby-sitter. The rule was that she had to be eleven before she could start baby-sitting:

(ruff draft)

Nead a babysitter?
Well you have one now.
My name is Laura I'm 11
and I love babies and older
Children such as 1-7.
The babies must be 2 mounths
and up
Pleas take this into
consideration.

Phone - 986-8013
Address 8396 W. Woodard Dr. 80227

       Sined
       Laura Reed

Laura was reminded that she couldn't baby-sit unless her mother was home.

(revision)

Need a babysitter?
Well you have one now.
My name is Laura
and I am 11 years old.

I love babies up to 2 mounts
and or up. I also like children
up to 1-7. Please take this
into consideration.
Untill 9 on weeknights. Untill 12 on
Friday & Saturday. My mother has to
be home while I babsit!
   Phone - 986-8013
Address - 8396 W. Woodard Dr. 80227
          Signed
          LAURA REED

Finally, Laura was asked if more parents might be convinced that she could handle all the details involved in babysitting if she paid very close attention to all the details in her writing. She—not so very patiently—tried one more time:

Need a babysitter.?

Well you have one now!
My name is Laura Reed
and I am 11 years old.
I love babies up to 2
months and or up. I also
like children up to 1-7
Please take this into
consideration.
Until 9 on weeknights. Untill
12 Saturdays and Fridays.
My mom has to be home
when I babysit!

Phone,- 986-8013
Add.- 8396 W. Woodard Dr. 80227
                    signed
                    Laura Reed

Laura's dad made fifteen copies of her advertisement, and she delivered it to parents in the neighborhood.

Direct Measures of Writing Ability

These measures help the teacher assess students' ability to

    achieve a purpose in relation to a specific audience;
    use language and style appropriate to a specific situation;
    organize and implement a set of ideas related to a topic; and
    approach a topic in a creative, interesting manner.

Four kinds of direct measures of writing ability are available to teachers:

Holistic scoring.
In holistic scoring, raters review a writing sample to arrive at an overall judgment. Although they may be influenced by the components of style, grammar, usage, and mechanics, raters do not pay specific attention to these components. Each paper is read by at least two raters, and then the two ratings are combined or averaged. For teachers who would like to know more about the holistic method of scoring writing samples, several references have been included in the bibliography (Cooper, 1977; Myers, 1980; Diederich, 1974).

Analytical scoring.
If you wish to assess the student's ability to work with one or more specific conventions of writing (for example, syntax, punctuation, organization, or sentence structure), you might be interested in learning about the analytical method. The factor or factors selected for assessment are isolated and scored individually by raters (Spandel and Stiggins, 1980).

T-Unit analysis.
T-units are independent clauses and any subordinate clauses or phrases that accompany them. Hunt (1977) has shown that the length of the T-unit used by children increases as they grow older and become more skilled as writers. He argues that analysis of T-units can

give teachers valuable information about the level of complexity of children's language.

Primary Trait scoring.
Primary trait scoring assesses the student's ability to fulfill an assignment. The student is given a writing task and is judged according to the degree to which he or she is able to meet the requirements of the task. The scoring method was developed by consultants for the National Assessment of Educational Progress (NAEP) for use in scoring student responses to items in their national writing assessments.

Of these four assessment procedures, I feel that the primary trait scoring system holds the greatest promise for meeting classroom teachers' needs. Because of this belief, I would like to treat it in some greater depth in the next few pages.

Primary Trait Scoring System

This system focuses on a specific characteristic of a student's writing. The student is given a specific assignment, such as playing a role, and is assessed on the ability to fulfill the assignment, in this case adopting and maintaining a role. Adopting the role is the *primary* trait in the assessment procedure. *Secondary* traits may also be assessed. These are traits that the teacher feels are important to the effectiveness of the paper, but they are not as critical as the primary trait.

When the primary trait scoring system is used to score a paper, the objective of the reader—whether it is another student or the teacher—is to determine to what degree the primary trait is present in the paper. A mystery story, for example, is *primarily* effective if it keeps the reader in suspense, so the reader must determine to what extent the story had that effect.

For teachers, the first step in developing an assignment that will be scored using the primary trait scoring system is to identify the primary trait to be assessed. The next step is to develop a scoring guide for that specific assignment. The NAEP used the following scoring guide for assessing "letters to a principal on solving a problem in school":

Score of paper	Characteristics of paper
1	Respondents do not identify a problem or give no evidence that the problem can be solved or is worth solving.
2	Respondents identify a problem and either tell how to solve it *or* tell how the school would be improved if it were solved.

3   Respondents identify a problem, explain how to solve the problem, and tell how the school would be improved if the problem were solved.

4   Respondents include the elements of a "3" paper. In addition, the elements are expanded and presented in a systematic structure that reflects the steps necessary to solve the problem. (Mullis, 1974)

After the teacher has decided on the definition of the primary trait, the ratings should move smoothly and quickly (Lloyd-Jones, 1977; Klaus et al., 1982).

My ninth-grader's teacher recently assigned students the task of writing a paper in which they were to tell the story of Cinderella from the stepmother's viewpoint. The teacher did not use the primary trait scoring system for assessment, but she easily could have. I would like to suggest ways in which that might have been possible.

First, in this case, the selection of the primary trait was inherent in the assignment—papers that were turned in had to make the reader believe that the character who was telling the story was the stepmother. A possible scoring guide might have been as follows:

Score of paper   Characteristics of paper

1   Respondents do not assume the role of the stepmother with any consistency.

2   Respondents assume the role of the stepmother, stepping out of it occasionally, and basically give the facts of the story.

3   Respondents consistently tell the story from the viewpoint of the stepmother, show sparks of creativity in using language, and give some life to the character and the story.

4   Respondents include the elements of a "3" paper but make the stepmother character come alive, so that the reader is drawn into the story. Touches of humor and expansion of the facts may be included.

Here are two papers which might be assessed using this scale. The first is the paper of a student enrolled in the ninth-grade class mentioned.

> Once upon a time in a land far away there lived my stepdaughter, Cinderella. She was a troublesome creature with an obscene fascination with mice. Because of this, she was roomed in the attic. I refused to have mice in my poor departed husband's home! She was constantly getting into trouble, so I kept her busy with housework.

One day we received an invitation to a ball at the palace (we being my two daughters and myself). I didn't even consider allowing Cinderella to come along. Surely she would trip on the carpet and make a fool of herself and us in front of the king and prince. She did ask to be allowed to go so I told her that if she could get her daily work done, she could.

The day arrived and with it a flurry of activity. Cinderella had tons of work and in addition to her daily chores, she had to help my wonderful daughters dress. When the carriage arrived we were walking out the door when down came that troublesome girl dressed in my beloved daughters' clothes. My girls tore her dress to rags and we walked out with a regal tilt to our heads.

At the ball, my girls were introduced to their majesties. The prince seemed to perk up just when he caught a glimpse of them coming up, after all those ugly girls with big hands and feet. Then a plain girl in a white flowing dress was introduced and the prince danced with her all evening. At exactly midnight, she ran from the palace and a rumor went around that she lost her slipper.

The next day, the Grand Duke came around with the slipper. I followed Cinderella to her room and locked her in, or else she would have made us all look extremely foolish. She doesn't take care of her appearance and certainly doesn't even attempt to have nice clothes.

Well, after greeting the Grand Duke, both my girls tried on the slipper. Neither of my daughters' feet fit the slipper, so we let the Grand Duke out. Suddenly, Cinderella ran down the stairs. She tried the slipper on. It fit.

She and the Prince were married and she hasn't visited once. The neighbors all said that it was a marriage made in heaven, and that they'll live happily ever after. I hope not. She doesn't deserve it, the ungrateful troublemaker.

In this paper, the student has achieved a fairly consistent image and an interesting twist on the image that Cinderella brings to mind for all of us. The stepmother is always in character, and there are touches of humor throughout the paper (for example, the stepmother's perception that the prince perked up when he caught a glimpse of her two daughters). The only trouble the student seemed to have was in the starting sentence, where she was determined to use the words, "Once upon a time in a land far away." The paper is probably a "4" paper.

This next paper was not written as a result of the same teacher's assignment.

Many years ago I married a man who had a daughter named Cinderella. My two daughters went with me to live at their house. We didn't like Cinderella and I wanted only the best for my girls, so I made Cinderella stay in the kitchen and do all the housework.

One day we got an invitation to the ball. The prince needed to find a wife. We were all so excited! I knew he would pick one of my girls. Cinderella wanted to go and I said she could if she got all her housework done but I didn't mean it.

On the day of the ball I gave Cinderella lots of extra work to do, but just as we opened the door to go she appeared on the stairs all dressed up. My daughters tore apart her dress and she ran out the door.

We went on to the ball and Cinderella cried in the garden. Her fairy godmother appeared and fixed her dress and sent her off to the ball.

At the ball we didn't recognize the beautiful girl in white. The prince wasn't even polite to my daughters. He just danced with her all night. At midnight she suddenly ran out the door and disappeared, except that she lost a slipper on the stairs as she fled.

The next morning the whole kingdom was in a dither. A messenger from the king came to the door and wanted to see my daughters. I locked Cinderella in her room.

My daughters tried and tried to get their feet into the slipper, but it was impossible. The messenger started to leave and suddenly there was Cinderella. Those mice again!

Her foot fit! And the prince married her and carried her off to live happily ever after. At least she's out of my hair. Now all I have to do is find a housekeeper.

The student has made an admirable attempt to keep in character. There are a few slips however—her knowledge of the fairy godmother, knowing that the kingdom was in a dither, how Cinderella lost her slipper. These are places where the student has slipped into the role of the omniscient narrator. The touch of humor at the end of the story is promising, and this student handled the beginning of the story in a more appropriate way than the other student. The paper is probably a "2" paper, but if this were the first draft, the teacher or peer editors could probably suggest ways in which the student could greatly improve the story.

Teachers who decide that they would like to use the primary trait scoring system will find help in a set of books developed by the National Assessment of Educational Progress in cooperation with CEMREL, Inc., a regional educational laboratory. *Composing Childhood Experience* and *Composing Adolescent Experience* (Klaus et al., 1982) offer teacher-evaluated examples of student writing and suggest ways to incorporate the method into assessment at the classroom level.

Informal Assessment of Writing Skills

Just as teachers have daily opportunities to assess development of children's speaking and listening skills, they, too, have continuing opportunities to assess progress in writing abilities. Because development of writing ability is an individualistic phenomenon, the teacher must find time frequently during class to work with each child and to have children work with each other. This is particularly important for students who are learning English as a second language.

An effective way to stay informed of children's progress and to assist them in their development is through individual conferences. Student/teacher conferences do not have to be long, and they can take place at any time during the various stages of the writing process. Following is an example from Marlene Harris' class of how conferencing might be combined with helping a student experience the writing process:

Harris kept an eye on Doreen throughout the day that Doreen had seen the dog die. Doreen seemed to feel okay about her conversation with Judy. At the end of the day, the teacher stopped Doreen and told her she was sorry that she had had such a sad experience and that she might want to talk with her Dad and brother that night to see if anything like that had ever happened to them.

Doreen came to school the next day and immediately told the teacher that she had talked to a neighbor downstairs. The neighbor told her that her dog had been hit by a car on the same street, and she wished that cars would be made to go slower on that street. The teacher suggested that Doreen talk with several other children in her small group that day and see if they think that they might be able to do something about it.

When the children talked that afternoon, they decided to start a petition to get the mayor of Chicago to change the speed limit. They developed the wording for the petition and confidently showed the passage to the teacher. She congratulated them on their idea and said that it would be interesting to find out if there was a way to get the city to make a change like that.

The teacher suggested that the children write a letter to the city's bureau of traffic and transportation to ask them for advice. Doreen drafted the letter and the other children helped her revise and edit it. The teacher reviewed it and offered several suggestions, two of which the children agreed with.

The children mailed the letter and waited for a response. It came two weeks later, with a kindly description of how complicated it would be to change the speed limit. Doreen headed a full-class discussion about whether they should get signatures on a petition anyway and send the petition directly to the mayor. The children decided that they should.

Two weeks later, the children had over 200 signatures on the petition. Again, Doreen drafted a letter, this time to the mayor. The children took the teacher's suggestions much more seriously this time.

The letter from the mayor's office took four weeks to reach the children. The mayor, too, said that changing the speed limit would be difficult to do. But she offered an alternative. Because children walk to school along that street, she had several signs placed that told traffic to slow down when school children were walking to and from school. The children cheered and decided to write a letter to thank the mayor.

Doreen's efforts were not the result of a specific writing assignment. Instead, they grew out of a need to understand her own feelings and to find out if she could have some control over the world around her. She gained confidence from the involvement of other children. Marlene Harris held at least six conferences with the children, none of which lasted more than two or three minutes. And Doreen and the other children went through all of the stages of the writing process—prewriting, drafting, revising, and editing—with continuing input from the teacher and other children. In addition, planning together, getting people to sign the petition, and discussing and resolving differences broadened their oral communication abilities.

Self-evaluation, where students assume responsibility for assessing their own writing and for deciding which pieces of writing they will share with the teacher and peers, can promote organization skills, self-reliance, independence, and creativity. Students can evaluate their various drafts as well as the final product, using teacher- and student-developed questions as a guide. Beaven (1977) suggests the following list of questions as a guide for students:

> How much time did you spend on this paper?
>
> (After the first evaluation) What did you try to improve, or experiment with, on this paper? How successful were you? If you have questions about what you were trying to do, what are they?
>
> What are the strengths of your paper? Place a squiggly line beside those passages you feel are very good.
>
> What are the weaknesses, if any, of your paper? Place an X beside passages you would like your teacher to correct or revise. Place an X over any punctuation, spelling, usage, etc., where you need help or clarification.
>
> What one thing will you do to improve your next piece of writing? Or what kind of experimentation in writing would you like to try? If you would like some information related to what you want to do, write down your questions.
>
> (Optional) What grade would you give yourself on this composition? Justify it. (p. 143)

Peer evaluation can involve just two students who read each other's writing or small groups of students, like those who worked with Doreen, who meet periodically to serve as a support group, offer suggestions on various drafts, and edit each other's work. Peter Elbow has developed what he calls the "center of gravity" response (1973), which is intended for formative response and feedback and can be used successfully by students to respond to one another's writing.

The "center of gravity" response asks the reader to go through four steps after reading a piece: (1) tell very quickly what you found to be the main points, main feelings, or centers of gravity; (2) summarize it into a single sentence; (3) choose one word from the writing which best summarizes it; and (4) choose a word that is not in the writing that best summarizes it. Students working with each other using this procedure will rapidly discover whether their writing is having the intended effect on the audience.

Beaven has also suggested a set of guidelines that can be used by peer editors working in a group:

> Identify the best section of the composition and describe what makes it effective.
>
> Identify a sentence, a group of sentences, or a paragraph that needs revision, and revise it as a group, writing the final version on the back of the paper.
>
> Identify one (or two) things the writer can do to improve his or her next piece of writing. Write these goals on the first page at the top.
>
> (After the first evaluation, the following question should come first.) What were the goals the writer was working on? Were they reached? If not, identify those passages that need improvement and as a group revise those sections, writing final versions on the back of the paper. If revisions are necessary, set up the same goals for the next paper and delete question 3. (1977, p. 149)

Many teachers may feel that the two procedures suggested above may not be appropriate for their students. They will, however, give teachers a point of departure, so that they can develop procedures that meet the needs of their own students. Most importantly, students will need careful guidance from the teacher before they routinely evaluate one another's work. Peer evaluation can be very effective if it is planned for carefully, because it gives students an opportunity to focus attention away from their teacher and to see how their writing affects members of their peer group.

A Final Note

Effectively assessing communication competence—children's ability to write, speak, and listen in ways that are appropriate to particular situations —depends on the role that the teacher is willing to play in class. If children are to expand abilities to speak and write for different purposes and for a variety of audiences, teachers must give them frequent opportunities to practice skills in an environment that invites them to take risks and that encourages them to accept failure as part of the process of learning and growing. Such an environment gives the teacher many opportunities for informal assessment of children's skills in a wide variety of situations.

This chapter has primarily focused on the importance of informal rather than formal procedures for assessing students' growth in speaking, listening, and writing skills. This is largely because formal assessment instruments in oral and written communication have not kept pace with the instructional needs and practices in today's classrooms. Some procedures, such as the primary trait scoring system, hold a great deal of promise, but their development has been slow.

Teachers may find themselves in a critical position over the next few years. It is not often that they have opportunities to influence the makers of tests. Right now, however, if higher authorities are going to mandate curriculum development, particularly in oral communication, teachers must demand that those authorities assume the responsibility for developing instruments that accurately assess the abilities of students, and that reflect classroom instruction. Moreover, the involvement of teachers, themselves, is vital to the usefulness of those tests for assessing communication competence.

References

Anderson, Linda M. "Classroom Management: Making Time to Learn Basic Skills." In *Basic Skills Issues and Choices, Volume I,* edited by Linda Reed and Spencer Ward. St. Louis: CEMREL, Inc., 1982.

Beaven, Mary H. "Individualized Goal Setting, Self-Evaluation, and Peer Evaluation." In *Evaluating Writing: Describing, Measuring, Judging,* edited by Charles R. Cooper and Lee Odell. Urbana, Ill.: National Council of Teachers of English, 1977.

Brown, Kenneth L. "Teaching and Assessing Oral Communication." Paper presented at the National Leadership Conference on Basic Skills, San Marcos, Tex., January 1982.

Brown, K. L.; Backlund, P.; Gurry, J.; and Jandt, F. *Assessment of Basic Speaking and Listening Skills: State of the Art and Recommendations for Instrument Development.* Volumes I and II. Boston: Massachusetts Department of Education, 1979.

Cooper, Charles R., and Odell, Lee, eds. *Evaluating Writing· Describing, Measuring, Judging.* Urbana, Ill.: National Council of Teachers of English, 1977.

Cooper, Charles R. "Holistic Evaluation of Writing." In *Evaluating Writing: Describing, Measuring, Judging,* edited by Charles R. Cooper and Lee Odell. Urbana, Ill.: National Council of Teachers of English, 1977.

Cooper, Charles R., and Odell, Lee, eds. *Research on Composing: Points of Departure.* Urbana, Ill.: National Council of Teachers of English, 1978.

Diederich, Paul B. *Measuring Growth in English.* Urbana, Ill.: National Council of Teachers of English, 1974.

Elbow, Peter. *Writing Without Teachers.* New York: Oxford University Press, 1973.

Holdzkom, David; Reed, Linda; Porter, Jane; and Rubin, Donald. *Research within Reach: Oral and Written Communication.* St. Louis: CEMREL, Inc., 1982.

Hunt, Kellogg W. "Early Blooming and Late Blooming Syntactic Structures." In *Evaluating Writing: Describing, Measuring, Judging,* edited by Charles R. Cooper and Lee Odell. Urbana, Ill.: National Council of Teachers of English, 1977.

Klaus, Carl; Lloyd-Jones, Richard; et al. *Composing Adolescent Experience.* St. Louis: CEMREL, Inc., 1982.

Klaus, Carl; Lloyd-Jones, Richard; et al. *Composing Childhood Experience.* St. Louis: CEMREL, Inc., 1982.

Larson, Carl; Backlund, Phil; Redmond, Mark; and Barbour, Alton. *Assessing Functional Communication.* Falls Church, Va.: Speech Communication Association and the ERIC Clearinghouse on Reading and Communication Skills, 1978.

Lieb-Brilhart, Barbara. "Standards for Effective Oral Communication Programs." In *Basic Skills Issues and Choices, Volume 2,* edited by Linda Reed and Spencer Ward. St. Louis: CEMREL, Inc., 1982.

Lloyd-Jones, Richard. "Primary Trait Scoring." In *Evaluating Writing: Describing, Measuring, Judging,* edited by Charles R. Cooper and Lee Odell. Urbana, Ill.: National Council of Teachers of English, 1977.

Lopate, Phillip. "Helping Young Children Start to Write." In *Research on Composing: Points of Departure,* edited by Charles R. Cooper and Lee Odell. Urbana, Ill.: National Council of Teachers of English, 1978.

Lundsteen, Sara W. *Listening: Its Impact on Reading and the Other Language Arts.* Urbana, Ill.: ERIC Clearinghouse on Reading and Communication Skills and the National Council of Teachers of English, 1979.

McCroskey, James C. "Oral Communication Apprehension: A Summary of Recent Theory and Research." *Human Communication Research* 4 (Fall 1977a): 78–96.

McCroskey, James C. *Quiet Children and the Classroom Teacher.* A Theory and Research Into Practice (TRIP) booklet. Annandale, Va.: Speech Communication Association and the ERIC Clearinghouse on Reading and Communication Skills, 1977b.

Mullis, Ina. "The Primary Trait Scoring System for Scoring Writing Task." Denver: National Assessment of Educational Progress, 1974.

Myers, Miles. *A Procedure for Writing Assessment and Holistic Scoring.* Urbana, Ill.: ERIC Clearinghouse on Reading and Communication Skills and the National Council of Teachers of English, 1980.

O'Hare, Frank. *Sentence Combining: Improving Student Writing without Formal Grammar Instruction* (Research Report No. 15). Urbana, Ill.: National Council of Teachers of English, 1973.

Rubin, Donald L.; Daly, John; McCroskey, James C.; and Mead, Nancy A. *A Review and Critique of Procedures for Assessing Speaking and Listening Skills Among Preschool through Grade Twelve Students.* Annandale, Va.: Speech Communication Association, in preparation.

Scriven, Michael. *Evaluation Thesaurus.* Second Edition. Inverness, Calif.: Edgepress, 1980.

Spandel, Vicki, and Stiggins, Richard J. *Direct Measures of Writing Skill: Issues and Applications.* Portland, Ore.: Center for Applied Performance Testing, Northwest Regional Educational Laboratory, 1980.

Stiggins, Richard J., ed. *Perspectives on the Assessment of Speaking and Listening Skills for the 1980's.* Portland, Ore.: Northwest Regional Educational Laboratory, 1981.

Contributors

R.R. Allen is a Professor of Communication Arts and Curriculum and Instruction at the University of Wisconsin–Madison. As a specialist in communication education, he has authored seven books and numerous articles relating to elementary, secondary, and college communication instruction. Professor Allen was President of the Speech Communication Association in 1979.

Marcia Farr is an Associate Professor of English in the Composition and Rhetoric Program at the University of Illinois at Chicago. She was formerly team leader for Research on Writing at the National Institute of Education where she developed and implemented a research program on the teaching and learning of writing. Her research and publications focus on nonstandard dialects and writing, early writing development, and the relationship between oral and written language.

Ken Kantor is an Associate Professor of Language Education at the University of Georgia. He is the author of articles in *Research in the Teaching of English, English Education, Language Arts, English Journal,* and *Theory into Practice,* as well as chapters in several book collections, and has presented papers at conferences of the National Council of Teachers of English and the American Educational Research Association. His primary areas of research interest are curriculum history and theory, developmental processes in composition, and classroom contexts for writing. Kantor is currently serving as chair of the NCTE Standing Committee on Research.

Robert Kellner died shortly after the completion of the manuscript for this book. He was Supervisor of English and Communication Arts for the State of Wisconsin, where he worked with public school districts on curriculum development, teacher evaluation, and grant writing. A former high school English and speech teacher and college composition instructor, Kellner also served as Dissemination Director for the Wisconsin ESEA Title IV program and for the Wisconsin Center for Innovative Programs.

Nancy S. Olson is currently Director of Publications for the American Society for Training and Development, Washington, D.C. She is former senior editor for the Association for Supervision and Curriculum Development and has written extensively on all aspects of the curriculum.

Linda Reed, at the time *Speaking and Writing, K–12* was initiated, directed federally funded projects in all areas of the basic skills and was the Associate Director of the School Improvement Group at CEMREL, Inc., a regional educational laboratory in St. Louis. She moved to CEMREL from NCTE, where she was the Assistant Director of the ERIC Clearinghouse on Reading and Communication Skills. Reed is currently a manager in the Marketing Department at NBI, Inc., an office automation company in Boulder, Colorado.

Donald Rubin is an Associate Professor in the Departments of Speech Communication and Language Education and in the Program in Linguistics at the University of Georgia. He has worked and published in the areas of the development of communicative competence, audience awareness in written communication, language variation, and instruction and assessment of speaking and listening skills. Rubin currently directs Project Synapse, a program supported by the Fund for Improvement of Postsecondary Education to improve the academic writing skills of basic writers through oral communication exercises.

Jana Staton is currently coordinating collaborative research projects with teachers at Gallaudet College and pre-college programs on the uses and benefits of dialogue journals for deaf students, and teaching inservice courses for District of Columbia and Arlington County public school teachers on the connections among thinking, writing, and personal development.

Charles Suhor is Deputy Executive Director of NCTE and Director of the ERIC Clearinghouse on Reading and Communication Skills. A former high school English teacher and K-12 supervisor, his publications include poetry, literature and composition textbooks, curriculum guides, and articles for various journals. Suhor's current interests include curriculum theory and practice, thinking skills, and technology.

Ann Jeffries-Thaiss is a registered nurse and childbirth educator with the American Society for Psychoprophylaxis in Obstetrics (ASPO). For the last three years she has been editor of *Potomac Potpourri,* the Virginia state newsletter of La Leche League International. She has published articles and poems in *The American Journal of Nursing, Perspectives in Psychiatric Care, Genesis,* and *The Maryland Woman's Journal.*

Christopher J. Thaiss is Director of the Plan for Alternative General Education at George Mason University and is Associate Director of the Northern Virginia Writing Project. Active in the development of school and college writing-across-the-curriculum programs since 1978, he also coordinates a national network of these programs, elementary to university. Thaiss has published a recent book, *Writing to Learn: Essays and Reflections on Writing Across the Curriculum* and articles on the writing process and in literary and dramatic history.

Barbara Wood is a Professor of Communication (University of Illinois at Chicago) and the author of many articles and books on how children learn communication skills. In school districts across the country, Professor Wood has conducted teacher-training workshops on integrating communication instruction into the curriculum. On the national level, she has promoted the concept of functional communication as the heart of a child's total educational program.